BARRY

TEXAN IDENTITIES

TEXAN IDENTITIES

Moving Beyond Myth, Memory, and Fallacy in Texas History

EDITED BY

Light Townsend Cummins
and
Mary L. Scheer
Foreword by Jesús F. de la Teja

Denton, Texas

Permissions:
University of North Texas Press
1155 Union Circle #311336
Denton, TX 76203-5017

The paper used in this book meets the minimum requirements of the
American National Standard for Permanence of Paper for Printed Library
Materials, z39.48.1984. Binding materials have been chosen for durability.

Library of Congress Cataloging-in-Publication Data

Names: Cummins, Light Townsend, 1946- editor. | Scheer, Mary L., 1949- editor. |
Teja, Jesús F. de la, 1956- writer of foreword. | Cummins, Light
Townsend. Texan identities.
Title: Texan identities : moving beyond myth, memory, and fallacy in Texas
history / edited by Light Townsend Cummins and Mary L. Scheer ; foreword
by Jesús F. de la Teja.
Description: Denton, Texas : University of North Texas Press, [2016] |
Includes bibliographical references and index.
Identifiers: LCCN 2016019950| ISBN 9781574416480 (cloth : alk. paper) | ISBN
9781574416589 (ebook)
Subjects: LCSH: Texas--Historiography. | Texas--History--19th century. |
Texas--History--20th century. | Collective memory--Texas. | Memory—Social
aspects--Texas. | Identity (Philosophical concept) | Cultural
pluralism--Texas.
Classification: LCC F385.2 .T49 2016 | DDC 976.4--dc23
LC record available at https://lccn.loc.gov/2016019950

The electronic edition of this book was made possible
by the support of the Vick Family Foundation.

A Grant from Texas State University assisted in the publication of this volume.

Dedicated to All Members of the History Faculty at Texas State University,
1903 to the Present and Victoria Hennessey Cummins and Richard L. Scheer

TABLE OF CONTENTS

List of Figures vii

Foreword
by Jesús F. de la Teja ix

Introduction: Texan Identities
by Light Townsend Cummins and Mary L. Scheer 1

Chapter 1: Line in the Sand; Lines on the Soul
by Stephen L. Hardin 29

Chapter 2: Unequal Citizens
by Mary L. Scheer 61

Chapter 3: The Texas Rangers in Myth and Memory
By Jody Edward Ginn 87

Chapter 4: On Becoming Texans
by Kay Goldman 121

Chapter 5: Ethel Tunstall Drought
by Light Townsend Cummins 155

Chapter 6: W. W. Jones of South Texas
by Patrick Cox 185

Chapter 7: *Delgado v. Bastrop*
by Gene B. Preuss 217

Contributors 251

Index 255

LIST OF FIGURES

Figure 1: John Wayne directing *The Alamo* (1960) 34

Figure 2: Davy Crockett 46

Figure 3: Rebuilt Independence Hall, Washington-on-the-
Brazos 63

Figure 4: Declaration of Independence and the Texas Constitution
of 1836, adopted March 17, 1836 74

Figure 5: Texas Rangers on Horseback, 1921 91

Figure 6: Cowboy Star Tom Mix (in white) with Texas Rangers at
Capitol in Austin, ca. 1925 111

Figure 7: Rabbi Jacob Voorsanger 135

Figure 8: San Antonio Turner Hall, late nineteenth century 140

Figure 9: Drought at the Art League Gallery 166

Figure 10: 1930 Portrait of Ethel T. Drought by Rosamund
Niles 179

Figure 11: W. W. Jones at his roll top desk 199

Figure 12: W. W. Jones in the center with his six
grandchildren 212

Figure 13: Minerva Delgado 221

Figure 14: Gus Garcia 225

Figure 15: The Contributors 251

Foreword

by Jesús F. de la Teja

This book of essays is both exceptional and important in a number of ways. First, it is an exploration of themes of increasing concern to historians. The introductory essay reminds us that identity, myth, and collective memory are all components of the story of Texas and how Texans see themselves. And, because of demographic changes in our state, questions of identity increasingly call to question who is a Texan. If the population projections are correct, more than half of the almost 28 million Texans in the state today are Asian, African American, and overwhelmingly Hispanic. The Texan identity, myths, and collective memories of yesteryear do not necessarily fit with their realities.

Second, this volume contributes to a growing body of work by university-trained historians of Texas reflecting on how the state's story has been told and who is telling it. It joins the ranks of Walter L. Buenger's and Robert A. Calvert's edited volume *Texas Through Time: Evolving Interpretations*, in which the editors critiqued their colleagues for failing to support a healthy reassessment of accepted truth: "Affected by a frontier heritage that is depicted as larger than life in both fiction and folklore, university professors translated into the official history of Texas what many citizens viewed as the unique experience of Anglo-Saxon males wrestling the wilderness from savage Indians and venal Mexicans."[1] It joins *Lone Star Pasts: Memory and History in Texas,* edited by Gregg Cantrell and Elizabeth Hays Turner who assert that "collective memoires, as wielded by powerful groups, have had a tendency to shape and define that which is acceptable, that which should be remembered, that which should be forgotten, and who may be allowed entrée into positions of economic or political ascendancy. Hence societal norms related to power, class, gender, and race may be redefined through cultural hegemonic forces as seemingly benign as memories of the past."[2] One example of this type of exploration of the intersection between power and memory is Paul H. Carlson's and Tom Crum's *Myth, Memory, and Massacre: The Pease River Capture of Cynthia Ann Parker*, in which the authors argue that the intentional misrepresentation of events served political and racist agendas, both for those involved and for future generations of Texans.

A third way in which this book is important is that it illustrates the ways in which historians of Texas seek to address new subject areas even as they continue to re-inspect traditional topics. While the Alamo and the Rangers remain the most iconic Texas history subjects, they are also the subject of considerable misrepresentation through myths, fallacies, and contesting collective memories. Other essays in this volume remind us that so much attention has been paid to a narrowly selected set of historical characters and events that Texans have come to suffer the effects of collective amnesia. We have forgotten that Texas was a cultural laboratory where, ironically, nineteenth-century German Jews could more easily participate in German cultural traditions than in Germany. In remembering political and military men, almost all of them white, our collective memory has left no room for women who were citizens and helped build the social and cultural institutions that make society worth fighting for. By highlighting a watershed event, for instance the district court decision that ostensibly ended the segregation of Mexican-American schoolchildren, we conveniently neglect the broader and more complex social, political, and economic aspects of the transformation Texas was undergoing in the mid-twentieth century. And, through the story of a South Texas rancher, the myth of the one-dimensional cattle baron can be exposed along with the misconception that urbanization and industrialization were the province of Houston, Dallas-Fort Worth, and San Antonio.

Fourth, on a personal level, in one way or another I know and have ties to each of the participants in the project. Some—Light Cummins, Mary Scheer, Steve Hardin, and Patrick Cox—have long been respected colleagues. Light succeeded me as State Historian of Texas, but preceded me in championing the early history of the Texas-Louisiana borderlands. Our interest in the Texas Revolution period, particularly the controversial role of Tejanos, has led me to a number of collaborations and joint appearances with Steve. Although I have known Patrick and Mary for many years, most recently we collaborated in a book of essays on prominent Texas historians. Other contributors to this volume—Gene Preuss, Kay Goldman, and Jody Ginn—were students at Texas State during my tenure there and have since become colleagues. Jody, the most recently minted Ph.D. (from the University of North Texas), has an interest in the mythology of the Rangers going back years before he became an M.A. student. Although he is the only member of the contributor group not to have written a thesis, he did work under my supervision on the historiography of Ranger treatment of Mexican Americans. Likewise, Kay Goldman brought her interest in Jewish businessmen in nineteenth-century Texas to her studies at what was still Southwest Texas State in the mid-1990s before going on for the Ph.D. at Texas A&M. Gene Preuss, who worked on his M.A. during my first couple of years as a junior faculty member in San Marcos, went on to complete doctoral work at Texas Tech after finishing a thesis on LBJ and education.

Which leads to the fifth and last reason why this volume is exceptional: all the contributors are, in fact, products of the M.A. history program at what we now call Texas State University. It is a program with a rich and successful tradition going back to 1938 when the school was still Southwest Texas State Teachers College. By the time co-editor and most senior contributor to this book, Light Cummins, earned his M.A. in 1972, the school had again changed its name; it was now Southwest Texas State University. Under this name six of the seven participants in this project graduated, the exception being Jody Ginn, who completed his studies after the school changed its name to Texas State University-San Marcos.

It should not surprise that when Light Cummins brought me his and Mary's idea for a collection of essays by these alumni, I was more than happy to entertain the idea of a symposium that could serve as a reunion to highlight the accomplishments of our graduates. The historians in this volume represent alumni from forty years of the Department of History's commitment to producing well-trained and productive scholars.

And, what better name could we choose for the gathering than "Views from the Hill: History, Myth, and Memory in Texas"? The "Hill" in the title of the symposium, which took place on January 31, 2015, refers to a nickname of the university based on its location on Chautauqua Hill, where the university's first building, now referred to as "Old Main," was constructed. When Southwest Texas State Normal School opened its doors on September 9, 1903, it did so in an edifice constructed on a site that the citizens of San Marcos had purposed to public education. As the Chautauqua movement waned, city leaders recognized the need for strengthening the area's educational resources and offered the state the eleven acres that had previously served as the site of the town's summertime education camps.

Despite the name changes, and enrollment growth fast approaching 40,000, Texas State University remains committed to public education today. The Department of History turns out dozens of bachelor's students every year who go into high school teaching across the state, and the

College of Education graduates the most teachers of any education program in Texas. The graduate program in History, which now includes a highly successful Public History program, continues to prepare M.A. students for doctoral institutions throughout the state and around the nation. The contributors to this volume are members of a proud history education tradition at "The Hill." My colleagues and I in the Department of History are proud of their accomplishments and their contributions to our ancient and vital profession.

Jesús F. de la Teja, Director

Center for the Study of the Southwest
Texas State University, San Marcos, Texas

NOTES

1. Walter L. Buenger and Robert A. Calvert, eds., *Texas Through Time: Evolving Interpretations* (College Station: Texas A&M University Press, 1991), xiv. In Buenger's most recent historiographical work, edited with Arnoldo De León, *Beyond Texas Through Time: Breaking Away from Past Interpretations* (College Station: Texas A&M University Press, 2011), he divides Texas historical writing into three groups, traditionalists, revisionists, and cultural constructionists. The first group is the most closely tied to the traditional interpretations that make up so much of the state's collective memory. The second group, Buenger argues, challenges those conceptions but on the pre-established categories of analysis that prevent truly new ways of interpreting the past. The latter group have come up with new interpretive schemes that address the state's past without concern for accepted norms. Gregg Cantrell and Elizabeth Hayes Turner, eds., *Lone Star Pasts: Memory and History in Texas* (College Station: Texas A&M University Press, 2007), 3.

2. Cantrell and Turner, *Lone Star Pasts: Memory and History in Texas*, 3.

TEXAN IDENTITIES

TEXAN IDENTITIES

MOVING BEYOND MYTH, MEMORY, AND FALLACY IN TEXAS HISTORY

by
Light Townsend Cummins and Mary L. Scheer

The question "what does it mean to be Texan?" is not a new one. Generations of Texans, everyday citizens, popular writers, academic historians, and other observers of the state have searched for answers to this vexing question. Just browse the shelves of any full service bookstore in Texas to confirm a tremendous number of titles published each year that deal in whole or in part with the subject. An online search of various Internet booksellers drives home the validity of this observation. This burgeoning literature is most often classified by those involved in the book trade under the rubric of *Texana*. It has proven to be very popular and likely will continue to be so well into the future.

The reasons for this are complex, with most of them rooted in the widespread assumption that Texas history is a colorful, unique, and expansive field of inquiry, filled with all sorts of narrative stories that provide good reading for a demanding public. Whatever the motivation, people do read these books, which are published in a variety of genres, from fiction, genealogy and journalism to folklore, popular histories, and academic history. The authors of this volume are all academic historians who conduct their historical analysis in an unbiased attempt to present the past in a non-polemical fashion. As such, they attempt to place their particular topic within a larger context that posits some sort of universalized commentary and truth about their specific subject. Their respective analyses seek to present past events, people, and occurrences as causal motivations for the present. Academic history, in addition to considering the history of the specific subject being examined, also includes what its practitioners call historiography, the study of what has already been written over time by other authors on a topic. Scholars who write academic history must relate their interpretations and explanations to the entire history of previous academic writing on the subject, explicitly justifying any new viewpoints they propose. Academic historians, then, are concerned equally with history and historiography as inseparable components in their research, writing, and interpretations.[1]

Academic writing about Texas history, as does all such historical scholarship, has an additional characteristic that forms one of the fundamental reasons for the existence of this volume of essays. Namely, historians writing in an academic frame of reference employ established interpretive perspectives that relate their individual research topics to specific analytical models, concepts of conceptualization, or explanatory constructs. They use these models and conceptualizations across academic history no matter what the specific topic each is considering. These interpretive modes become the structural framework for the writing of academic history. Academic historians, as part of their understanding of historiography, agree on what specific interpretive constructs and intellectual frames of reference should apply to their writing. Such interpretive norms are therefore common standards of analysis, enabling them to look at relatively small, specific parts of the historical experience and relate it directly to the whole of history. For Texas, most of these interpretive concepts come from the larger enterprise of academic writing on United States history since the state can most easily be seen as a subset of that larger canvass of historical analysis. This volume rests on the assumption that Texas has distinctive identities that define "what it means to be Texan." It also relies upon the reality these identities flow from myth and memory, some of which are truthful and some of which are historical fallacies.

Each contributor to this volume provides in some fashion an answer to seminal questions routinely asked by academic historians and others writing about the history of the state: What does it mean to be Texan? What constitutes a Texas identity and how may such change over time? What myths, memories, and fallacies contribute to making a Texas identity, and how have these changed for Texas? Are all the myths and memories that define Texas identity true or are some of them fallacious? Is there more than one Texas identity? Academic historians believe the answers to these questions lie in the study of Texas history. They are not alone in this frame of reference. Conceptualizations of identity, along with the role of myth, and memory in creating them, are also analytical constructs routinely used to analyze the larger history of the United States from the colonial period to the modern era. It is within the analytical concepts of identity, myth, and memory that historians have much to say about the Texas historical experience. Each of the essays in this volume therefore validates the assumption that Texas does have a history worthy of special commentary. In that regard, many Texans believe that the state's history has singular attributes, and its past has distinctiveness, which legitimizes looking at Texas history from the standpoint of focused historical analysis. These perceptions relate directly to the concepts of identity, myth, and memory, most often expressed—at least in the general culture of the state if not in its academic history—by stereotypes that have become iconic representations of what it means to be Texan.

Each of the essays in this volume will, in its own fashion, address one or more of these concepts in its respective analysis of particular events, places, and people in Texas history. They will explain how their topics are related to Texas identity, myth, and memory and how, for the most part, their conclusions are representative examples—as focused and particularized topical studies—of the manner by which many present day academic historians are altering these interpretive constructs. Because each essay is a topical case study, however, there is no common approach to dealing with myth, memory, and fallacy as component parts of Texan identities. Some of the essays concentrate on exposing fallacies out of which established Texas myths have been constructed, while others deal with how memory shapes popular understandings of the Texas historical experience as reflected in widely held identities. Other essays expand on traditional and increasingly outdated interpretations of the Anglo-American myth of Texas by considering little known, if not generally obscured, roles played by women, racial minorities, and specific stereotypes such as the cattleman.

A discussion of the intellectual conceptualizations of identity and its relationship to myth, memory, and fallacy as employed by Texas historians is necessary to provide context to the respective essays. Each of these three analytical and interrelated attributes has been the subject of a voluminous theoretical literature over the last generation of scholarship in all areas of history, a theorizing engaged in across the board by historians of the United States, Europe, and Latin America. The interest of Texas historians in these concepts as explanatory considerations for the history of the Lone Star State flows directly from this internationally based literature. In many respects the work of the French *Annales School* of historiographical interpretation began these developments in the decades prior to World War II. These historians of France dispensed with the traditional political and economic frames of reference that permeated much of the academic historical writing in the west. Concerned with the broader aspects of social history, they fashioned a concept that they styled *mentalités*. This term referred to identifying historically what people believed about themselves at a given time in the past. In part, these historians were asking "what does it mean to be French?" or "what does it mean to be European?" Within a generation, the *Annales* viewpoint had become popular in historical writing in other parts of the world, including the United States. American historians began to fashion various analytical concepts that could be employed to address the component parts of *mentalités* in considering United States history, although they universally refrained from using the French term in describing their efforts. This brought them to study the parameters of identity, myth, and memory as valid subjects of analysis co-equal with long-established political, economic, diplomatic, military, and other widely accepted frameworks of historical analysis. In part, the historians of the United States influenced by *mentalités* were asking "what does it mean to be American?" For many historians, the answer to this question lay at the juncture of identity with myth and memory. [2]

Of these three related concepts, identity is a compelling category of analysis useful to historians of Texas. Identity is shaped by myth and memory. Although the idea of identity has long been favored as an intellectual concept by historians of the United States, especially those concerned with the development of geopolitical nationalism, a much wider spectrum of scholarship during recent decades has embraced it as an analytical tool for examining the historical process. This has been the case in large part because academic historians have increasingly been influenced by methodologies borrowed from other disciplines in the social sciences, especially sociology. There is a significant sociological scholarship that engages in defining, assessing, and studying the notion of identity as it relates to human existence, social groupings, and the structures of society. "An identity," as one preeminent introductory study to this literature notes, "is the set of meanings that define who one is when one is an occupant of a particular role in society, a member of a particular group, or claims particular characteristics that identify him or her as a unique person." In essence, sociologists are asking the question: "What does it mean to be who you are?"[3]

Given this perspective, United States historians have understandably found identity-based analytical models useful in writing about regional, ethnic, religious, economic, gendered, linguistic, and other denominative groups they perceive as having played roles as historical entities. Historians thus ask: "Who were the people in these groups and what beliefs brought them together?" Scholars writing about the American Revolution helped lead the way in posing such questions. This was the case because of their deep interest in learning why some colonists embraced an identity as "American" and some did not. Further, they wanted to know what role an American identity played in the decision to revolt against Great Britain. Recent studies of the Revolutionary era have established identity formation as one of the most important, if not the transcendent force at work, in creating the new nation. Given the fact that sociologists readily concede people can have multiple identities, as long as they are complimentary to one another, United States colonial historians agree that there existed simultaneously a state-based identity, as well as a national one during the late eighteenth and early nineteenth centuries. Americans of the Revolutionary generation also saw themselves as both Americans and as Virginians, New Yorkers, Georgians, Pennsylvanians, or as identities related respectively to all the other new states.[4]

The mentality of being an American therefore did not preclude English speakers in the United States during the early nineteenth century from adopting complementary self-conceptualizations regarding other identity groups to which they eventually belonged. Identity formation, it seems, was not set in stone, but changed and adapted to new conditions. "Identity was a historical process," historian Kathleen Wilson has noted about the creation of an American self-identification, "rather than an outcome, a negotiation between individual conceptions of self and collectivity and their social valence."[5]

By the second decade of the nineteenth century, this process had continued to the point that many of the white residents of the former plantation colonies had also become southerners, in addition to being Americans, even as many of them moved westward to the Mississippi River and beyond. Nonetheless, they also remained Alabamians, Tennesseans, and other state-based identities too as they solidified their southernism. Historian Christopher Morris has provided a closely reasoned analysis of how and why these people defined themselves as southerners, while Light T. Cummins has demonstrated the manner by which English-speakers did the same when they moved into Spanish territory in the lower Mississippi valley and to areas along the Gulf Coast.[6]

It was this migratory impulse that brought the first English speakers from the United States into Texas as legal residents during the 1820s. It can be argued that, much as their forebears had been doing for two generations in the older states, they analogously fashioned an identity for themselves that made them into Texans, with a substantial number of them also being Americans and southerners. Andrea Kökény has explained: "Texians gradually started to regard themselves as a group having a separate identity. At the same time, they never wholly forgot about their native land."[7]

This was an Anglo-American identity. At least from the viewpoint of these new "Texans," a perspective no doubt based in the racial and religious norms of that era, there was no room for those of African, Hispanic, or Native American background in the identity they fashioned. This identity would also reject across the generations of its dominance in Texas those who were not Protestants or whose native language was not English. One's place in the political, economic, and social order also determined identity, such as that of women who were outside the male sphere of power and politics that defined Texan identity as masculine. This Anglo-American Texas identity in Texas thus became patriarchal. As the same time, identities subordinate to the predominating Anglo-American identity also took hold in Texas, especially among native speakers of Spanish. "The decision to become Mexican or American or Texan was not only a question of placing or imagining oneself within one collectivity," as Andrés Reséndez has observed of the state's Hispanic population, "most critically it involved choices about the organization of the economy, the contours of the political system, and religious and moral values."[8] Other non-Anglo groups in Texas have also faced similar choices. Nonetheless, it must be noted that the Anglo-American identity took center stage during the nineteenth century in determining what it meant to be Texan.

One of the first written expressions of this Anglo-American, southern-based identity came when Henderson Yoakum, a faculty member at Austin College before the Civil War, published a two-volume *History of Texas* in 1856. English-speaking migrants from the United States won control of Texas (in the process fashioning their identity) in Yoakum's historical opinion because they were more highly evolved than their Spanish-speaking rivals, specifically representing better natural adaptations in a cultural sense than those of Hispanic background. This interpretation continued well into the twentieth century as fundamental to the dominant Texas identity. In 1903, George P. Garrison wrote an influential volume entitled *Texas: A Contest of Civilizations*. In it, Professor Garrison noted it was the cultural and economic superiority of English speakers from the United States that gave the state its identity in a way that provided definitive political, economic, and cultural distinctiveness.[9]

History is in large part written by the victors. For that reason by the early decades of the twentieth century, the Anglo-American identity had become the dominant narrative for defining in the public mind the entire historical experience that was Texas. It permeated the popular culture of the state and nation to the extent that by the 1930s it constituted a "branding" of the state across the entire country, if not the world. The idea of branding is both "a process and an image." According to Leigh Clemons branding is the means by which "the idea of the Lone Star—the mainstream white, male Texas—is created as a commodity." Branding therefore involves the presentation of attributes, characteristics, and qualities inherent in a person, place, or product in such a way as to assign a set of values to it whenever it is evoked. The Anglo-American identity of Texas, certainly by the time of World War II, had become the primary focus in characterizing the Lone Star State as a distinctive place.

This could be seen in motion pictures, in the world of popular music, in magazines and novels, and even in the writings of Texas intellectuals who analyzed the state. In the latter case, it dominated the publications of three writers who eventually became an acclaimed literary triumvirate for Texas. Their writings came to embody intrinsically the Anglo-American identity of Texas: J. Frank Dobie, Roy Bedichek, and Walter Prescott Webb. Although none of them explicitly addressed the concept of identity in their body of work about Texas, their books can be seen as the epitome of written expression rooted in Anglo-American conceptualization of Texas identity. Bedichek wrote about the land and the state's natural environment, always with a main eye on Anglo Texans as they interacted with the landscape. Dobie chronicled the folklore of the state, with special reference to the frontier, rural areas, and the cattle culture from an Anglo frame of reference that sometimes depreciated the Hispanic. Walter P. Webb emerged as the preeminent academic historian in the state as he focused on its Anglo-American development with special attention afforded to groups such as the Texas Rangers.[10]

By the 1970s the mainstay parameters of this male Anglo-Texas identity embodied a complex array of attributes. Grounded in a rural, agrarian viewpoint, cast within the heritage of an almost limitless frontier and coupled to a patriarchal view of historical development, it stressed the role of men in fashioning Texas history. A fierce devotion to individuality, entrepreneurship, personal liberty, and the search for prosperity proved to be qualities celebrated in this identity, especially since Texas had proved itself as a land of economic promise to those who embraced this identity.

Today the reality of a singular Anglo identity of Texas has changed drastically. The question "what does it mean to be Texan?" can no longer be answered in masculine, Anglo-centric terms. The present-day Lone Star State is more urban, more multi-cultural, and far more diverse than the place where Dobie, Bedichek, and Webb lived. More Texans, by far, drink water from plastic bottles than they do from backyard wells. Many Texans routinely refer to ballplayers running the bases at a stadium in Arlington as Texas Rangers, rather than law enforcement officers. Multiple identities are modifying and supplanting the traditional Anglo identity that has for so long characterized it. In our own times, historians have come to understand that any society involves multiple and sometimes competing identities. It is possible for one person to have an adherence to several different identities in hierarchical fashion. A single individual living in Houston, for example, can identify as an American, a Texan, and a Houstonian, along with an array of other characteristics including being Hispanic, African-American, male, or female. Religious and educational parameters, among many others, also help to shape one's identity given the circumstances of self-definition. It must therefore be stressed that today academic historians contend there is no single, monolithic identity in determining what it means to be Texan. There are multiple identities at work in making such a determination. For that reason the essays in this volume assume the existence of Texas identities in a pluralistic manner, something earlier generations of scholarship sometimes simplified by a concentration on a male Anglo-American frame of reference. It is also important to understand that identities change across time and place as they are reconstructed in the face of new social and cultural realities.

Texas identities cannot be considered in isolation from myth or memory. Myth and memory are the building blocks out of which a people's common identity is constructed. Of the latter two analytical concepts, myth is more closely tied to the notion of identity across long and extended time frames. Myths have powerful endurance as they are repeated over and over, sometimes across generations of retelling. They determine how we see the world from a fundamental perspective. Scholars have been dealing with the cultural phenomenon of myth for almost as long as academic research and writing has existed in the western European intellectual tradition. In the eighteenth and nineteenth centuries, many of these studies concentrated on ancient civilizations, especially the Roman and Greek worlds. These scholars of myth studied the classical pantheons of gods, attendant theocratic beliefs, and the related sacred mythologies used by the ancients to explain and foster group identity. In so doing there came to exist early in the scholarly literature a definition of myth that centered on its religious, sacred dimensions.[11]

By the late nineteenth century, however, the study of myth had expanded to include a larger perspective than sacred belief. It incorporated folk tales, legends, other verbal aspects of cultural reference, and common social rituals, all of which had secular dimensions but which also served the same basic purposes as religious mythology. Many of these "folk myths," unlike the sacred, had their roots in history as perceived by the group, drawing upon actual events from the past. From the viewpoint of history, however, these secular folk myths presented interpretations of the past that were not entirely true in recounting what happened, but neither were they fictional either.[12] Myths are composed of canonical stories, traditions, and recountings of events, sometimes drawn from history, used to define and disseminate social values by ionic reference. They are often repeated narratives, stories, and representations of an almost semi-religious nature. They are well-known to most members of a given society and mold how its members see themselves at a fundamental level. For historians, such myths thus constitute a category of explanatory concept embodying the basic characteristics that form particular identities. They are fundamental, canonical, and symbolic narratives of a reverential nature that exist beyond debate as fundamental, iconic, and denominating cornerstones of an identity. Myth in this meaning of the term has been embraced by scholars as an academic concept employed to analyze a given society and culture.

The word myth, however, also has a popular, related definition that is also relevant to defining identity. Instead of the well-developed academic meaning of the term as a fundamental explanatory narrative, myth can also be a fallacy, a misconception, mistake, or historical untruth. Such fallacies can bolster larger mythic narratives of meaning and cohesion for a given society in a very effective manner. In fact, the component parts of the overriding, comprehensive myths that people use to bolster their identities often do contain fallacies in any society or culture. Mythic untruths are as important as mythic truths in understanding the formation of identities in history. "Historical myths and legends are needful in establishing national identity and stimulating patriotic pride," historian Thomas A. Bailey had noted, and "false historical beliefs are so essential to our culture that if they did not exist, like Voltaire's God, they would have to be invented."[13] The British scholar Percy S. Cohen highlights this definition when he writes: "Myths, on this view, are erroneous beliefs clung to against all evidence. The term is then synonymous with fallacy."[14] Although untrue, such fallacies serve the same purpose as truthful mythic narratives. Veracity and fallacy are often intertwined in the making of myths. As one character in the motion picture *The Man Who Shot Liberty Valance* says in an often-quoted line, "When the truth becomes legend, print the legend."

Myths are therefore a combination of fallacies and truthful events from the past filtered through the value structures of a given society to elevate selected parts of its identity-based narratives to a transcendent status. Once so elevated, these crafted interpretations became set-piece renditions or practice rituals used to explain who a people are, where they came from, and what their society means to them. Such myths, both truth and fallacy, employ stylized representations of people, historic places and events from the past, and ceremony to reinforce a group's values, ideals, beliefs, and attributes of their common identity. Myths educate new members while they reconfirm the culture's validity for others already belonging to the group. The rise of anthropology as an academic discipline in the early twentieth century greatly accelerated the study of secular myths rooted in historical occurrences. The late Claude Lévi-Strauss pioneered in developing Anthropology into a form of analysis that considered a people's belief systems and myth as significant areas of study. Much modern theory about the role of secular myth drawn from a people's common history relies on his insights.[15]

Texas, of course, has a highly developed array of secular myths, revered physical places, iconic historical personages, and transcendent occurrences drawn from a shared past upon which Texan group identities in the state are based. These do not come from the realm of fiction, but instead have their foundation in a commonality of history shared by all who consider themselves Texans. In a sense, the mythic ideals and symbols drawn from this common past have been "deified" in a secular manner to represent attributes that define the outlines of group identity. They constitute a sort of cultural shorthand by which Texans order their shared value assumptions as criteria for creating group identity. As Louise Cowan has pointed out, some of these are creation myths that explain how Texas came to be for the people who see themselves as Texans. [16]

For the historically dominant narrative myth of Anglo-Texas, many of these idealized narratives and icons revolve around Manifest Destiny, along with the events and places of the Texas Revolution, most especially the Alamo, the massacre at Goliad, and the Battle of San Jacinto. The Anglo-Texan myth began with the land—a promised land of vast resources, abundant wealth, and limitless opportunities. A man named Moses—Moses Austin—beckoned his people to follow his lead westward and heed the Old Testament command "to be fruitful, to multiply, and to establish dominion over the earth." As God's chosen people, Anglos were destined to conquer and settle the continent, including Mexican-held Texas. Confident their calling was divine, their cause was righteous, and their victory foreordained over the forces of evil, Anglo-Texans, by right, would inherit the earth. Thus, the battle of the Alamo, an American Thermopylae, assumed mythic proportions as sacred ground, sanctified by sacrifice, and with a narrative replete with highly defined heroes and clear-cut villains. [17]

dominion

Popular culture has interpreted the Alamo as both history and myth. It says much that one of the earliest motion pictures made in the United States with a storyline was about the Alamo, filmed in San Antonio during 1911 by the French movie pioneer Georges Méliès. In a later, more

well-known motion picture, John Wayne masterfully encapsulated the
Alamo myth with a short speech from his 1960 film *The Alamo* when
he said: "Republic. I like the sound of the word. Means that people can
live free, talk free, go or come, buy or sell, be drunk or sober, however
they choose. Some words give you a feeling. Republic is one of those
words that makes me tight in the throat." Wayne obviously conflated the
battle of the Alamo with the concepts of republican and representative
government, constitutional structures not likely to have been on the
minds of anyone who fought on either side of the fortress walls during
that fateful day in March 1836. John Wayne can certainly be excused for
doing this because, as a preeminent filmmaker, he knew that myth is
often more compelling than the history on which it is based.

Anthropologists observe that myths can also flow from shared experiences that are not directly related to a common past. Such popular myths
reinforce the mythic parameters of shared history. For that reason the
mythic status accorded to the Texian defenders of the Alamo has also
been attributed to later individuals in Texas history. These new heroes
also embodied the values of courage, love of freedom, independence,
forthrightness, self-reliance, ruggedness, and entrepreneurial spirit that
form part and parcel of the Texas myth. As such they have become some
of the state's most enduring icons. Most of them, as did John Wayne,
would have liked the word republic. One need look no further than the
mythic status of the Texas Rangers as a law enforcement organization
and the role it has played in defining the historical meanings of the state.
For the Civil War generation, figures such as Ben McCullough, Tom
Green, and Dick Dowling joined the myth of being Texan. The cattle
frontier produced Richard King, Charles Goodnight, Jesse Chisholm,
some of whom appear by name in the pages of novels such as Larry
McMurtry's *Lonesome Dove* series, itself based in large part on the Texas
myth, blending historical fact and pure fiction. This phenomenon has
continued into the twenty-first century, drawing its sources from the
realms of politics, oil, business, sports, entertainment, and a host of others
who became members of this mythic panoply.

adept at myth-making

myth of the building

Physical objects can also become imbued with mythic standing when defined in the popular view as value-ladened symbols relating to the formation of group identity. They have iconic meaning as part of the mythology of being Texan. An array of tangible objects, public activities, and recreational pursuits has therefore become distinctly symbolic of the Texas ethos in a mythic way. Indeed, the shape of Texas itself is one of these icons, seen all across the state in hundreds of thousands of highway markers and road signs. The outlines of the state also appear on beer bottles and food labels, neon advertising signs and business logos, and in countless other places. Silhouettes of the horns on a longhorn cow or the outline of the Alamo chapel's roofline serve much the same role as mythic icons in the state's popular culture, as do the image of the five-pointed Lone Star so closely associated with the state and its history. Paintings of bluebonnets, the silhouette of a cowboy on a cutting horse along with boots, a ten-gallon hat, and a strand of twirling rope also serve such functions.

Attending a Texas rodeo evokes much the same reaction as an icon endowed with Texan identity. For many modern Texans, attending a Friday night high school football game in the fall also evokes, at some level, solidarity with the myth of Texas. This is also true on Saturdays for Texas universities and other days of the week for professional gridiron contests by NFL teams in the state. It is not accidental that some of these football teams, along with others from sports such as baseball, have names that equate them directly with historical iconography. Team names such as the Cowboys, Spurs, Texans, and others flow directly from the mainline mythology associated with Texas history.

Like myth, the concept of memory is also a significant determinant of a people's identity. Memory intrinsically involves history because it is rooted in the actual events of the past. Memories, however, can ebb and flow to a greater extent than myth. As one scholar has noted, myths are memories on steroids. Memory is also more flexible and prone to change than myth. It changes with time and as the times change, memory alters the manner by which it defines identities. Memories can be the firsthand memories by individuals or the recalled memories adopted by a group. As in the case with myth, shared or collective memory helps explain to a given group of people why their society has become the way they understand it to be. Memory can be defined as the explicit exposition of what a people know anecdotally, informally, generally, and popularly about their history. As the widely held, consensus view of the past, it is part of the socialization process into a culture. However, unlike myth, public memory does not elevate certain parts of the past to heroic or transcendent status that serve as iconic symbols of fundamental group values. Instead, as its name indicates, it is what a people remember about their past and how they see their society as its product. Memory, however, is not benign, judgment-free, or even accurate in its representation of the past. Instead, collective memory is a complex narrative that involves remembering some things that came before, while demanding that other things be forgotten. For example, those who today embrace the Confederate battle flag as tangible memory of their southern heritage from the 1860s choose to forget its emblematic image as a symbol adopted by individuals of a later historical era who were opposed to racial integration during the 1960s, and *vice versa* for those who reject it for that latter reason. Philosopher and sociologist Maurice Halbwachs has noted: "As a living imagination, collective memory is continually reshaped by the social contexts into which it is received. The more powerful the context, the more imposing its memories will be."[18]

Although people cherish public memory, it does change over time as the culture evolves. Memory, therefore, is not written in stone as inviolate belief to the same extent as myth, but is instead socially constructed at points in time and changes more easily. This is the case because memory is a product of various institutions and centers of opinion-making in a given culture. People learn the content of public memory in school when they take history classes, go to museums, visit historical sites, participate in civic celebrations, attend theatrical productions, go to the movies, or watch television. "Collective memory," historians Gregg Cantrell

Coim - memory
foundation - myth.
stone

and Elizabeth Hayes Turner have reminded us, "is constructed through such activities as the writing and teaching of history, the celebration of holidays, the creation of art, the building of monuments, and museums, and the preservation of historic sites gives a society its identity and helps to define its values." They also note that "studying how a society remembers its history, therefore, usually tells us much more about that society's present identity and values than it does about the historical events being remembered."[19] And, of course, memory can also contain fallacies as much as does myth.

Memory is as much a part of popular culture as it is explicitly a component of historical understanding. The lessons presented by memory are therefore brokered choices, reflecting a view of the past that represents conscious determinations about what is worth knowing or, on the other hand, what is useful to forget. In that regard, the parts of the past omitted from public memory are just as important for understanding it as what remains. In other words, as historian Randolph B. Campbell has pointed out, memory is often as much about "forgetting as remembering." Public memory is often dependent upon commercial, political, philanthropic, and interest group support for its existence. For that reason, collective memory can be a sanitized, non-controversial, non-offensive, and confirming presentation of history that serves some of the same general purpose as myth, but with a less exalted and reverential status. Memory, in this respect, is often times a mechanism of social control defined by those elements in a society who hold power. Memory thus becomes a way to help maintain and ensure that dominance. Fitzhugh Brundage, one of the leading historians about memory in the history of the American South, explains that "the depth and tenacity of a historical memory within a society may serve as one measure of who exerts social power there." As such, it can explain a good deal about who has power in a given culture, why they have it, and how public memory has been fashioned to justify that situation of dominance. It is therefore not surprising that academic history, which is an enterprise not tied to reconfirming memory, occasionally runs afoul of the public consensus when it arrives at different conclusions than collective memory in explaining what happened in the past and why.[20]

Academic history rests primarily on archival research and presents its conclusions within a historiographical nexus, while memory chiefly maintains its viability by not departing from the complex cultural consensus of which it is a part. This relationship gives academic historians a special interest in public memory because they can study it as part of the historical process. "Memory has become a pressing problem for history itself," historian Patrick Hutton notes. "Since the 1980s, historians have focused more directly on the relationship between memory and history as an historiographical problem." This has certainly been the case for scholars who write academic history about Texas. The last twenty years of historical scholarship in Texas history have witnessed an explosion of studies analyzing historical memory, commenting on its relationship to academic history, and scrutinizing the way by which dominant sectors in the state have shaped its context. Historians who have examined the outlines of historical memory in Texas have, not surprisingly, concluded that it has enjoyed a strong commonality with myth. Historical memory in Texas was for many generations formulated in what historian Walter Buenger has called a "top down" approach to the past, one that reflected the viewpoints of politically conservative elites. He has explained explicitly how this traditional public memory in Texas mostly "told the story from the elite perspective, tended to conserve and protect the cultural and political power of the elite by quieting controversy in politics and in society at large, and emphasized that history could turn a profit." It has tended to be "a linear history that stressed wars, generals, captains of industry, political leaders, and white males." If one is to believe Buenger, and academic historians do, this long-standing collective memory for Texas has been the story of white, Anglo-Saxon, mostly protestant, agrarian, self-reliant, democracy-loving frontier folk who came to Texas in the antebellum era to carve out their fortunes. They were an individualistic and entrepreneurial people who always had an eye for the chance to improve themselves, along with Texas as a whole. This public memory

don't
complicate, (for us)
thing.

was absolutely optimistic in its basic undertone, while it told a story of
cooperation instead of conflict without recognition of ambiguity in the
past. These viewpoints, so ingrained in this version of public memory
in Texas, have continued with popularity in some quarters well into
the twenty-first century in such a manner as to lionize elites, deprecate
violence, ignore racism, and whitewash or ignore contradictory parts of
the past while it downplayed the role of minorities and women. [21]

This traditional conceptualization of public memory in Texas has
changed drastically in circles of academic history during recent decades
for two important reasons. First, there have always been multiple, coun-
tervailing, contradictory memories held by Texans of Hispanic, African, or
other racial backgrounds, along with those from various religious groups
and women in the state. For generations, these particularized memories
remained sublimated and could be found only inside the boundaries
of their specialized identity groups. In recent decades, these memories
have come to the forefront of public recognition by means of the same
institutions that once created the older, elite-based and Anglo-centric
view of Texas. The teaching of history in the schools, the publication of
history textbooks, the newer museum exhibitions, the creation of public
sculptures or other works of art, the implementation of folklife festivals,
and related social mechanisms have created a diversified, collective
memory that increasingly includes historical notice—on their own terms
—of racial, gendered, and religious minorities previously peripheral to
the traditional collective memory. That process is still incomplete and,
at least to the present time, the various versions of what will probably
be a new, all-encompassing collective memory for Texas still remain
atomized. How this new public memory will be formed, especially as it
relates to what it means to be Texan, is still to be determined.

Second, traditional public memory in Texas is changing because the
content of academic history no longer supports or sustains it. A landmark
analysis of this historiographical trend and its impact on public memory
occurred with the 2007 publication of a book of essays entitled *Lone Star*

Pasts: Memory and History in Texas, edited by Gregg Cantrell and Elizabeth Hayes Turner. Eleven distinguished historians contributed analytical essays to this volume, each of which examines the relationship between public memory and the academic studies being produced in recent decades. They found a disconnection between memory and academic history. Today, much academic history is written from the "bottom up." It considers what is sometimes called the "underside of history," meaning an emphasis on the exploited, the downtrodden, and others who failed to achieve the optimistic promise embodied in the traditional public memory. For example, the cowboy has been an integral component of Lone Star memory. He is remembered as a genuine legend, embodying many admirable traits such as self-reliance, ruggedness, and a strong work ethic, one "who had ridden through a golden moment in American [and Texan] history." Historian Jacqueline M. Moore's study of Texas cowboys of the late nineteenth century, however, has shown they had much in common with the factory workers of the northeast. Both groups, one working on the open land and the other in factories, were laborers who furthered the industrialization of the United States. Additionally Moore's analysis of the Texas cattle kingdom revealed that cattlemen were primarily capitalists, similar to the factory owners of the Gilded Age. This viewpoint was completely ignored or forgotten in the traditional public memory of Texas. Much writing on Texas history by academic historians across a wide variety of topics and subjects, each in its own fashion, has echoed in analogous fashion the questioning perspectives in Moore's book about Texas cowboys and cattlemen. The myth of the cowboy eventually overshadowed considerations of memory and gender embodied in the multiple identities about which Moore wrote in her analysis of gender, masculinity, myth, and memory on the cattle frontier.[22]

Given the complex relationship that academic history has with identity, myth, and memory, the authors who have contributed essays to this volume examine their respective historical topic as each relates in some fashion to the complexities of myth, memory, and fallacy in forging some aspect of Texan identities. They are case studies. Each essay explicitly notes how its topic either supports or detracts from the generally accepted myths, memories and/or identities embodied in answering the question "what does it mean to be Texan?" Some essays raise historical questions about how specific myths and memories, rooted either in truth or fallacy, have fashioned Texas identities, while others point out historical events or persons whose eventual inclusion in a new consensus might change the future nature of identity in Texas. However, it falls outside the focus of this volume to provide the reader with a full, itemized description of what it means to be a Texan in a comprehensive fashion that gives an expository and textbook-like elucidation of identity formation in Texas history. The emerging scholarship on this question is not evolved to the point of being a full synthesis. The contributors have had freedom with the structure of this volume to choose their topics and determine how each relates to the common themes of this volume. As Texas novelist and journalist George Sessions Perry observed: "It is manifest that nobody is going to write all about Texas in any one book." That is true for this volume as well. [23]

There is an additional point of commonality embodied in this volume that inspired our initial interest in developing this group of essays. With a growing population during the twentieth century, the history profession expanded and the locus of scholarship on Texas moved away from its earlier academic center—the University of Texas at Austin. A newer generation of scholars, educated across the region at other universities in the state, began to make their mark. This study represents such change both in the earlier degree-granting center of historical lineage and in the broader perspectives and interpretations offered by the authors. As noted in the foreword to this book, each of the contributors to this volume holds an M.A. in history from Southwest Texas State University, now Texas State University, and all of them also later earned a Ph.D. in Texas history. They began their graduate studies on "The Hill," as the campus of that university is popularly known. All of us see this volume as a way to repay, at least in part, the debt of gratitude we owe stemming from our respective years of graduate study at Texas State University. In that regard the editors and contributors wish to express their appreciation to Professor Jesús F. de la Teja, Director of the Center for the Study of the Southwest, and to Professor Mary Brennan, Chair of the History Department. They graciously hosted a symposium at Texas State University on January 31, 2015, at which we read preliminary versions of the essays contained in this volume. In addition Texas State University generously provided funds that helped to underwrite the publication of this book. As editors of this book, we express our admiration and appreciation to our fellow alumni of the Texas State history department who contributed essays to this volume. Each of them is an established scholar who has mastered an enviable specialty regarding the topics about which they have chosen to write in the pages that follow. For that reason, as editors, we have been determined to let them speak for themselves without imposing a common historical voice or rhetoric on their essays. We believe what they have written is powerful in itself and something the imposition of a stylistic uniformity on our part would have diminished.

In the final analysis all of the historians involved in this anthology hope a fuller understanding of Texas history will emerge from the essays in the book. In the past the interpretive constructs of identity, myth, fallacy, and memory that tie this manuscript together have often been used to obscure history, by ignoring multiple Texan identities, perpetuating time-worn myths, repeating historical fallacies, and denying divergent memories. The seven essays below all provide, in one form or another, an answer to the question "What does it mean to be Texan?" By moving beyond myth, memory, and fallacy in Texas history, these observations hopefully will advance a newer and less parochial conceptualization of Texas, recognizing the state's complexities, incorporating its development within a larger context, and providing a more usable past for a broader range of Texans. In closing, all of us who have written essays for this book would like to dedicate this volume to the historians at Texas State University who have served in the history department and trained generations of historians over the decades starting from the first year of classes at San Marcos in 1903 down to the present time. Additionally,

Light Cummins, as co-editor, wishes to acknowledge his wife Victoria Hennessey Cummins in the dedication of this volume. Mary Scheer, as co-editor, also would like to dedicate this anthology to her husband Richard L. Scheer, who comforts her when she is afflicted and afflicts her when she is comfortable.

NOTES

1. For a survey of academic literature dealing with Texas history, see: Bruce Glasrud, et al., *Discovering Texas History*; Patrick L. Cox and Kenneth E. Hendrickson, Jr., *Writing the Story of Texas* (Austin: University of Texas Press, 2013); Walter L. Buenger and Arnoldo de León, eds., *Beyond Texas through Time: Breaking Away from Past Interpretations* (College Station: Texas A&M University Press, 2011); Walter L. Buenger and Robert A. Calvert, eds., *Texas Through Time: Evolving Interpretations* (College Station: Texas A&M University Press, 1991); Light Townsend Cummins and Alvin R. Bailey, Jr., *A Guide to the History of Texas* (Westport, CT: Greenwood Press, 1988).

2. Historian Daniel Little has defined mentalités as "a broad shared set of ideas, representations, and values within a given people." This is a concept closely related to identity. Daniel Little, *New Contributions of the Philosophy of History* (New York: Springer, 2010), 195; Richard Mowery Andrews, "Some Implications of the Annales School and Its Methods for a Revision of Historical Writing about the United States," *Review* (Fernand Braudel Center), vol. 1, no. 3/4 (Winter-Spring 1978), 165-83; Laurence Veysey, "The New 'Social History' in the Context of American Historical Writing," *Reviews in American History*, vol. 7, no. 1 (March 1979): 1-12; T. C. R. Horn and Harry Ritter, "Interdisciplinary History: A Historiographical Review," *The History Teacher*, vol. 19, no. 3 (May 1986): 427-448.

3. John Breuilly, *Nationalism and the State* (Chicago: University of Chicago Press, 1982), 1-4; Peter J. Burke and Jan E. Stets, *Identity Theory* (New York: Oxford University Press, 2009), 3.

4. Michael Zuckerman, "Identity in British America," in Nicholas Cannay and Anthony Padgen, eds. *Colonial Identity in the Atlantic World, 1500 to 1800* (Princeton, N.J.: Princeton University Press, 1989), 115-158; Dror Wahrman, "The English Problem of Identity in the American Revolution," *American Historical Review*, vol. 106, no. 4 (October 2001): 1236–1262.

5. Kathleen Wilson, ed., *A New Imperial History: Culture, Identity, and Modernity in Britain and the Empire, 1660-1840* (Cambridge, U.K.: Cambridge University Press, 2004), 6.

6. Christopher Morris, *Becoming Southern: The Evolution of a Way of Life, Warren County and Vicksburg, Mississippi, 1760-1860* (New York: Oxford University Press, 1995); Light Townsend Cummins, "Oliver Pollock and the Creation of an American Identity in Spanish Colonial Louisiana" in Gene Smith and Sylvia L. Hilton, eds., *Nexus of Empire: Negotiating Loyalty and Identity in the Revolutionary Borderlands, 1760s-1820s* (Gainesville, Fla.: University Presses of Florida, 2011).

7. Andrea Kökény, "The Construction of Anglo-American Identity in the Republic of Texas, as Reflected in the 'Telegraph and Texas Register,'" *Journal of the Southwest*, vol. 46, no. 2 (Summer 2004): 298.

8. Andrés Reséndez, "National Identity on a Shifting Border: Texas and New Mexico in the Age of Transition, 1821-1848," *Journal of American History*, vol. 86, no. 2 (September 1999): 687-88.

9. Carroll Van West has noted Yoakum manifested a "dogmatic faith in American superiority on the North American continent." Carroll Van West, "Democratic Ideology and the Antebellum Historian: The Case of Henderson Yoakum," *Journal of the Early Republic*, vol. 3, no. 3 (Autumn 1983): 336; H. Yoakum, *History of Texas from its First Settlement in 1685 to its Annexation to the United States in 1846* (Austin: Steck, 1935 reprint of 1856 edition). George P. Garrison, *Texas: A Contest of Civilizations* (New York: Houghton Mifflin, 1903); Llerena Friend, "A Dedication to the Memory of George Pierce Garrison: 1853-1910," *Arizona and the West*, vol. 17, no. 4 (Winter, 1975): 305-308.

10. Mark E. Nackman, *A Nation within a Nation: The Rise of Texas Nationalism* (Port Washington, NY: Kennikat Press, 1975); Leigh Clemons, *Branding Texas: Performing Culture in the Lone Star State* (Austin: University of Texas Press, 2008), 95. These three literary figures were greatly lionized by the time of their respective deaths, last of which occurred with Dobie's passing in 1964. Although an assessment of their voluminous writings lies well beyond the focus of this essay, see the following for an appreciation of their place in the history of Texas writing. Ronnie Dugger, ed., *Three Men in Texas: Bedichek, Webb, and Dobie* (Austin: University of Texas Press, 1967) and William A. Owens, *Three Friends: Roy Bedichek, J. Frank Dobie, and Walter Prescott Webb* (Garden City, N.J.: Doubleday and Company, 1969).

11. The best known of these is *Bulfinch's Mythology*, which has held a central place in the study of classical mythology since its first publication in the 1850s. Thomas J. Bulfinch, *Bulfinch's Mythology* (New York: Barnes and Noble, 2006. reprint of 1857 edition); Carl J. Richard, *The Golden Age*

of the Classics in America (Cambridge, Mass: Harvard University Press, 2009), 32-34.

12. Geoffrey Stephen Kirk, *Myth: Its Meaning and Functions in Ancient and Other Cultures* (Berkeley, Ca.: University of California Press, 1970), 36.

13. Thomas A. Bailey, "Mythmakers of American History," *The Journal of American History*, vol. 55, no. 1 (June 1968): 5.

14. Percy S. Cohen, "Theories of Myth," *Man*, vol. 4, no. 3 (September 1969): 337.

15. James Boon and David Schneider, "Kinship vis-à-vis Myth Contrasts in Levi-Strauss's Approach to Cross-Cultural Comparison," *American Anthropologist*, vol. 76, no. 4 (October 1974): 799-817.

16. These concepts are developed in a landmark volume: Robert F. O'Connor, *Texas Myths* (College Station: Texas A&M University Press, 1986).

17. Michael L. Collins, "Statehood, 1845-1860," in *The Texas Heritage*, 4th ed., edited by Ben Procter and Archie P. McDonald (Wheeling, Ill.: Harlan Davidson, Inc., 2003), 87.

18. Gregg Cantrell and Elizabeth Hayes Turner, "A Study of History, Memory, and Collective Memory in Texas," in Cantrell and Turner, eds., *Lone Star Pasts: Memory and History in Texas* (College Station: Texas A&M University Press, 2007), 1-14; Maurice Halbwachs, *The Collective Memory*, trans. by Francis and Vida Ditter (New York: Harper & Row, 1980), 78-106; Nathan Wachtel, "Memory and History: An Introduction," *History and Anthropology*, vol. 2 (1986): 207-24; Patrick Hutton, *History as an Art of Memory* (Hanover, N.H.: University Press of New England, 1993), 73-90; Nathan Wachtel, "Memory and History: An Introduction," *History and Anthropology*, vol. 2 (1986): 207-24.

19. Gregg Cantrell, "The Bones of Stephen F. Austin: History and Memory in Progressive-Era Texas," *Southwestern Historical Quarterly*, vol. 108, no. 2 (Oct., 2004): 148.

20. Randolph B. Campbell, "History and Collective Memory in Texas: The Entangled Stories of the Lone Star State, in Cantrell and Turner, eds., *Lone Star Pasts*, 270-282; W. Fitzhugh Brundage, "No Deed But Memory," in W. Fitzhugh Brundage, ed., *Where These Memories Grow: History, Memory, and Southern Identity* (Chapel Hill: University of North Carolina Press, 2000), 9-10; Edward T. Linenthal, "Struggling with History and Memory," *Journal of American History*, vol. 82, no. 3 (December 1995): 1100.

21. Patrick Hutton, "Recent Scholarship on Memory and History," *The History Teacher*, vol. 33, no. 4 (August 2000): 534; Walter L. Buenger, "'The Story of Texas'? The Texas State History Museum and Forgetting and Remembering the Past," *Southwestern Historical Quarterly*, vol. 105, no. 3 (January 2002): 487, 490-91.

22. See Cantrell and Turner, eds., *Lone Star Pasts*; Patrick Dearen, *The Last of the Old-Time Cowboys* (Plano: Republic of Texas Press, 1998) 9; Jacqueline M. Moore, *Cow Boys and Cattle Men: Class and Masculinities on the Texas Frontier, 1865-1900* (New York: New York University Press, 2009).

23. George Sessions Perry, *Texas: A World in Itself* (New York: McGraw-Hill, 1942), vii.

CHAPTER 1

LINE IN THE SAND; LINES ON THE SOUL

THE BATTLE OF THE ALAMO IN MYTH, MEMORY, AND HISTORY

by
Stephen L. Hardin

Editor's Note: The Alamo lies at the center of the Texas myth. It also holds a place essential to the memory of Texas. Few Texans, if any at all, would fail to mention the Alamo as one of the most significant icons of what it means to be a Texan. It has been perhaps the most essential part of the myth and memory that created the Anglo-American identity of Texas. The Alamo myth embodies in its inherent values most of what many Texans hold dear in defining their identity: freedom, independence, strength of action, sacrifice for the general betterment, and a host of other parameters of character or good judgment that comprehend the world view of Texas identities. We are all continually admonished to "Remember the Alamo." Anyone painting a picture of the Alamo myth in all its manifestations would require an extremely large canvass upon which to work. As noted by

Stephen L. Hardin, entire books have been written on the myth and memory of the Alamo and its impact on shaping Texas identities. The following essay takes a less sweeping and more finely focused view of the Alamo myth by examining some of the smaller, component fallacies that have been perpetuated regarding historical events related to the Alamo story. Some of these fallacies, slow to be corrected and almost impossible to expunge from public memory, have traditionally composed the building blocks of the larger, all-encompassing, and broad-ideological role the Alamo has played in defining both the Texas and the American identity. Professor Hardin's purpose is not to smite those who over time have been untruthful in fashioning Alamo narratives, but to highlight the sometimes imperceptible dividing line between truth and fallacy in the fashioning of myth and memory. After all, great narratives are composed of smaller tales, each told as a meaningful component of the complete myth. Does it matter some of these regarding the Alamo are fallacies? Probably not because the realistic possibility of relegating them to the storehouse of history has long passed. It is, however, essential that historical fact be separated from fallacy. That is the purpose of the following essay.

There is a rich academic literature touching on the myth and memory of the Alamo, including works by authors such as Holly Benchley Brear, Richard R. Flores, James Crisp, and others. These studies analyze the role the Alamo has played in determining the American character since the fateful battle of 1836. In particular, Brear finds the story of the Alamo to be "the creation myth" for Texas.[1] In that regard, it is almost impossible to overstate the impact that the Alamo has had on determining identities in Texas and across the nation as a whole. Flores has noted: "The Alamo, as a major feature of cultural memory, references not only aspects of 1836 but the social and historical moment of its remembering as well."[2] Myth has so enshrouded every aspect of the Alamo story that it becomes difficult— not impossible, but difficult—to separate the fanciful from the factual. The essay that follows examines the Alamo below the level of its all-encompassing cultural influence across time as a conceptual and large-scale myth, concentrating on the fallacies embodied in component parts of the Alamo story, the latter likely caused by a desire to extol the doomed defenders beyond the point that evidence merited. For that reason, some parts of the Alamo narrative fall into the category of fallacy. Yet, newer myths also evolved, often produced by politically correct trends that sought to undermine treasured traditions, and changing the meaning of the battle. Like older myths, documentation often failed to support them.[3]

It is useful to define terms. When discussing the role of myth in Texas history, contentious question-and-answer sessions invariably ensue. Predictably, a fuming member of the audience asks a question like this one: "Tell me, Dr. Hardin, when you talk about the Alamo myth, are you claiming that those brave men didn't actually die there, or that it's just a fairy story someone made up?" That is one definition of "myth"—"an unfounded or false notion"—but *not* the one at play today. No, the operating definition is, "a usually traditional story of ostensibly historical events that serves to unfold part of the world view of a people or explain a practice, belief, or natural phenomenon." The battle of the Alamo is a perfect example of this second definition.

When Texans shouted "Remember the Alamo," were they urging people to recall a catastrophic defeat? Was it an appeal for contemplation and caution, so Texans never again suffered such a loss? No, of course not. What began as a cry for vengeance became one of pride and exultation. Outsiders, those who fail to understand Texas culture and deny Texas exceptionalism, find it curious that natives celebrate a crushing slaughter. They fail to understand that the defenders' last stand transcended mere history, becoming both symbol and icon. It represented to Texans and many Americans "a people fighting against tyranny and arbitrary rule and for personal liberty and the rule of law." Or, to state it more succinctly, Texans and Americans constructed a myth that became universally recognized and extolled as emblematic of Texan identity.[4]

Hardly had the smoke cleared over the old mission before Texians began to describe the episode in mythic terms. Less than three weeks after the battle, a Texas newspaperman employed extravagant language to pay homage to the fallen defenders:

> Spirits of the mighty, though fallen! Honors and rest are with ye: the spark of immortality which animated your forms, shall brighten into a flame, and Texas, the whole world, shall hail ye like the demi-gods of old, as founders of new actions and as patterns of imitation![5]

Notwithstanding all that President Andrew Jackson had on his plate —issues with Indian removal, the Second Seminole War, the upcoming presidential election—he felt himself moved to reply to the nine-year-old Jackson Donelson. He was the son of Andrew and Emily Donelson, the president's closest living relatives. From his boarding school, young Jackson had written his "Uncle" Andrew mourning the fall of the Alamo. On April 22, 1836 (the day following the Texian victory at San Jacinto), the "Old Hero" responded to the boy:

> Your sympathies expressed on hearing of the death of those brave men who fell in defense of the Alamo displays a proper feeling of patriotism and sympathy for the gallant defenders of the rights of freemen, which I trust will grow with your growth . . . and find you always a strong votary in the cause of freedom.

Old Hickory voiced the feelings of most Americans. Although Texas had not yet joined the American union, "those brave men" had died in defense of American values and traditions—"in the cause of freedom."[6]

Four years later, Texians had codified this rhetoric. Upon visiting San Antonio, Texas, booster A. B. Lawrence waxed elegiac:

> Will not in future days Bexar be classic ground? Is it not by victory and the blood of heroes, consecrated to liberty, and sacred to the fame of patriots who there repose upon the very ground they defended with their last breath and last drop of generous blood? Will Texians ever forget them? Or cease to prize the boon for which these patriots bled? Forbid it honor, virtue, patriotism. Let

every Texian bosom be the monument sacred to their fame, and
every Texian freeman be emulous of their virtues. [7]

Thus, almost immediately the battle lost its factual content, ceased
to be a calamitous military defeat, becoming instead a paradigm of
"honor, virtue, and patriotism." The myth made acceptable that which
was inherently intolerable. It consoled Texans, assuring them that the
sacrifice of Travis and his men had not been in vain.

No surprise then that Texans began to embellish the narrative. No
praise of the fallen defenders could be too effusive; no estimations of
slain *soldados* at the foot of Jim Bowie's sick bed could be too high;
no presumptions of Mexican malice could be too excessive. In 1860
Reuben Marmaduke Potter, an American citizen living in Matamoros
during the Texas Revolution, wrote the first historical account of the
fall of the Alamo, depicting the siege as "a great heroic epic." Artists
such as Henry A. McArdle and Robert Jenkins Onderdonk elevated the
Alamo defenders to mythic status, painting "noble Anglos" fighting
"treacherous Mexicans," on their canvasses. By the end of the nineteenth
century the parable also became the central scene of a Lone Star morality
play, a melodrama in which slain champions served as primordial types.
Consider, for example, this paradigm of purple prose contained within
a popular textbook:

> The Mexicans, bleeding, wounded, and shattered, hesitated to
> renew the attack, but the stern command of Santa Anna and the
> flashing sabers of the cavalry, forced them on. By tens, by hundreds,
> they swarmed up the ladders. Down fell the first, down, down
> went the second, crushing all beneath them, while the Texans
> stood like gods waiting to let others feel their mighty strength.[8]

Such perceptions survived the romantic nineteenth century and thrived
even into the mid-twentieth century. In 1960, actor and director John
Wayne described his film *The Alamo* as "the story of 185 men joined
together in an immortal pact to give their lives that the spark of freedom
might blaze into a roaring flame. It is the story of how they died to the last

man, putting up an unbelievably gallant fight against an overwhelming enemy; and of the priceless legacy they left us."[9]

Figure 1. John Wayne directing *The Alamo* (1960)

Courtesy of Bettman/Corbis

Wayne unintentionally identified the problem with the mythic Alamo. The traditional story was, indeed, "*unbelievably*" gallant. Nevertheless, those of a certain age who grew up with the Walt Disney version—who wore coonskin caps and sang "Da-vy, Davy Crockett," until it drove parents to distraction—are frequently aggrieved when some historian tells them that their childhood hero may not have gone down swinging ol' Betsy *a la* Fess Parker. They are chagrined when their children and grandchildren, who did not grow up with Fess Parker and John Wayne, fail to share their enthusiasm for the tale. The bombast and lack of credibility that accompanies most of the mythic accounts tends to alienate younger people who, quite rightly, demand to examine the evidence. [10]

One of the newer fallacies suggests that despite "the desperate bravery of the garrison at the Alamo," Bowie and Travis were foolish to attempt to hold a post of no military significance. The battle should never have been fought and "their contribution to the strategy of the Texas Revolution was nil or negative." Those who hold this view tend to examine the battle only in tactical terms. To fathom the encounter fully one must appreciate its strategic context.[11]

Any general worthy of his epaulettes could have read a map. In 1836, two major roads led into Texas from the Mexican interior. The first was the Atascosito Road, which stretched from Matamoros on the Rio Grande northward through San Patricio, Goliad, Victoria, and finally into the heart of Austin's colony. The second was the Old San Antonio Road, a *camino real* that crossed the Rio Grande and wound northeastward through San Antonio de Béxar, Bastrop, Nacogdoches, and San Augustine before crossing the Sabine River into Louisiana.

Yet what was manifest to Mexican General Antonio López de Santa Anna was equally clear to Texian leaders, who took steps to block these vital transportation arteries. Two forts barred these approaches into Texas and each functioned as a frontier picket post, ready to alert the Anglo settlements of an enemy advance: Presidio La Bahía at Goliad and the Alamo at San Antonio. James Clinton Neill took charge of the Béxar garrison. Some ninety miles to the southeast James Walker Fannin, Jr. subsequently commanded at Goliad. Both Neill and Fannin determined to stall the centralists on the frontier. Still, they labored under no delusions. Without speedy reinforcements, neither the Alamo nor Presidio La Bahía could long stand.

The self-styled "Napoleon of the West" sought to emulate the French emperor. Santa Anna planned to strike swiftly, hurl his columns along parallel roads, and achieve strategic surprise. Ignorant of his intentions, the rebels dispersed their meager forces against the threat of multiple

Mexican advances. Santa Anna, keeping the Texians guessing, would concentrate his battalions to deliver a hammer blow where the enemy was weakest.

The generalissimo anticipated ensnaring the rebels in a strategic pincer movement. On February 16, he crossed the Rio Grande near modern-day Eagle Pass with the bulk of his army and rumbled toward San Antonio. The following day, General José Urrea forded more than three hundred miles downriver at Matamoros with about five hundred infantry and cavalry. Barreling up the Atascosito Road, his mission was to retake Goliad.[12]

San Antonio de Béxar was the linchpin of Santa Anna's stratagem. "Béxar was held by the enemy," he explained, "and it was necessary to open the door to our future operations by taking it." Once he had reduced the Alamo, the town could serve as a supply depot, a stopover for weary *soldados*, and a springboard against rebel enclaves further east. Some critics have argued that once he had surrounded the Alamo, he could have simply monitored the garrison and continued his campaign. Yet what sort of commander would allow an enemy garrison to remain just outside his base of operation and sit astride his central line of communication? [13]

His officers, however, whispered that other issues might have influenced Santa Anna's plans. Some observed that Goliad, which controlled the entire Texas coastline, was actually of more strategic importance than Béxar. Even so, Béxar was the *political* hub of Tejas, a consideration of enormous symbolic importance.

Although Travis had initially objected to his posting, once there he began calling Béxar the "key of Texas." Curiously, Santa Anna and Travis selected similar metaphors to describe the town's strategic importance. Like Neill and Bowie, Travis came to realize that the best way to protect Texian families was to stop the enemy at San Antonio. One may argue the tactics of the battle, but to assert that San Antonio de Béxar was of no strategic significance is absurd.[14]

Another component fallacy that has perpetuated the Texas myth is that Travis and Bowie disobeyed Houston's orders to abandon the Alamo and blow it up. On January 17, 1836, General Sam Houston wrote Governor Henry Smith that he had ordered Colonel James Bowie and a company of volunteers to San Antonio. Traditional misunderstanding of the letter's contents created one of the most persistent canards of the Alamo story.[15]

For the careful reader, Houston's own words clarify the issue: "I have ordered the fortifications of the town of Béxar to be demolished, and, *if you think well of it*, I will remove all the cannon and other munitions of war to Gonzales and Copano, blow up the Alamo and abandon the place, as it will be impossible to keep up the Station with volunteers. [T]he sooner I can be *authorized* the better it will be for the country" [Emphasis added].[16]

Houston clearly wanted to raze the Alamo and withdraw, but it is likewise obvious that he was asking Smith's consent to do so. Smith and the council could concur upon few issues, but on this occasion both the governor and the council agreed they must maintain the Alamo and the San Antonio River line.

On January 19, Bowie rode into the Alamo. What he saw impressed him. The old mission had begun to look like a real fort. Neill's arguments and leadership electrified Bowie. He declared that he and Neill had resolved to "die in these ditches" before they would surrender so valuable a post. Bowie's letter confirmed the governor's view of the defensibility of the Alamo. Smith and the council had already concluded that Texian forces must hold Béxar, and Bowie's judgment only strengthened this determination. Rejecting Houston's plan, Smith prepared to funnel reinforcements and provisions to the Alamo.[17]

Above all others, one document refutes the often-repeated assertion that Bowie and Travis disobeyed their orders to "abandon and then blow up the Alamo." On January 21, responding to Houston's advice to Governor Smith in the January 17 dispatch, members of the council directed that an "express be sent immediately to Bejar, with orders from

the acting Governor [James W. Robinson] countermanding the orders of
Genl. Houston, and that the Commandant be required to put the place
in the best possible state for defense, with assurances that every possible
effort is making to strengthen, supply and provision the Garrison, and in
no case to abandon or surrender the place unless in the last extremity."
Even if Houston had sent orders to abandon the post—and, once again,
no evidence exist that he actually did—this directive from the legally
constituted civilian government rendered them null and void.[18]

Contrary to the facts, Houston did not dispatch "direct orders" to
abandon the Alamo, only to have Neill and Bowie ignore them. In brief,
Houston had asked for permission to evacuate the post. The politicians
considered his request; the answer was an unequivocal "No." Even after
the Texian government fell apart, both Governor Smith and the council
directed Neill to stand his ground. While Houston thought it prudent,
there was never an actual directive for Neill and Bowie—and later, Travis
—to evacuate the fort. To the contrary, the instruction they *did* receive
demanded that they defend it to the "last extremity."[19]

Many assume that the Alamo defenders knew from the beginning that
they were doomed. As John Wayne wrote, "[Alamo defenders] joined
together in an immortal pact to give their lives that the spark of freedom
might blaze into a roaring flame." But Travis did not enter the fort to
enjoy a glorious death, but to hold it until reinforcements arrived. He
made that clear in his famous letter of February 24: "Then, I call on you
in the name of Liberty, of patriotism & everything dear to the American
character, to come to our aid, with all dispatch." He was not, as many
have asserted, delusional.[20]

As the siege continued and none of the promised aid appeared, Travis
became anxious, then angry. On March 3 he wrote to the delegates of the
Independence Convention then assembled in the Town of Washington:

> Col. Fannin is said to be on the march to this place with reinforce-
> ments. But I fear it is not true, as I have repeatedly sent to him for
> aid without receiving any. . . . I look to the colonies alone for aid;

unless it arrives soon, I shall have to fight the enemy on his own terms. I will, however, do the best I can under the circumstances.[21]

Later the same day, Travis revealed even more bitterness in a letter to his friend Jesse Grimes: "I am determined to perish in the defense of this place, and my bones shall reproach my country for her neglect."[22]

This prompts an obvious question: Why did Texian leaders ignore Travis's repeated calls for assistance? Texans dislike admitting it, but the provisional government that should have—and could have—organized relief efforts had fallen apart because of its bickering, dissension, and discord. On March 1, when Texian delegates finally assembled in the town of Washington to organize a new government, it was too late for the men besieged inside the Alamo. They were as much victims of political malfeasance as of enemy bayonets. Having received "assurances that every possible effort is making to strengthen, supply and provision the Garrison," Travis found it difficult to accept that his superiors had placed him and his men in harm's way only to forsake them through sheer ineptness and indifference. Even so, it happened.[23]

Travis was not, as some have insisted, a zealot with a death wish. The men of the Alamo were not part of an obsessive death cult, nor were they bent on ritual suicide. Such fanaticism was not part of their cultural tradition. The defenders were citizen soldiers. They may have been willing to die for their country, but that was never their aspiration. They fervently prayed that such a sacrifice would prove unnecessary.

It never occurred to them to join "in an immortal pact to give their lives." That knowledge makes their sacrifice *more*, not less, heroic. When their political leaders neglected them, Travis and his garrison did as they promised. They fought the enemy on "his own terms" and did the best they could "under the circumstances." What more could anyone possibly ask of them? [24]

One of the most cherished aspects of the Alamo myth, Travis drawing his sword and placing a line in the sand, is also one of the most incredible.

Here is the timeline: French immigrant Louis "Moses" Rose left the Alamo on or about March 3. After many hardships, he made his way to East Texas and took refuge in the home of Abraham and Mary Ann Zuber, where he related his story. The Zubers had a son, William Physick, who was fifteen years of age in 1836, but away from home serving in the Texian army. Over the years he learned the tale of the mysterious visitor from his parents. Not until 1872, thirty-five years after an event he did not witness, did he publish his account of Rose's escape in the *Texas Almanac* wherein he related the story of Travis's line.

Zuber's account was highly detailed. Even at the time, many wondered how he could have known the exact wording of Travis's speech. On September 14, 1877, Zuber wrote to the Adjutant General of the State of Texas responding to his critics. In this letter Zuber confessed to fabricating the speech, but claimed he had based it on information Rose had provided his parents, which over the years they had passed along to him. He further admitted that he had concocted one paragraph out of whole cloth: "I found a deficiency in the material of the speech, which from my knowledge of the man, I thought I could supply. I accordingly threw in one paragraph which I firmly believe to be characteristic of Travis, and without which the speech would have been incomplete."[25]

As historian Walter Lord observed, "Zuber never said what the passage was, but the omission itself is significant. The line [in the sand] was the crux of the whole speech—the center of the controversy. If his concoction ('without which the speech would have been incomplete') was not the line, it seems he would have said so, for this was the one thing everyone wanted to know." The dramatic announcement of their inevitable doom appeared to have been an element that he "threw in" as "characteristic of Travis."[26]

It is true that survivors Susanna Dickinson Hanning and Enrique Esparza also referenced the line in the sand tale, but not until long after Zuber had published his article and the public had embraced it. Mrs. Hanning botched the story completely. As she told it, Travis invited those who wished to *leave* to cross the line. Even more damning, she has this pivotal event take place on the first day of the siege. Despite all the inconsistencies, many could not let the fable go. As one crotchety Texan argued: "Is there any proof that Travis didn't draw the line? If not let us believe it, even though it possibly may be legendary and based on an offer that any who wanted to leave could do so." [27]

That is not the way history works—at least not professional, academic history. History is not something that *might* have happened or we *wish* had happened. History is what documents prove *did* happen. By that standard the tale of Travis drawing a line in the sand does not even come close.

Nowadays most Alamo scholars reject the legend. In *Texian Iliad*, the current author gently dismissed it, stating, "According to legend, [Travis] drew a line in the dust with his saber, inviting all those who were resolved to stay and die with him to cross. Evidence does not support the tale, but apparently Travis did gather the men for a conference." In 1998, William C. Davis was far more emphatic in his rigorously researched *Three Roads to the Alamo*. "Nothing in this story stands up to scrutiny," he insisted. "So far as this present work is concerned, the event simply did not happen, or if it did, then something much more reliable than an admittedly fictionalized secondhand account written thirty-five years after the fact is necessary to establish it beyond question." Nevertheless, the use of a line in the sand, according to Randy Roberts and James S. Olson, was "hardly novel." Southerners often utilized the method for voting and Travis was certainly drawn to dramatic flourishes. Recently the line myth received a patron when James Donovan, author of *The Blood of Heroes*, professed to believe it had actually occurred. Even so, in his afterward he admitted that he had based his faith upon "secondhand and third hand, or circumstantial" evidence. This is hardly a ringing endorsement. Indeed, those are the same complaints professional historians have had with the line parable since Zuber first introduced it in 1872. [28]

Another fallacy easy to refute is that the Texians' valiant defense of the Alamo bought Sam Houston "precious time" to gather his army and defeat Santa Anna. Houston biographers carefully documented the general's movements and, as Walter Lord observed with eloquent understatement, "Sam Houston . . . was strangely inactive during most of the siege." On February 23, the day the Alamo siege began, Houston was not even with the army. He was in East Texas negotiating with the Cherokees as an emissary of the deposed Governor Smith. On February 29 he arrived in the Town of Washington where he served as a delegate at the Independence Convention. On March 4 the delegates re-confirmed him as commander of the Texian army. On March 6 Houston promised "if mortal power could avail," he would personally lead a detachment to "relieve the brave men in the Alamo." Ironically, the Alamo had already fallen earlier that same morning. On March 11, Houston finally joined the army at Gonzales. Obviously, the stand of Travis and his men had not bought Houston the "precious time" he required to raise and train the Texian army.[29]

Even so, the thirteen-day siege *did* delay Santa Anna's advance through Texas. Without the Alamo siege, he would have likely routed the members of the Independence Convention before they finished writing a constitution for the Republic of Texas. The siege produced political dividends, but Houston did not begin his military duties until after the Alamo had fallen.[30]

The breached wall fallacy also remains current in the Alamo story. "[An artillery] battery finally brought about what Santa Anna had been trying to accomplish for eleven days. A sizable breach was battered in the east end of the plaza's north wall." This passage appears in John Myers's 1948 book *The Alamo*. Published in 1955, Frederic Ray's *The Story of the Alamo: An Illustrated history of the Siege and Fall of the Alamo* affirmed: "By March 5th, Mexican cannon had breached the north wall." Moreover, the "breach" story also appeared in more highbrow treatments including Lon Tinkle's bestseller *13 Days to Glory: The Siege of the Alamo*, published in 1958. Tinkle even included an illustration of the compound showing the "breach" in the north wall. The exception was Walter Lord's *A Time to Stand*. He made no mention of a breach and his illustration of the compound depicted the north wall standing intact.[31] Hollywood reinforced the breach-in-the-wall tale. Both 1955's *The Last Command* and 1960's *The Alamo* included scenes that showed the wall crumbling during the March 6 assault and Mexican troops flooding through. Throughout the 1950s and 1960s, most Texans accepted the breach in the wall as gospel.[32]

Curiously, contemporary accounts failed to reference any breach. As late as March 3 Travis could boast, "I have fortified this place, so that the walls are generally proof against cannon balls; and I shall strengthen the walls by throwing up dirt." Eyewitness Mexican reports recount the difficulty they had climbing *over* the north wall but none recalled a yawning hole in it—a detail they surely would have mentioned.[33]

How did the "breach-in-the-wall" become entrenched in the public imagination? Tinkle's *13 Day to Glory* provides a clue. In a note to the bird's-eye-view of the compound, Tinkle revealed that it was "based on sketches by Lt. J. Edmund Blake in 1845 and Lt. Edward Everett in 1846 and on the map drawn by Capt. R. M. Potter after his visit to the Alamo in 1841." Of course, all of those officers sketched the Alamo as it appeared *after* the battle; none knew what it looked like during the 1836 siege.[34]

They were likely unaware that following the battlefield disaster at San Jacinto, General Vicente Filisola had ordered General Juan José Andrade to demolish the Alamo and evacuate Béxar. After the March 6 assault, Andrade and his men had remained in San Antonio with instructions to renovate the fort for a future Mexican garrison. Now with the Mexican army in full retreat, Filisola ordered Andrade to dismantle the compound so that it would never again provide safe haven for the enemy. On May 22 Dr. Joseph Barnard, a captive American physician, noted, "They [Andrade's troops] are now busy as bees *tearing down walls*, &c." In the years following 1836, many tourists visited the Alamo and commented on its ruined condition. Blake, Everett, and Potter no doubt saw a "breach" and assumed Santa Anna's cannon had created it. Yet it is almost certain that Andrade's picks and sledgehammers produced the "sizeable breach" in the north wall.[35]

The three waves of Mexican attack on that fateful morning also falls into the category of fallacy. Many traditional accounts of the battle assert that on March 6, Mexican assault troops required three separate attacks to overwhelm the Alamo's defenses. The May 25, 1836, edition of the Frankfort, Kentucky, *Commonwealth* ran a highly detailed recounting of the final assault with "some particulars" that Susanna Dickinson supplied. "The enemy three times applied their scaling ladders to the wall; twice they were beaten back," the article recounted. "But numbers and discipline prevailed over valor and desperation. On the third attempt they succeeded, and then came over '*like sheep*.'" Anna J. H. Pennybacker's *A New History of Texas for Schools* transferred this version to generations of Texas schoolchildren. Then the movies took up the tale, most notably in 1955's *Davy Crockett, King of the Wild Frontier*. By 1960, when singer-songwriter Marty Robbins released his "Ballad of the Alamo," with lyrics that "twice he charged, then blew recall. On the fatal third time, Santa Anna breached the wall and he killed them one and all," the fable was well ensconced in the popular imagination.[36]

The Widow Dickinson was responsible for this old canard. In 1876, during her interview with the Adjutant General's Office, she recalled:

> On the morning of 6th Mch. about daylight enemy threw up signal rocket & advanced & were repulsed. They rallied & made 2nd assault with scaling ladders, first thrown up on E. side of Fort. Terrible fight ensued. Witness retired into a room of the old church & saw no part of the fight—Though she could distinctly hear it.[37]

Later, in an 1881 interview for the San Antonio *Daily Express*, the number of attacks had changed:

Three times [the Mexican assault troops] were repulsed, and the two cannon, planted high upon the ramparts, carried dismay with their belches of fire and lead.[38]

All of Mrs. Dickinson's accounts offer complications. In the first place, she was illiterate. Consequently, all of her accounts take the form of answers to questions posed to her by others. Her testimony to the Adjutant General's Office is hastily scribbled notes by an unknown party. Reporters heavily edited nearly all her interviews. Clearly, neither of these methods was conducive to an accurate recollection of an historical event. Additionally, the lengthy period between the incident and her recounting of it was also cause for concern. Her testimony to the Adjutant General's Office came forty years after the event; her *Daily Express* interview was an additional five years later. She recalled two attacks in 1876, yet in 1881, she claimed that the defenders repulsed the Mexican assault troops "three times." Did that mean that their *fourth* attack was successful?

Shielded in the church sacristy along with the other non-combatants, Mrs. Dickinson was in the worst possible location to view the battle. Indeed, the unnamed reporter in the 1881 *Daily Express* article admitted as much. "[Mrs. Hanning] says she can give but a little of the struggle, as she was in a little dark room in the rear of the building."[39]

This is a quandary with her recollections; what she asserts in one, she contradicts in another. The most incriminatory feature of Mrs. Dickinson's multiple-attack story is that none of the other witnesses corroborates it. Joe, Travis's body servant, was standing by his master on the north wall and was certainly in a better position to see the assault than Mrs. Dickinson. Yet he never mentioned separate Mexican attacks. Nor did any of the Mexican participants—not Juan Almonte, not Ramón Martínez Caro, not Vincenté Filisola, not José Enrique de la Peña, not José Juan Sanchez-Navarro, and not Antonio López de Santa Anna.[40]

So far removed from the event, it is impossible to reconstruct what Mrs. Dickinson believed she might have seen, much less what she might have heard. Most likely the clamor of four Mexican assault columns hitting the walls at different times reached her startled ears and she interpreted them as separate attacks. Nevertheless, it is clear that her multiple repulse fable does not survive scrutiny.

Many still cling to the fiction that Alamo defenders died fighting to the last man. This fallacy demands too much of human nature. When the tide of battle turns against them, nearly all soldiers succumb to the instinct of self-preservation. The defenders of the Alamo were no exception.

Figure 2. Davy Crockett

Courtesy Briscoe Center for American History, University of Texas at Austin

Credible Mexican sources reveal that some of the defenders attempted to surrender. José Enrique de la Peña recalled that during the struggle for the long barracks, a few defenders "poked the points of their bayonets through a hole with a white cloth, the symbol of ceasefire, and some even used their socks." When the Mexican assault troops poured over the north and west walls, as many as eighty defenders sought to escape by bounding through the gun emplacements at the northeast corner of the cattle pen, over the wall of the horse corral, and, finally, over the south wall palisade and through the abatis. Now outside the fort, they ran for cover, but lancers commanded by General Joaquín Ramírez y Sesma intercepted them. In his post-battle report, he testified to the escapees' "desperate resistance" and lauded the Texians for selling "their lives at a very high price," but all but one died under the lethal lances. One escapee burrowed deep into the heavy brush and refused all demands to come out. Finally, the cavalrymen shot him where he crouched.[41]

Not just Peña, but several eyewitness Mexican accounts, confirm that *soldados* took six or seven defenders captive. General Manuel Fernández Castrillón interceded with Santa Anna to spare their lives but, turning on his heel, His Excellency ordered their immediate deaths. Proper soldiers, those who had actually fought in the battle, balked at obeying such a barbarous order. Yet members of the generalissimo's personal staff, those who had not taken an active part in the assault, drew their swords and hacked the helpless prisoners to pieces. An overwhelming body of evidence asserts that Congressman David Crockett was among these unfortunate defenders murdered at Santa Anna's direct command.[42]

No, the defenders did not fight to the last man. Rather, Santa Anna ordered his staff lackeys to kill them to the last man and therein rests a delicious irony. Had Santa Anna been willing to take prisoners he would have robbed the battle of its moral power; Americans would remember the Alamo only as a terrible debacle; Hollywood would have had no interest in making movies about a military disaster; and few today would express any curiosity in a long forgotten defeat. Whatever mythic mojo the battle contains is because it was a *last stand*. And who was responsible for making sure it was one? Santa Anna.

In the public imagination the Alamo church has always looked the same. This too is a fallacy that makes for a mythic icon. In popular culture venues illustrators have depicted the church consistently. Nearly all of these representations share two common traits: at least some variation of the arched gable—what most folks call the Alamo "hump"—and the inclusion of the upper windows. Yet these features did not appear until the US Army took possession of the building between 1850 and 1852. The arched gable was the creation of Bavarian-born architect John Fries and local stonemason David Russi.[43] The army added a second floor inside the building and cut a pair of windows to provide sunlight. Oddly, after all the care Fries and Russi lavished on the gable, army engineers did not attempt to mirror the Spanish style of the lower windows. Consequently, the army-installed upper windows assumed a utilitarian, even jerry-rigged, appearance. Some found the alterations to the façade repugnant. Lieutenant Edward Everett, who had earlier sketched the church in ruins, protested: "I regret to see . . . that tasteless hands have evened off the rough walls, as they were left after the siege, surmounting them with a ridiculous scroll, giving the building the appearance of the headboard of a bedstead." [44]

Remarkably, it was not until John Lee Hancock's 2004 film, *The Alamo*, that Hollywood depicted the church without upper windows and the "ridiculous scroll." Production designer Michael Corenblith carefully researched all the post-battle sketches and the only existing daguerreotype before the army "Taco-Belled" it to reproduce an accurate facsimile of the 1836 original. It was an astonishing achievement; he re-created the church—down to the size and shape of the stones in the facade—with absolute fidelity. Nevertheless, Corenblith exasperated many purists when he moved his church forward some eighty feet to "make the icon accessible throughout the plaza, so that the audience understands where they are at all times."[45]

Even so, recent research suggests that even Corenblith got it wrong. Alamo scholar and illustrator Gary Zaboly asserted that reliance on the post-1836 sketches and the daguerreotype has led historians astray. He argued that Colonel José Juan Sánchez-Navarro's sketch—the only one drawn during the 1836 siege—indicated a completely different roofline from the post-battle illustrations. Zaboly maintained that the large "gouges" that are prevalent in the post-1836 sketches, the 1849 daguerreotype, and consequently the set of the 2004 film were—like the so-called "breach" in the north wall—the result of General Andrade's after-battle demolition. During the battle the western-facing façade of the church was likely more rectangular, with a straight, unbroken, roofline. Zaboly even declared that the roofline was likely crenelated. Debate concerning the 1836 appearance of the church will continue, but it is certain that the upper windows and the iconic "hump," so frequently represented in popular culture, were absent.[46]

It is imprudent to attribute an event as complex as the Texas War for Independence to a single cause, yet increasingly many do. Consider, for example, the following observation: "In retrospect, rather than a fight for liberty, the 1835 Anglo-led revolution was a poorly conceived southern land grab that nearly failed." No mention of land speculation, no mention of the Constitution of 1824, no mention of the dissolution of Mexican federalism, no mention of ethnocentrism, no mention of efforts to install a centralist regime in Texas, no mention of Santa Anna's vow to rid Texas of all "perfidious foreigners,"—no, according to this persistent cant the Texas Revolution was all about slavery. Period.[47]

Documents from the period, however, refute this fallacy. For example the "Declaration of the People of Texas," issued on November 7, 1835:

> Whereas, General Antonio Lopez de Santa Ana, and other military chieftains, have, by force of arms, overthrown the Federal Institutions of Mexico, and dissolved the social compact which existed between Texas and the other members of the Mexican

Confederacy; the good People of Texas, availing themselves of their natural right. SOLEMNLY DECLARE . . .

The following eight articles delineated their intentions and principles—but never mention slavery.[48]

The Alamo garrison was extremely cosmopolitan. It strains credulity to claim that James Brown of Pennsylvania, or John Flanders of Massachusetts, or John Hubbard Forsyth of New York, or Gregorio Esparza of Texas and especially Daniel Bourne from England, Lewis Johnson from Wales, Henry Courtman from Germany, and Charles Zanco from Denmark would have risked their lives for a "southern land grab." Further, Travis's open letter at the Alamo to "the People of Texas & all Americans in the world" contained no hint of slavery. He explained the Texan position and then challenged his countrymen to come to his aid "in the name of Liberty, of Patriotism, & every thing dear to the American character."[49]

Slavery was part of the toxic stew that led to war—but not the principal ingredient. Randolph B. Campbell, who literally wrote the book on Texas slavery, should have the last word: "The immediate cause of the conflict was the political instability of Mexico and the implications of Santa Anna's centralist regime for Texas. Mexico forced the issue in 1835, not over slavery, but over customs duties and the general defiant attitude of Anglo-Americans in Texas."[50]

Myth is an unalienable part of the Alamo story. Even if it were possible, efforts to purge the mythic content would prove unwise. As with Washington and the cherry tree, Travis and the line in the sand is a homily that conveys a vital lesson. It is part of a shared national experience and constitutes a valuable cultural touchstone in defining both the Texas and American identity. It will certainly do children no harm to hear it and it may even do them some good. Ponder the wisdom of C. S. Lewis: "Since it is so likely that children will meet cruel enemies, let them at least have heard of brave knights and heroic courage. Otherwise you are making their destiny not brighter but darker."[51]

Understand and appreciate the myths; understand and appreciate the historical reality. But graze them in different pastures. Hazards arise for both individuals and societies—not when they treasure national myths —but when they begin to *mistake* those myths and their component fallacies for history.

Myth reflects history; it does not verify it. The warped image it provides is that of fun house mirrors, one that reveals more about the modes and motives of those who constructed, and continue to embrace, the myths. Nevertheless, when one strips away the layers of legend, fabrication, and fallacy, what is left is still grandly heroic. Further, by analyzing our mythologies and our sacred narratives, we can recognize how they shape social hierarchies and Texas identities, thereby allowing others to claim their past. Chauvinism may have steered A. B. Lawrence's fervent pen, but he was not wrong. The Alamo story is remarkably complex but, at its core, it remains one of "honor, virtue, and patriotism."

SELECTED BIBLIOGRAPHY

Brear, Holly Beachley. *Inherit the Alamo: Myth and Ritual in an American Shrine.* Austin: University of Texas Press, 1995.

Crisp, James. *Sleuthing the Alamo: Davy Crockett's Last Stand and Other Mysteries of the Texas Revolution.* NewYork: Oxford University Press, 2005.

Donovan, James. *Blood of Heroes: The 13-Day Struggle for the Alamo—and the Sacrifice That Forged a Nation.* New York: Little, Brown and Company, 2012.

Flores, Richard R. *Remembering the Alamo: Memory, Modernity, and Master Symbol.* Austin: University of Texas Press, 2002.

Hansen, Todd, ed. *The Alamo Reader: A Study in History.* Mechanicsburg, PA: Stackpole Books, 2003.

Hardin, Stephen L. *Texian Iliad: A Military History of the Texas Revolution.* Austin: University of Texas Press, 1994.

Long, Jeff. *Duel of Eagles: The Mexican and U.S. Fight for the Alamo.* New York: William Morrow and Company, Inc., 1990.

Lord, Walter. *A Time to Stand.* New York: Harper & Brothers, 1961.

Roberts, Randy, and James S. Olson. *A Line in the Sand: The Alamo in Blood and Memory.* New York: The Free Press. 2001.

Tinkle, Lon. *13 Days to Glory: The Siege of the Alamo.* New York: McGraw-Hill Book Company, Inc., 1958; reprint, College Station: Texas A&M University Press, 1985.

Winder, Richard Bruce. *Sacrificed at the Alamo: Tragedy and Triumph in the Texas Revolution.* Abilene: State House Press, 2004.

Zaboly, Gary S. *An Altar for Their Sons: The Alamo and the Texas Revolution in Contemporary Newspaper Accounts.* Buffalo Gap, TX: State House Press, 2011.

NOTES

1. Holly Beachley Brear, *Inherit the Alamo: Myth and Ritual in an American Shrine* (Austin: University of Texas Press, 1995), 151. For additional academic studies dealing with the Alamo and its place in fashioning a touchstone for Texas identity see: Richard R. Flores *Remembering the Alamo: Memory, Modernity, and Master Symbol* (Austin: University of Texas Press, 2002); James Crisp, *Sleuthing the Alamo: Davy Crockett's Last Stand and Other Mysteries of the Texas Revolution* (New York: Oxford University Press, 2005).

2. Flores, *Remembering the Alamo*, p. xvi. Flores believes that much of the myth and memory associated with the Alamo rests with glorying Anglo-American identity over that of Mexican, to the point that it codifies the "social relations circulating at the beginning of the twentieth century."

3. The late Walter Lord was the first to approach the mythic Alamo in a scholarly, or even-handed manner. In his classic *A Time to Stand*, he included an addendum to his narrative titled "Riddles of the Alamo." In this section he lassoed many of the sacred Texas cows with enormous skill, sensitivity, and audacity. Long before Carmen Perry and Dan Kilgore published their work, Mr. Lord dared suggest that David Crockett might have died *after* the battle and that William Barret Travis probably did *not* draw the legendary line in the sand. More than half a century later, Lord's book remains indispensable. Walter Lord, *A Time to Stand* (New York: Harper & Brothers, 1961), 198-212. Seven years later, Lord contributed an article to an anthology in which he expanded upon "Riddles of the Alamo." Students of the mythic Alamo ignore it at their peril. Walter Lord, "Myths and Realities of the Alamo," in Stephen B. Oates, ed., *The Republic of Texas* (Palo Alto, CA: American West Publishing Company and Texas State Historical Association, 1968), 18-25.

4. Randy Roberts and James S. Olson, *A Line in the Sand: The Alamo in Blood and* Memory (New York: The Free Press, 2001), 142, 181-182.

5. Telegraph and Texas Register (San Felipe de Austin, Tex.), Vol. 1, No. 21, Ed. 1, Thursday, March 24, 1836. The Portal to Texas History, http://texashistory.unt.edu/ark:/67531/metapth47891/m1/3/

6. Andrew Jackson to Jackson Donelson, April 22, 1836, quoted in Pauline Wilcox Burke, *Emily Donelson of Tennessee* (2 vols., Richmond, Virginia: Garrett and Massie, 1941), 2:97.

7. [A. B. Lawrence], *Texas in 1840, or The Emigrant's Guide to the New Republic; Being the Result of Observation, Enquiry and Travel in That Beautiful Country, by an Emigrant, Late of the United States, With an Introduction by the Rev. A. B. Lawrence, of New Orleans* (New York: William W. Allen, 1840; reprint, Austin: W. M. Morrison Books, 1987), 220.

8. Dan Kilgore and James Crisp, *How Did Davy Die? And Why Do We Care So Much?* (College Station: Texas A&M University Press, 2010), 84-92; Anna J. H. Pennybacker, *A New History of Texas for Schools, Also for General Reading and for Teachers Preparing Themselves for Examination* (Austin: Mrs. Percy V Pennybacker, 1900), 142.

9. John Wayne letter in Thomas J. Kane, ed., *The Alamo* (N.P.: Sovereign Publications, 1960), unnumbered pages. This is the movie souvenir book for John Wayne's epic film. Film studios sold these in theatre lobbies ("lobby book" was another common term for such publications) during the road show engagements of A-list feature films.

10. On December 15, 1954, Americans heard "The Ballad of Davy Crockett" for the first time when the television miniseries *Davy Crockett* aired as part of the "Disneyland" program. Disney composer George Bruns wrote the music; Thomas W. Blackburn crafted the lyrics. San Angelo, Texas, native Fess Parker won the plum role of Davy Crockett and also starred in four other episodes.

11. H. W. Brands, "The Alamo Should Never Have Happened," Texas Monthly online, http://www.texasmonthly.com/story-should-never-have-happened; Lay historian Jeff Long best represented this view. Jeff Long, *Duel of Eagles: The Mexican and U.S. Fight for the Alamo* (New York: William Morrow and Company, Inc., 1990), 218.

12. For an expanded discussion of the strategy of the Texas War for Independence see the author's *Texian Iliad: A Military History of the Texas Revolution* (Austin: University of Texas Press, 1994), passim.

13. Antonio López de Santa Anna, *Manifesto Relative to His Operations in the Texas Campaign and his Capture*, in Carlos E. Castañeda, ed., *The Mexican Side of the Texan Revolution* (Dallas: P. L. Turner Company, 1928; reprint, Austin: Graphic Ideas, 1970), 12-13.

14. William Barret Travis to Henry Smith, February 16, 1836, in John J. Jenkins, ed., *The Papers of the Texas Revolution, 1835-1836*, 10 vols. (Austin: Presidial Press, 1973), 4:368.

15. Marshal De Bruhl, *Sword of San Jacinto: A Life of Sam Houston* (New York: Random House, 1993), 186; Houston's biographers were especially egregious in promoting this unfounded tale. See, for example, Marquis

James, *The Raven: A Biography of Sam Houston* (Indianapolis: The Bobbs-Merrill Company, 1929), 227; John Hoyt Williams, *Sam Houston: A Biography of the Father of Texas to Henry Smith, February* (New York: Simon & Schuster, 1993), 131; De Bruhl, *Sword*, 177, 179, 186-188. Never one to miss an opportunity to misconstrue sources, Jeff Long also piled on this bandwagon. Long, *Duel of Eagles*, 119.

16. Sam Houston to Henry Smith, January 17, 1836, in Jenkins, ed., *PTR*, 4:46-47.

17. James Bowie to Henry Smith, February 25, 1836, in ibid, 4:236-2238.

18. D. C. Barrett, J. D. Clements, Alexander Thomson, and G. A. Pattillo to Acting Governor James Robinson, January 31, 1836, in ibid., 4:204-206

19. The author discussed this issue with more depth in *The Alamo 1836: Santa Anna's Texas Campaign* (Oxford, UK: Osprey Publishing, 2001), 28-29.

20. John Wayne letter in Kane, ed., *The Alamo*, 1; Travis to the Public, February 24, 1836, in Jenkins, ed., *PTR*, 4:423; lay historian Jeff Long best expressed the view that the Alamo commander had lost his grasp on reality. Long, *Duel of Eagles*, 189-190.

21. Travis to Convention, March 3, 1836, in Jenkins, ed., *PTR*, 4:502-504.

22. Travis to Grimes, March 3, 1836, in ibid, 4:504-505.

23. D. C. Barrett, J. D. Clements, Alexander Thomson, and G. A. Pattillo to Acting Governor James Robinson, January 31, 1836, in ibid., 4:204-206; Richard Bruce Winders explores this controversy with sensitivity and acumen in *Sacrificed at the Alamo: Tragedy and Triumph in the Texas Revolution* (Abilene: State House Press, 2004), 82-110.

24. Travis to Convention, March 3, 1836, in Jenkins, ed., *PTR*, 4:502-504.

25. William P. Zuber quoted in Lord, *A Time to Stand*, 203.

26. Lord, *A Time to Stand*, 203-204.

27. Susanna Dickinson Hanning interview, [San Antonio] *Daily Express*, April 28, 1881, quoted in Todd Hansen, ed., *The Alamo Reader: A Study in History* (Mechanicsburg, PA: Stackpole Books, 2003), 51-54. The following are Mrs. Hannings own words, or at least her words as embellished by the *Daily Express* reporter. Frankly, they sound far too grandiose to be those of an illiterate frontier woman: "THE MEXICAN BUGLES WERE SOUNDING. The charge of battle, and the cannon's roar was heard to reverberate throughout the valley of the San Antonio. But about one hundred and sixty sound persons were in the Alamo, and when the enemy appeared, overwhelmingly, upon the environs of the city to the west, and about where the International depot now stands, the Noble

Travis called his men, drew a line with his sword and said: 'My soldiers, I am going to meet the fate that becomes me. Those who will stand by me, let them remain, but those who desire to go, let them go—and who crosses the line that I have drawn, shall go!'" Again, note that in this version Mrs. Hanning has Travis drawing the line on the *first* day of the siege and requesting those who *wished to leave* to cross over; J. K. Beretta to Editor, *Southwestern Historical Quarterly*, 43 (October, 1939), 253

28. Hardin, *Texian Iliad*, 136; Roberts and Olson, *Line in the Sand*, 156-157; William C. Davis, *Three Roads to the Alamo: The Lives and Fortunes of David Crockett, James Bowie, and William Barret Travis* (New York: HarperCollins, 1998), 731-732, n. 99. In this content endnote, Davis offers a cogent argument against the line myth. In his chapter, "Afterword—Moses Rose and the Line," Donovan presented a lengthy, spirited, but ultimately unconvincing defense of the line myth. James Donovan, *Blood of Heroes: The 13-Day Struggle for the Alamo—and the Sacrifice That Forged a Nation* (New York: Little, Brown and Company, 2012), 351-374. Yet, even Donovan appeared unsure: "There are historians who will complain that much of the evidence is hearsay, or circumstantial, or that post-1873 journalists may have inserted such details into their 'interviews,' especially with Mrs. Hanning and Enrique Esparza. They will say that there is no direct evidence that Moses Rose escaped from the Alamo, or that he was even there, or that he was even the same individual, if he ever existed, as the Louis/Lewis Rose abundantly documented in the Nacogdoches records—and there is even less documentation for the story of the line that Travis drew. Those historians would be technically correct." What an amazing admission this is. As a lay historian, Donovan, of course, is free to believe anything he desires. This is an indulgence professional historians do not have. The rules of their profession require them to follow clear lines of evidence, reject unconfirmed tittle-tattle or circumstantial testimony, and voice the niggling criticisms that buffs find so annoying. Indeed, the current author stands fast with those historians Donovan mentions, those who "complain" about the nature of the unsubstantiated rumor and sheer invention that undergirds the line-in-the-sand legend.

29. Remarkably, the entire screenplay of John Wayne's epic 1960 film is online at http://johnwayne-thealamo.com/forum/viewtopic.php?t=43 (accessed September 4, 2014); Lord, *A Time to Stand*, Sam Houston image caption, unnumbered page. For Houston's activities during this critical period, see James L. Haley, *Sam Houston* (Norman: University of

Oklahoma Press, 2002), 120-122. [Charles Edwards Lester], *The Life of Sam Houston (The Only Authentic Memoir of Him Ever Published)* (New York: J. C. Derby, 1855), 90-91.

30. Bruce Winders, the historian and curator of the Alamo, makes the point succinctly. Winders, *Sacrificed at the Alamo*, 134;

31. John Myers, *The Alamo* (New York: E. P. Dutton & Company, Inc., 1948; reprint, New York: Bantam Books, 1966), 142; Frederic Ray, *The Story of the Alamo: An Illustrated History of the Siege and Fall of the Alamo* (N.P.: privately printed, 1955), unnumbered pages; Lon Tinkle, *13 Days to Glory: The Siege of the Alamo* (New York: McGraw-Hill Book Company, Inc., 1958; reprint, College Station: Texas A&M University Press, 1985), 193; Lord, *A Time to Stand*, bird's-eye-view of the 1836 Alamo compound printed on endpapers.

32. *The Last Command*, videocassette, directed by Frank Lloyd (1955, Los Angles: NTA Home Entertainment, 1984; *The Alamo*, videocassette, directed by John Wayne (1960, Los Angeles: MGM/UA Home Video, Inc., 1992).

33. Travis to Convention, March 3, 1836, in Jenkins, ed., *PTR*, 4:502-504; José Enrique de la Peña described the Mexican assault troops' heroic efforts to scale the north wall: "General [Martín Perfecto de] Cos, looking for a starting point from which to climb, had advanced frontally with his column to where the second and third were. All united at one point, mixing and forming a confused mass. Fortunately the wall reinforcement on this front was of lumber, its excavation was hardly begun, and the height of the parapet was eight or nine feet; there was therefore a starting point, and it could be climbed, though with difficulty. But disorder had already begun; officers of all ranks shouted but were hardly heard. The most daring of our veterans tried to be the first to climb, which they accomplished, yelling wildly so that room could be made for them, at times climbing over their own comrades. Others, jammed together, made useless efforts, obstructing each other, getting in the way of the more agile ones and pushing down those who were about to carry out their courageous effort. A lively rifle fire coming from the roof of the barracks and other points caused painful havoc, increasing the confusion of our disorderly mass. The first to climb were thrown down by bayonets already waiting for them behind the parapet, or by pistol fire, but the courage of our soldiers was not diminished as they saw their comrades falling dead or wounded, and they hurried to occupy their places and to avenge them, climbing over their bleeding bodies. The sharp reports of

the rifles, the whistling of bullets, the groans of the wounded, the cursing harangues of the officers, the noise of the instruments of war, and the inordinate shouts of the attackers, who climbed vigorously, bewildered all and made this moment a tremendous and critical one." José Enrique de la Peña, *With Santa Anna in Texas,* trans. and ed. by Carmen Perry, new introduction by James Crisp (College Station: Texas A&M University Press, 1975; Expanded Edition, 1997), 48-49. Mexican assault troops surely would not have subjected themselves to all that horror if they could have simply strolled through a gaping hole in the north wall.

34. Tinkle, *13 Days to Glory,* caption to the drawing, "The Alamo Under Fire," in illustrations following p. 128.

35. J. H. Barnard, *Dr. J. H. Barnard's Journal: A Composite of Known Versions of the Journal of Dr. Joseph H. Barnard, One of the Surgeons of Fannin's Regiment, Covering the Period from December, 1835 to June 5, 1836,* edited and annotated by Hobart Huson (N. P.: privately printed, 1950), 43; for years, researcher and illustrator Gary S. Zaboly has studied Andrade's demolition of the Alamo. See his extensive sidebar, "Andrade Demolishes the Alamo," in his *An Altar for Their Sons: The Alamo and the Texas Revolution in Contemporary Newspaper Accounts* (Buffalo Gap, TX: State House Press, 2011), 347-349.

36. Russian-born composer Dimitri Tiomkin partnered with P. F. Webster on the music and lyrics to "The Ballad of the Alamo" for John Wayne's 1960 film. Although Tiomkin employed the music as part of the soundtrack, viewers of the film only heard a sampling the lyrics in the final scene. Most Americans never heard all the lyrics until Marty Robbins released his spirited version; *Davy Crockett, King of the Wild Frontier,* DVD, directed by Norman Foster (1955; Burbank: Buena Vista Home Entertainment, 2004). Susanna Dickinson quoted in [Frankford, Kentucky] *Commonwealth,* May 25, 1836, in Hansen, ed., *Alamo Reader,* 75; Pennybacker, *New History of Texas,* 142. With characteristic hyperbole, Mrs. Pennybacker described the three attacks:Santa Anna's troops advanced to the attack. The Texans received them with a terrible volley of musketry and artillery. Back rushed the Mexicans before that fire of death. Again they, advanced, planted their ladders and tried to mount. The fury and despair nerved the arms of Travis's men, and again they hurled back the foe.

37. Mrs. Joseph Hanning interview, September 23, 1876, Adjutant General's Office, (RG-401), Strays—Alamo Dead and Monument, Texas State Library and Archives, in Hansen, *Alamo Reader,* 47.

38. Susanna Hanning interview, [San Antonio] *Daily Express*, April 28, 1881, in ibid, 53.

39. Ibid.

40. The following newspapers quoted Joe in their reports of the battle: [New Orleans] *Commercial Bulletin*, April 11, 1836; *Memphis Enquirer*, April 12, 1836; [Washington, D.C.] *National Intelligencer*, [Frankfort, Kentucky] *Commonwealth*, May 25, 1836. All of the above cited articles appear in Hansen, ed., *Alamo Reader*, 70-76. Like Mrs. Dickinson, Joe was illiterate. Thus, all of Joe's statements come from individuals who allegedly reported what he said. Juan N. Almonte, "The Private Journal of Juan Nepomuceno Almonte, February 1–April 16, 1836," *Southwestern Historical Quarterly* 48, no. 1 (July 1944); Ramon Martinez Caro, *Verdera Idea de la Primera Campaña de Tejas y Sucesos Icurridos Después de la Accion de San Jacinto*, English language translation in Castañeda, ed., *Mexican Side of the Texan Revolution*, 92-164; Vicente Filisola, *Representacion Dirigida Al Supremo Gobierno por el General en Gefe del Ejercito Sobre Tejas*, English language translation in ibid, 164-209; José Juan Sanchez-Navarro, *La Guerra de Tejas: Memorias de un Soldado*, ed. By Carlos Sanchez Navarro (Mexico, D.F.: Editorial Polis, 1938); Santa Anna, *Manifiesto Que de Sus Operaciones en la Campana de Tejas y en Sus Conciudadanos el General Antonio Lopez de Santa Anna* (Veracruz: Imprenta Liberal a cargo de Antonio María Valdes, 1837), English language translation in Castañeda, ed., *Mexican Side of the Texan Revolution*, 2-91.

41. Peña, *With Santa Anna in Texas*, 51; Joaquín Ramírez y Sesma, after-battle report, Expediente, XI/481.3/1149, Archivo Historico Mexicano Militar, Mexico, D.F., quoted in Davis, *Three Roads to the Alamo*, 562.

42. Of all the Alamo controversies, none generates more dissension than the circumstances surrounding the death of David Crockett. Indeed, during the 1990s, explaining how Davy died became something of a cottage industry. Crisp's "Introduction" in the 1996 expanded edition of Peña's *With Santa Anna in Texas* provides a concise and erudite summary of the debate. Peña, *With Santa Anna in Texas*, 1996 Expanded Edition, xi-xxv. Crisp's "Introduction" makes this the best edition.

43. Thomas "Ty" Smith, "The U.S. Army and the Alamo, 1846-1877," *Southwestern Historical Quarterly* 118 (January 2015): 273.

44. Susan Prendergast Schoelwer with Tom W. Gläser, *Alamo Images: Changing Perceptions of a Texas Experience* (Dallas: DeGolyer Library and Southern Methodist University Press, 1985), 35-36; Edward Everett quoted in *ibid*.

45. Michael Corenblith quoted in Frank Thompson, *The Alamo: The Illustrated Story of the Epic Film* (New York: Newmarket Press, 2004), 26.

46. Gary Zaboly, *An Altar for Their Sons: The Alamo and the Texas Revolution in Contemporary Newspaper Accounts* (Buffalo Gap, Texas: State House Press, 2011), S14-S28.

47. Gary Clayton Anderson, *The Conquest of Texas: Ethnic Cleansing in the Promised Land, 1820-1875* (Norman: University of Oklahoma Press, 2005), 5. See also James W. Russell, "Slavery and the Myth of the Alamo," George Mason University History News Network website, http://hnn.us/article146405 [accessed May 30, 2014].

48. "Declaration of the People of Texas, In General Convention assembled," November 7, 1835, in Jenkins, ed., *PTR*, 2:346-348.

49. For thumbnail biographical sketches of every known member of the garrison, see Bill Groneman, *Alamo Defenders—A Genealogy: The People and Their Words* (Austin: Eakin Press, 1990); William Barret Travis to the People of Texas and All Americans, February 24, 1836, in John H. Jenkins, *PTR*, IV:423.

50. Randolph B. Campbell, *An Empire for Slavery: The Peculiar Institution in Texas, 1821-1865,* (Baton Rouge: Louisiana State University Press, 1989), 48.

51. C. S. Lewis, "On Three Ways of Writing for Children," the entire 1946 article appears online at http://mail.scu.edu.tw/~jmklassen/scu99b/chlitgrad/3ways.pdf (accessed August 21, 2014). The quotation appears on page five.

CHAPTER 2

UNEQUAL CITIZENS

WOMEN, RIGHTS, AND MYTH IN
THE TEXAS CONSTITUTION OF 1836

by
Mary L. Scheer

Editor's Note: Although recent scholarship has provided a more inclusive answer to the question "what does it mean to be Texan?" the persistent Anglo-Texas male myth continues to limit the scope and progress of Texas women's history. This dominant narrative, which defines Texans as white and masculine, constructed a limited identity that marginalized women and other groups. In this case study, Mary L. Scheer applies legal and gender analysis to the proceedings and outcomes of the Texas Constitutional Convention of 1836, showing that the Anglo male identity left its imprint on the Republic years. Beginning with an all-male constitutional convention and ending with the surrender of Texas independence in favor of annexation, the founders of the Republic crafted a government that upheld male prerogatives and denied women equal citizenship. However, a careful reading of the constitution reveals that, at least on paper, women were part of the polity entitled to certain political rights, including the vote. Given the nature of the times, these provisions no doubt applied only to white women, with little if any cognizance given to those of Hispanic origin. Although these lawmakers never intended it, society never expected it, and women never asked for it, Texas white women from 1836 to 1845 could, but did not, exercise their full rights. Since the historical record is silent whether women actually took advantage of the constitutional provision or under what circumstances, the focus of this essay therefore rests on a legal analysis of the founding document of the Republic. Yet this loophole, which ended in 1845, has gone unnoticed, attesting to the continued influence of the Texas myth that blinds scholars and others from asking gendered question of the past and fully integrating women into the story of Texas.

On March 1, 1836, the elected delegates of the people of Texas, in general convention, assembled at Washington-on-the-Brazos to declare independence and adopt a constitution for the Republic of Texas (1836-1845). Only one house in the town of about one-hundred residents was deemed suitable for their deliberations—a two-story frame building that was "weather-boarded with clap boards." Built as a commercial establishment, the house fronted on the south side of Main Street. Without doors or windows, the unfinished building utilized cotton cloth stretched across the openings to keep out the chilling spring winds and rain. A long, rough table on the first floor extended "from near the front door to near the rear wall," containing the papers and documents needed for the meeting. Spectators freely entered the lower chamber at will and "stood at convenient posts of observation, [and] listened to the deliberations." Then they quietly retired, "silent and at respectful distances," allowing the delegates to complete their business and others to enter and witness the historic proceedings.[1]

For seventeen days the fifty-nine elected delegates labored under extreme conditions of discomfort, fear, and haste. On the first day the convention opened, a "norther" blew across Texas, causing the temperature to plummet to thirty-three degrees Fahrenheit. Since the meeting house was made of wood without insulation or windows, it offered little protection from the elements. Far more serious was the distinct possibility that the delegates would be unable to complete their business before having to evacuate eastward. Rumors that the enemy was nearby created excitement and alarm among the townspeople and the delegates. On one occasion thieves, whose purpose was to frighten away the population, rode into town shouting that "the Mexican army was within a few miles of the town and advancing." Such an alarm was contagious and "every family but one in Washington fled to the river." Amidst these conditions the delegates struggled to complete the difficult task, in a crowded amount of time, and on issues of vital importance to the future of an independent Texas.[2]

Figure 3. Rebuilt Independence Hall, Washington-on-the-Brazos

Photo courtesy Richard L. Scheer

Until recently scholars of most traditional accounts of the framing of the Texas Constitution of 1836 formulated their respective historical interpretations of the convention based on the political, economic, and legal contests among the delegates. Debates over land titles, slaves, elections, and debts dominated the narrative. One of the earliest was Rupert N. Richardson's essay entitled "Framing of the Constitution of the Republic of Texas," which provided detailed discussion of the members, the land question, the various drafts, and the adoption of the constitution. While important, these issues focused solely on the public sphere—in land offices where titles were recorded, on auction blocks where men bought and sold slaves, and at the ballot box where political decisions were made—all areas from which women were explicitly excluded. If women were recognized as part of the polity in these narratives, it was indirectly through their domestic status as wives and mothers or in gender-neutral language so that they might be encompassed by the constitution's provisions.[3]

In a 1991 article, "Texas Women: History at the Edges," historian Fane Downs famously wrote that the "suffocating Texas macho myth" had limited the scope and progress for Texas women's history. In a state where male, Anglo-American identity has dominated the public mind, the "ethnocentric and gender-skewed narrative" of Texas history burdened Texas women with a popular bias that marginalized their contributions. By obscuring the roles of all Texans except Anglo males, the Texas myth left little room for "others" to claim rights and full citizenship. In other words the iconic representations of "what does it means to be Texan?"—masculine, white, individualistic, larger-than-life, and heroic —did not apply to those who did not share in these attributes, such as women and other groups. Their historical experiences were not part of the mainstream narrative about Texas. Their identity and claims on society were not legitimized. And the public remembrances of their unique history were either omitted or forgotten. Thus, within the context of this Texas myth, the proceedings at Washington-on-the Brazos have commonly been depicted as the story of fifty-nine white male delegates declaring independence, overthrowing an autocratic dictatorship, and crafting a new, "free" republican form of government—the Republic of Texas (1836-1845). This traditional viewpoint, so ingrained in myth and memory, has served to preserve the long-standing, male Anglo-centric answer to the question: "What does it mean to be Texan?"[4]

As a consequence, little gender analysis has been applied to the events of March 1–17, 1836. Like the US constitution, no women participated in the writing or ratification of the new constitution or held office in the Republic. Without a female presence or a voice—even a private one such as Abigail Adams in 1776—Texas women played no direct political role in the drafting of the document. Nevertheless, Texas women were citizens of the proposed Republic and entitled to equal rights under a Lockian social compact between the government and the governed. In fact the preamble to the Texas constitution declared that "We, the people of Texas" establish a government for the "general welfare," one that would "secure the blessings of liberty" for themselves and their posterity. In reality, of course, Texas was never a nation in which all citizens were "free" or equal. From the very beginning, only a select few—white Anglo men—enjoyed those privileges under the Republic, leaving women and other groups subordinate and unequal.[5]

Before the constitutional convention could convene on March 1, an election of delegates had to be held. The Council under the Provisional Government therefore passed a resolution calling for an election and then an assembly to meet on March 1, 1836, to determine "the form of government to be adopted." Reflecting the prevailing local, political, and social arrangements of the day, the election procedures and composition of the electorate was to be consistent with "the same manner" that elections had previously been conducted. Unfortunately, the selection of members to previous governing bodies had been flawed, with various factions viewing the process as either unrepresentative or those chosen as "unsuitably credentialed." As a consequence, such assertions cast a shadow of uncertainty regarding claims whether delegate selection to the upcoming Washington meeting would represent "a gathering authorized by the people."[6]

What then was "the same manner" in which previous elections were held? Who comprised the electorate with the right to vote? Who could hold office? Who would wield power in the new government? Answers to those questions require an examination of the legal and constitutional precedents prior to 1836. Beginning with the Mexican Constitution of 1824, to which the Anglo colonists were subject, the government left "the qualifications of the electors" to the individual legislatures of the states. Thus, for Texans, the Constitution of the State of *Coahuila y Tejas, 1827,* determined "the same manner" of previous elections. Its Article 24 stated that "none but citizens who are in the exercise of their rights can vote for popular employments (officers) in the state. . . ." The document further limited office holding to citizens of twenty-five years of age who were inhabitants of the state with "residence in it for two years immediately before the election." Additional provisions were made for foreigners born outside "the Territory of the Federation" or "in any other part of the Territory of America." In both cases of voting and office holding, only "citizens" were eligible if they met the additional requirements. *Coahuiltejanos* (citizens of *Coahuila y Tejas*), then, under the Constitution of *Coahuila y Tejas* with political rights were comprised of all native-born men, but also citizens from other states, their children, and qualified immigrants "legally domiciled in the state." Presumably, at least in theory, the last three groups included both eligible men and women. In practice, however, those who write constitutions rarely craft a perfect document, free of inconsistencies and ambiguities, leaving them open to interpretations and subject to societal norms. Thus, while Hispanic women certainly held important legal rights at the time, prevailing customs and gendered assumptions limited the franchise in Mexico to men only. Nevertheless, the Constitution of *Coahuila y Tejas* was the most operant governing document that Texans encountered in defining their political rights as either inhabitants or citizens of *Coahuila y Tejas*.[7]

The next constitutional precedent that provides a clue about the conduct of elections was the proposed State of Texas Constitution, 1833, separating Texas from the Mexican state of *Coahuila*. This proposal by a committee chaired by Sam Houston emerged from meetings held in San Felipe from 1832-1833 in reaction to escalating grievances between Texas and Mexico. In this document eligible voters, unless previously disenfranchised (such as the insane, paupers, bonded servants, etc.) included "every male inhabitant of the age of twenty-one years, who shall be a citizen of the state, and shall have resided for the last six months, immediately preceding the day of election, within the precinct, or district." Although Mexico rejected it as a dangerous step toward secession and independence, the proposed constitution served as a model for the type of government and electorate desired by the Anglo-Texans, one in which eligible white males would exercise exclusive power.[8]

By the fall of 1835, as relations between the two sides broke down, the long-smoldering resistance dissolved into armed rebellion. Texans then formed three political bodies, presumably chosen according to the requirements laid out in 1833, which stipulated only male electors. On October 11, 1835, they formed a Permanent Council that lasted only three weeks. The Consultation, a second governmental body, followed this short-lived government. The long-awaited Consultation, although not completely representative of all Texas districts, gathered in San Felipe and on November 7, 1835, approved a "Texas Declaration of the Causes for Taking up Arms against Santa Anna." It also endorsed the creation of a Provisional Government, comprised of a governor, lieutenant governor, and a Council with one member from each municipality. But for the next two months the forces of division and disorder reigned, while the Provisional Government dissolved into chaos. Looking to replace this bickering and quarreling government, the people of Texas sought answers from the upcoming meeting scheduled for March 1 in Washington.[9]

Elections to the constitutional convention took place in each district on "the first day of February, 1836." According to "The Resolution Calling for the Convention of March 1, 1836," all "free white males *and* Mexicans opposed to a Central Government" could vote. Anticipating challenges to voting rights, the Council also enfranchised "all the Citizen Volunteers in the Army" through proxy procedures, to vote for candidates in their home districts. The language used in this resolution was significant. With the words "free white males," black slaves, Indians, and women were at once excluded from political participation, while soldiers and Mexican men who aided in the revolution were enfranchised. This resolution signaled the changing attitudes toward independence by late 1835, but it also reflected the racial discrimination and societal prejudice toward certain groups. While election questions about a candidate's loyalty, personality, residency, and position on independence could and did arise, challenges to disenfranchisement based on sex, race, or enslavement would not. So while the Texas Revolution and the subsequent independent Texas government might overthrow an autocratic regime and establish a republican form of government, it clearly had no intention of wrenching apart the social fabric.[10]

Once elected, the male delegates who assembled at Washington-on-the-Brazos uncritically accepted the patriarchal and unequal assumptions of the day. A majority of the men—fifty-two of the final fifty-nine delegates—were recent arrivals from the United States, especially the South. Most possessed only brief experience with Texas affairs and retained strong ties to their Jeffersonian-Jacksonian heritage. This meant that the new Texas leadership not only reproduced many of the basic features of the U.S. Constitution, but also left intact the social and gendered arrangements of that era. In the 1830s, with the rise of Jacksonian America and a market economy, this meant that men and women increasingly lived in separate spheres—men in the public world of politics and business and women in the domestic realm of home and family. At the same time, men and women constructed their identities based on the patriarchal attitudes in place with men's position as heads of household and women's roles as the guardians of home and family. Thus, while men pursued more worldly activities, women cultivated certain feminine ideals that would enhance their roles as wives and mothers. The true woman was to be "pious, pure, submissive and domestic," thereby protecting her from the corrupting influences of public life.[11]

But the tenets of "true womanhood" were often far from uniform or transparent in a frontier setting such as the Republic. In an unstable and fluid environment such as Texas, some women were able to contest and transform entrenched gender roles into public purposes. Rather than strict spheres separating the sexes, boundaries were often permeable. Women managed homesteads, protected their families from intruders, and demonstrated self-reliance by overcoming "their fears, insecurities, and sense of alienation." Despite certain liberating tendencies, however, Texas customs and culture remained basically masculine in orientation. Traditional patterns of gender relations, often referred to as the doctrine of separate spheres for the sexes, were absorbed, transported, replicated, and at times modified by conditions on Mexican-Texas soil.[12]

Along with their gendered notions of society, the male delegates also modeled their new Republic on the recent expansion of the suffrage under Jacksonian Democracy. Previously, large numbers of propertyless men were disenfranchised, but by eliminating property requirements for political participation, the white male franchise greatly increased. Since only a few women held or controlled property anyway, now the only impediment to white Texas women voting was their sex. As historian Rosemarie Zagarri observed, women "were excluded simply because they were women—not because they lacked sufficient property, education, or virtue." This shift from a "property-based to a gender-based prerogative" served to maintain existing social hierarchies and a patriarchal system that favored men. In short, Texas women, like those in Jacksonian America, were disfranchised, unequal citizens who were denied any direct role in government.[13]

A careful reading of the Texas Constitution of 1836 reveals, however, that the founders of the Republic, at least on paper, acknowledged that women were part of the polity with certain political rights and privileges, including the right to vote. This surprising contradiction between the intentions of the delegates to treat women apolitically and their legal and constitutional actions at the Washington convention was not due to any egalitarian ideals, but to a unique set of military and procedural circumstances at the time. First, in their rush to complete their deliberations and flee before the Mexican troops arrived, the men who drafted the Texas constitution inadvertently empowered Texas women with direct political rights. Second, the numerous drafts of the document over seventeen days of debate created inconsistencies and confusion, opening a path toward equality that was never intended. Third, through the use of gender-neutral language in the document, women were encompassed by its provisions—either at some future date or at the time. And fourth, the committee on style, responsible for the final wording of the constitution, failed to bring uniformity and agreement to its content and phraseology, resulting in ambiguity and unanticipated results. As a consequence, either through haste, oversight, or imprecise language, the new nation under the Republic of Texas actually bestowed direct political rights on women, allowing them, at least on paper, "all the privileges" of citizenship, even the vote. Although these lawmakers never intended it, society never expected it, and women never asked for it, Texas women from 1836 to 1845 could, but did not, exercise their right to full citizenship.[14]

As the convention began to take up the matter of constructing a government, the specter of war hung ominously over the proceedings. During the spring of 1836 thousands of families joined in the Runaway Scrape, the mass exodus eastward away from the advancing Mexican army towards safety across the Sabine River. This primarily female episode became "a full-scale rout," spreading like a prairie fire across Texas. Many women and families fled their homes, experiencing "profound hardships and privations." They lost their possessions and some even lost their lives in the process. William Barret Travis's desperate appeal for help from the Alamo and rumors of an imminent attack also added to the "sense of military urgency," threatening adjournment even before any government could be established. Aware of the general and widespread panic, the delegates, many with families of their own exposed to danger, debated a general emergency relief policy in the final days. Failing to adopt one, the members rushed to complete their work in the early morning hours of March 17. Without time for lengthy deliberations or careful proofing, they hastily approved the document, adjourned, and then dispersed in all directions to gather their families who were "exposed and defenseless" against the advancing Mexican troops.[15]

Under duress to complete their task, the delegates worked daily on several drafts of the constitution. According to William Fairfax Gray, a recent immigrant from Virginia who attended most of the meetings and recorded much of the day-to-day activities, progress was slow with "much altered and amended." His diary, along with the official *Journals*, provides "the best account of the proceedings" and documents the "harried deliberations" that confronted the delegates. On March 2 Gray wrote that the delegates got down to work and quickly appointed a committee consisting of "one member from each municipality who was appointed to draft a constitution." By March 7 Gray reported that a first draft was introduced, but it was an "awkwardly framed arrangement" with bad phraseology, containing "general features much like that of the United States." On the last full day of the meeting, amid "confusion and irregularity" Gray concluded that the final document was a "good one on the whole," but still needed "much alteration and revision to make it respectable in language and arrangement."[16]

One source of the "confusion and irregularity" was the gender-neutral language employed throughout the Texas Constitution of 1836. Such usage of universal language was not uncommon in the early nineteenth century and widely employed by another document—the U.S. Constitution, which served as a model for the delegates. Several words were used interchangeably to refer to "citizens" or the "people" of Texas. For example, "persons," "population," "head of a family," "individuals," "inhabitants," and "electors" occurred regularly throughout the document. Persons, population, head of a family, individuals, and inhabitants surely referred both to men and women. For example, widows were considered as heads of families and men, women, and children of both sexes were certainly inhabitants of the state. "Electors," as well, were gender-neutral, referring to both sexes, excluding neither. Such wording surely caused ambiguity and confusion, standing in sharp contrast to those instances where the delegates could and did utilize gender-specific language.[17]

The language of the Texas Constitution of 1836 was not consistently gender-neutral throughout the document. In two instances the delegates utilized the word "male," which unambiguously refers to the male sex. Art. IV, Sec. 11 referred to the right of petition by "one hundred free male inhabitants" of a territory prior to its division into counties. Then, in the Schedule, Sec. 3, it stated that "every male citizen who is, by this constitution, a citizen . . . shall be entitled to hold any office, or place of honor, trust, or profit under the republic." These specific references to sex allowed men to exercise those rights exclusively, while excluding them from women. Clearly, the delegates understood how to discriminate by sex and did so for specific purposes, when they chose; alternately, they also utilized sex-neutral terms in those cases when they chose not to do so.[18]

Unlike the word "male," which was sex specific, the words "female," "woman," or "women" do not appear in the Texas Constitution of 1836, or other constitutions of that period. Some scholars have argued that the omission of women, if not intentional, then simply reflected the prevailing gender bias of a patriarchal society. Others have suggested that the absence of women and the emphasis on gender-neutral language was actually intentional, leaving the door open so that women might be encompassed by its provisions. They cite that the language of the eighteenth-century Enlightenment typically employed "man" (individual) or "men" (mankind), as well as masculine nouns and adjectives, to stand for all of society, especially concerning "natural rights." For example, the words "man" or "men" occurred six times in the Texas Constitution. The first occurrence was in the General Provisions, Sec. 10, which provided that "every single man of the age of seventeen and upwards" could receive a "third part of one league of land." Since few Texas women at that time remained single and, unless widowed, were not heads of household eligible for land grants, this provision most likely was restricted to single males. The other five instances, however, occurred in the Declaration of Rights, and concerned the natural rights of "all men" or "every man," that "shall never be violated" by government. Applying a general rule of construction of contracts, statutes, and constitutions, the word "men," listed under this bill of rights, implicitly acknowledges women, otherwise they would be entitled to "privileges or emoluments" denied to men. Further, if women were denied these basic rights, then women such as Rebecca Finley and Nancy Walker, citizens of the Republic, would never have been entitled to a "remedy by due course of law" for damages they had incurred at the time.[19]

Adding to the turbulent conditions and awkward, confusing construction of the document were the numerous drafts, largely done by a committee of the whole. This process required that parts of the document be adopted section by section, with few members present having ever read the constitution in its entirety. As a result errors and inconsistencies crept into the final draft. So on March 14 the convention referred the constitution to a committee of five to resolve discrepancies and correct all "errors and phraseology." Thomas J. Rusk of Nacogdoches, a signer of the Texas Declaration of Independence who took "a keen interest in every issue that was raised" during the Convention, chaired this committee on style. Apparently, due to his standing and ability among the delegates, he was "more responsible than any other man for the final wording of the instrument." But faced with the press of time and threatened dissolution, the Convention rushed to complete the final draft, adding several last-minute refinements and amendments even after it was submitted. Gray's diary entry of March 16 recorded the great confusion and sense of peril in the final hours as some members left the meeting even before final approval. As a result the next day, after the constitution was finally adopted in the early morning hours, some issues and language construction still remained unresolved.[20]

Figure 4. Declaration of Independence and the Texas Constitution of 1836, adopted March 17, 1836

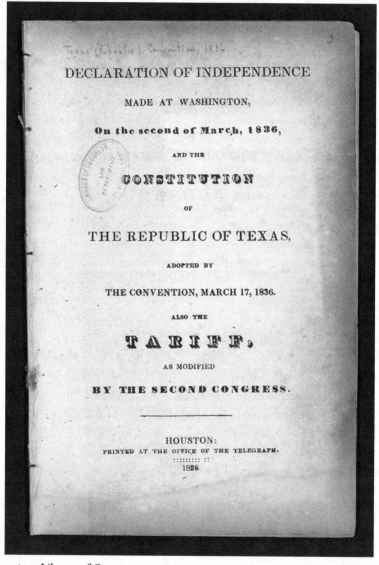

Courtesy Library of Congress

The first test of the new constitution was to establish a regular government following the victorious battle of San Jacinto on April 21, 1836, which secured Texas independence. An *ad interim* government under President David G. Burnet and his cabinet had proclaimed the first Monday of the following September as the date for the first legitimate vote by "the free and independent people of Texas." Based on the provisions of the soon-to-be ratified constitution, the nation's first congress and president would be "elected by the people." But who specifically were "the people" entitled to vote? An early draft indicated that "every free white male citizen" composed the electorate, but this was revised on a motion by Thomas J. Gazley of Bastrop. No debates or discussion exists to explain the change in wording, as defined in Art. VI, Sec. 11, of the Texas Constitution of 1836, which determined "the people" eligible to vote under the Republic. It stated:

> Every citizen of the republic who has attained the age of twenty-one years, and shall have resided six months within the district or county where the election is held, shall be entitled to vote for members of the general congress.

Only those persons, according to General Provisions, Sec. 1, "convicted of bribery, perjury, or other high crimes and misdemeanors" would be excluded from holding public office, exercising the right of suffrage, and serving on juries.[21]

With the phrase "every citizen of the republic," the delegates to the Constitutional Constitution unambiguously framed the right to vote in gender-neutral terms. Whereas earlier constitutions and resolutions utilized gender-specific language such as "male inhabitants" and "all free white males," proving that Texans could and did discriminate on the basis of sex, the final draft of the 1836 Constitution only restricted suffrage based on citizenship, age, residency, and certain disqualified groups. Further, those citizens eligible to vote could not be deprived of their privileges or "disfranchised, except by due course of the law of the land."[22]

So who were citizens of the Republic entitled to vote? The General Provisions, Sec. 10 of the constitution, provides the answer:

> All persons (Africans, the descendants of Africans, and Indians excepted) who were residing in Texas on the day of the declaration of independence, shall be considered citizens of the republic, and entitled to all the privileges of such.

Clearly, the word "persons" did not connote one sex or the other and the definition of citizenship, with its all-encompassing privileges, was not confined to men—white or Hispanic—alone. Further, the delegates only excluded slaves, Indians, and those not residents of Texas on March 2, 1836, from citizenship. Again, the fact that the delegates did not specifically exclude Anglo women as they did other groups, substantiates that they were citizens of the Republic with "all the privileges of such," including voting, as provided under Art. VI, Sec 11.[23]

Did the enfranchisement of Texas women represent the actual intentions of the framers in 1836? What reasons might explain such a revolutionary concept eighty-two years before Texas women first officially voted? Was this a genuine innovation that simply passed unnoticed? No evidence or debates indicate that empowering Texas women was the intentional action by the delegates or a radical realignment of social and political hierarchies. At the same time, no women were known to have interpreted it in such a manner by attempting to vote. Instead, it most likely resulted from several causes: oversight during the "harried deliberations" of the chaotic seventeen-day convention, the use of imprecise, gender-neutral language, multiple drafts, and the entrenched gendered assumptions of the time that prevented the male delegates—or even the male voters, who later overwhelmingly approved the constitution—from seriously considering female political participation. Nonetheless, for almost ten years Texas women constitutionally held direct political rights, including suffrage, which were neither intended, acknowledged, nor revoked by due process under the Republic. Then in 1845 this loophole ended. When Texas joined the Union as the twenty-eighth state, the new constitution stipulated that only "free male persons" could vote.[24]

So if Texas women constitutionally possessed direct political rights under the Texas Constitution of 1836, why did they fail to exercise those rights and why has no one noticed? There are several reasons for the failure of women to exercise their full political rights under the Republic. The most significant was the long-standing gender biases, expressed through customs and mores, which dictated that women were by nature weaker and inferior to men, dependent on male family members for protection and survival. The patriarchal family structure followed the prevailing "natural order" between the sexes, assigning men to the competitive male arena of politics and power, and women to the more passive female sphere of home and family. Women, therefore, came to stand for those citizens who did not need or possess direct political rights; as such they were incapable of representing themselves. This meant that they need not vote, hold office, serve on juries, and, if they were married, they could not control property, write a will, or expect custody of their children. Far from equal status, women had no recourse but to leave governing to white male officials who would exercise power in the new Republic and leave the maintaining of order and harmony within the family to husbands as heads of household.

Along with the prevailing gender norms of Texas society, the legal system under the Provisional Government and the Republic of Texas generally disadvantaged women. As early as November 1835 the Provisional Government declared that all judges would decide legal cases according to English common law, a system with which Anglo colonists had greater familiarity. Therefore, in March of 1836 the drafters of the Texas Constitution formally incorporated English common law as "the rule of decision" for the new government. Art. IV, Sec. 13, of the constitution stated that, "congress shall, as early as practicable, introduce, by statute, the common law of England." With the passage of the Act of January 20, 1840, this meant that under common law a woman's legal position was based on her marital status. Known as the doctrine of coverture, it bestowed few rights on married women, whose legal existence was virtually suspended during the marriage. Thus, a single woman, or *feme sole*, might own and control her property, while a married woman, or *feme covert*, was "covered" or controlled by her husband. Since few women remained single on the Texas frontier, most female legal identities then were subsumed under that of her husband. So fundamental and axiomatic were these legal patterns that during the proceedings of the Texas constitutional convention, the question of women's political participation never arose. Women might be part of the polity, but they were unequal citizens with no direct role to play in government [25]

Nevertheless, in one instance the Act of January 20, 1840, benefited women. Growing out of the existing Spanish and Mexican law, and over-laid with English common law, this provision defined marital property and granted women substantial property rights. It allowed a wife to keep her separate property while also sharing in the wealth of community property. But it also allowed husbands to retain power to manage all of the property during the marriage, with certain restrictions from wasting or selling assets without the wife's consent. Legislators at the time viewed it as a way to protect the family from creditors and women becoming a burden on society. Thus, the same men who wrote the Texas constitution and served as legislators during the Republic, recognized women's legal—even mental—capacity to make economic decisions concerning property. In doing so they also provided a path for women to identify with the nation, even if only on unequal terms. [26]

At the same time the definition of rights in the nineteenth century was a gendered one. While society recognized the universality of "natural rights" for men and women, they applied the concept differently to the sexes. Women's rights were non-political, implying certain "duties and obligations" related to the traditional feminine roles of wife and mother. Men's rights, on the other hand, were political and economic, providing "individual liberty and personal autonomy" in the public realm. So when the delegates in 1836 recognized female citizenship, one that provided certain rights and privileges, even inadvertently, they were not proposing women's direct participatory role in politics. Instead, women's rights were limited and apolitical in nature, confined to the domestic sphere, which in turn, would provide them with "benefits" in terms of material support and physical protection.[27]

Few women on the Texas frontier challenged their political subordination. The uncertainties and burdens of pioneer life, along with the lack of material comforts and time-consuming daily chores, left little time or resources to do so. There was no comparable Abigail Adams in Texas at the time to warn against placing "unlimited powers into the hands of husbands." There were no women such as the unmarried female property owners of New Jersey who for three decades (1807-1837) could and did vote. And on the Texas frontier there were few places for women to gather, learn from each other, or act in concert to demand their rights. While a few women like Jane Long, Angelina Peyton Eberly, and Pamelia Mann occasionally demonstrated "resilient spirits and strong muscles," by resisting prescribed gender norms and confronting male authority, there was no demand for direct political rights. Those challenges to inequality would have to wait another twenty years until the Constitutional Convention of 1868-1869. Even then the woman's question died for lack of support. So, while the harsh and dangerous conditions of living on a frontier often mitigated the model of separate spheres for the sexes, requiring women to perform typically male duties, the family circle, centered on the home and family, remained the locus of the female world.[28]

Finally, the brevity of the Texas revolutionary experience (October 1835-April 1836), according to historian Paul Lack, limited the degree to which the political order and the social fabric would be wrenched apart. The sudden military success at San Jacinto, while securing Texas independence, did not result in shifts in power or property, leaving the radical potential of the revolution and the new nation unfulfilled. No reign of terror emerged, no large-scale slave rebellions arose, and only one serious threat by the Tejano community in Nacogdoches occurred to undermine the Texas government. At the same time white Texas women, who were in a better position than *Tejanas* to exercise rights, made no demands on the new government. Nor were there any organized efforts for equal citizenship. So, together with the short duration of the revolution, the subsequent conservative constitution, the long-standing patriarchal assumptions and gender norms, a legal system that disadvantaged women, the gendered definition of rights, and the harsh realities of frontier living, collectively prevented Republic women from claiming full rights as equal citizens.[29]

So if women during the Republic possessed, but did not exercise, direct political rights, including the franchise, why has no historian noticed? The answer lies with the state of the historical academy and the continued influence of the Texas myth. Histories about the Republic of Texas continue to embody much that was heroic, legendary, and mythic. Texans still boast, inaccurately, that Texas was the only state in the Union to have been an independent nation. Popular histories and textbooks often characterize the Republic years as a masculine, often-troubling period of nation-building, with larger-than-life male figures such as Sam Houston. Popular culture equates the Republic with John Wayne's speech in the film *The Alamo* when he said: "Republic, I like the sound of the word. Means that people can live free, talk free, go or come, buy or sell, be drunk or sober, however they choose." And collective memory frequently celebrates "this young, rising, and interesting Republic," while forgetting those excluded from full participation. As a result, beginning with the all-male constitutional convention until its surrender of independence in favor of annexation, the male, macho Anglo-Texan identity has left its imprint on the Republic years. In short the Texas myth has been so pervasive in constructing a limited identity of what it means to be Texan that no one questioned or noticed whether Republic women, who were also citizens and builders of Texas, legally held political rights.[30]

Nonetheless, the increase in recent scholarly production, focused on the historical experiences of Texas women, has helped dispel some of the traces of "the suffocating Texas macho myth." As a result women's history has begun to move away from the "edges," but still far from the mainstream of Texas history. Only by moving beyond the traditional Anglo Texan myth, asking different questions about our past, and integrating multiple identities such as women into the story of Texas, will we no longer accept out-of-hand that Republic women were subordinate helpmates with limited rights, but understand that they were unequal citizens entitled to exercise their full political rights and privileges, including the vote, but did not. [31]

SELECTED BIBLIOGRAPHY

Andreadis, Harriette. "True Womanhood Revisited: Women's Private Writing in Nineteenth-Century Texas." *Journal of the Southwest* 31 (Summer 1989): 179-204.

Boswell, Angela. *Her Act and Deed: Women's Lives in a Rural Southern County, 1837-1873.* College Station: Texas A&M University Press, 2001.

Carroll, Mark. *Homesteads Ungovernable: Families, Sex, Race, and the Law in Frontier Texas, 1826-1860.* Austin: University of Texas Press, 2001.

Caughfield, Adrienne. *True Women and Westward Expansion.* College Station: Texas A&M University Press, 2005.

Downs, Fane. "Texas Women: History at the Edges" in Walter Buenger and Robert A. Calvert, eds. *Texas Through Time: Evolving Interpretations.* College Station: Texas A&M University Press, 1991.

Furman, Necah Steward. "Texas Women vs the Texas Myth" in Ben Procter and Archie McDonald, eds. *The Texas Heritage.* St. Louis, Mo.: Forum Press, 1980.

Gray, William Fairfax. *The Diary of William Fairfax Gray: From Virginia to Texas, 1835, 1836.* Houston: n.p. 1909.

Henson, Margaret. *Anglo-American Women in Texas, 1820-1850.* Boston: 1982.

Lack, Paul D. *The Texas Revolutionary Experience: A Political and Social History, 1835-1836.* College Station: Texas A&M University Press, 1992.

Myers, Sandra L. *Westering Women and the Frontier Experience, 1800-1915.* Albuquerque: University of New Mexico Press, 1982.

Scheer, Mary L., ed. *Women and the Texas Revolution.* Denton: University of North Texas Press, 2012.

Stuntz, Jean A. *Hers, His, and Theirs: Community Property Law in Spain and Early Texas.* Lubbock: Texas Tech University Press, 2005.

Richardson, Rupert N. "Framing the Constitution of the Republic of Texas." *Southwestern Historical Quarterly* (January 1928): 191-220.

NOTES

1. The author is indebted to her husband Richard L. Scheer for providing legal and constitutional assistance, as well as unflagging support. His suggestions and expertise have strengthened this essay. *Galveston Daily News*, June 24, 1900; William Fairfax Gray, *The Diary of William Fairfax Gray: From Virginia to Texas, 1835, 1836* (Houston: n.p., 1909; reprint 1997), 112.

2. *Galveston Daily News*, June 24, 1900; Gray, *Diary*, 112, 115; Rupert N. Richardson, "Framing the Constitution of the Republic of Texas, *Southwestern Historical Quarterly* (Jan. 1928): 192-193.

3. The Constitution of the Republic of Texas, March 17, 1836, in Ernest Wallace, David M. Vigness, and George B. Ward, eds. *Documents of Texas History* (Austin: Texas State Historical Association, 2002), 100-106; Richardson, "Framing the Constitution," 191-220.

4. Fane Downs, "Texas Women: History at the Edges," in Walter Buenger and Robert A. Calvert, eds., *Texas Through Time: Evolving Interpretations* (College Station: Texas A&M University Press, 1991), 100.

5. Preamble, The Constitution of the Republic of Texas, March 17, 1836.

6. For a full discussion of the election and composition of the delegates see Lack, *The Texas Revolutionary Experience: A Political and Social History, 1835-1836* (College Station: Texas A&M University Press, 1992), 75-85. See also Sec. 3, "The Resolution Calling for the Convention of March 1, 1836," in Vigness and Ward, eds., *Documents of Texas History*, 94; Lack, *The Texas Revolutionary Experience*, 4.

7. Like women elsewhere, Mexican women were unequal citizens and did not gain the suffrage until 1953. Title 3, sec. 9, Constitution of the Mexican United States, 1824; Art. 18 and Art. 24, Constitution of the State of *Coahuila y Tejas*, 1827; Ron Tyler, et al., eds., *The New Handbook of Texas* (Austin: Texas State Historical Association Press, 1996), 2:286.

8. *Coahuila y Tejas* was originally divided into three departments: Coahuila, Nuevo León, and Texas. By 1833 Texans objected to the lack of representation, trial by jury, and schools, as well as the control by Saltillo, later Monclova, the capitals. They therefore proposed to form a separate state of Texas. Art. 23, 29, and 41, The Proposed Constitution for the State of Texas, 1833, in Vigness and Ward, eds., *Documents of Texas History*, 80-85; Tyler, et al., eds., *The New Handbook of Texas*, 2: 291.

9. For a discussion of the leading causes of the Texas Revolution, see Lack, *The Texas Revolutionary Experience*, 3-37. "The Texas Declaration of Causes for Taking Up Arms Against Santa Anna," November 7, 1835, in Vigness and Wards, eds., *Documents of Texas History*, 91; Lack, *The Texas Revolutionary Experience*, 44–45.

10. Sections 2 and 3, "The Resolution Calling for the Convention of March 1, 1836," in Vigness and Wards, eds., *Documents of Texas History*, 94; Lack, *Texas Revolutionary Experience*, 76–86, 259.

11. The other seven delegates were from England, Ireland, Canada, Scotland, and three from Mexico. Anne Carroll Smith Rosenberg, "Beauty, the Beast and the Militant Woman: A Case Study in Sex Roles and Social Stress in Jacksonian America," *American Quarterly* (1971): 563; See also Barbara Welter, "The Cult of True Womanhood, 1820-1860," *American Quarterly* 18 (Summer 1966): 151-174.

12. Julie Jeffrey, "Permeable Boundaries: Abolitionist Women and Separate Spheres," *Journal of the Early Republic* 21, no. 1 (Spring 2001): 79-93; Ann Patton Malone, *Women on the Texas Frontier: A Cross-Cultural Perspective* (El Paso: Texas Western Press, 1983), 14-19; Mark M. Carroll, *Homesteads Ungovernable: Families, Sex, Race and the Law in Frontier Texas, 1823-1860* (Austin: University of Texas Press, 2001), 101-102. Angela Boswell, *Her Act and Deed: Women's Lives in a Rural Southern County, 1837-1873* (College Station: Texas A&M University Press, 2001), 5; Sandra L. Myres, *Westering Women and the Frontier Experience 1800-1915* (Albuquerque: University of New Mexico Press, 1982), 5-8. Caughfield, *True Women and Westward Expansion* (College Station: Texas A&M University Press, 2005) and Harriette Andreadis, "True Womanhood Revisited: Women's Private Writing in Nineteenth-Century Texas" *Journal of the Southwest* 31 (summer 1989): 179-204.

13. Tyler, et al., eds., *The New Handbook of Texas*, 6:1046-1047; Rosemarie Zagarri, "The Rights of Man and Woman in Post-Revolutionary America," *William and Mary Quarterly*, vol. 55, no. 2 (April 1998): 227–228.

14. See Gray, *Diary*, March 1-17, 1836. Richardson, "Framing the Constitution," 208-209.

15. Light Townsend Cummins, "Up Buck! Up Ball! Do Your Duty!: Women and the Runaway Scrape," in *Women and the Texas Revolution*, ed. by Mary L. Scheer (Denton: The University of North Texas Press, 2012), 153-154, 176; Gray, *Diary*, 122-125; H.P.N. Gammel, Journals of the Convention, *Laws of Texas*, I (Austin: 1898), 900-901; Lack, *The Texas Revolutionary Experience*, 222-228.

16. The Journals of the Convention use the date March 9 for the first draft. Gammel, Journals of the Convention, I: 859; Richardson, "Framing the Constitution," 192-193; Fairfax, *Diary*, 115-124.

17. Jan Lewis, "Women Were Recognized in the Constitution," *Journal of the Early Republic* 15 (fall 1995): 359-387; The Constitution of the Republic of Texas, 1836.

18. Art IV, Sec. 11 and Schedule, Sec. 3, The Constitution of the Republic of Texas, 1836.

19. General Provisions, Sec 10, and Declaration of Rights, 1-17, The Constitution of the Republic of Texas, 1836; Jean Stuntz, *Hers, His, and Theirs: Community Property Law in Spain and Early Texas* (Lubbock: Texas Tech University Press), 141; Lewis, "Women Were Recognized in the Constitution," 359-387.

20. The other members of the committee were: T. J. Gazley, Robert Hamilton, James Gaines, and Stephen Everett; Tyler, et al., eds., *The New Handbook of Texas*, 5: 721-722; Richardson, "Framing the Constitution,"196, 208-209; Gray, *Diary*, 122-124; Gammel, Journals of the Convention, I: 832; Sam Houston Dixon, *The Men who Made Texas Free* (Houston: Texas Historical Publishing Co., 1924),180-186.

21. A possible explanation for the change of the definition of the electorate in 1836 from "every free white male citizen" to "every citizen of the republic" was objection to the word "white," which would potentially also exclude Mexicans. Art. III, Sec. 2, Art. VI, Sec. 11, General Provisions, Sec 1, The Constitution of the Republic of Texas, 1836; Hammel, Journals of the Constitution, I: 864, 883.

22. See the Proposed State of Texas Constitution, 1833 and "The Resolution Calling for the Convention of March 1, 1836" for examples of the use of the word "male"; Right 7, Declaration of Rights, The Constitution of the Republic of Texas, 1836.

23. Art. VI, Sec. 11 and General Provisions, Sec. 10, The Texas Constitution of the Republic of Texas, 1836; *Journals of the Convention* (Austin: Miner & Cruger, 1845), 54.

24. In "The Constitution of Texas, 1845," by Frederic L. Paxson, *Southwestern Historical Quarterly*, 18 (April 1915), 389-392, the author discussed changes between the 1836 and 1845 constitutions. While he detailed necessary changes as Texas moved from independence to statehood, he failed to notice or comment that the insertion of "free male persons" into the 1845 document meant important changes for women in the electorate between the two constitutions. Art. III, Sec. 2, The Texas Consti-

tution of 1845 in Vigness and Ward, eds., *Documents of Texas History,* 149-159. See also *Journals of the Convention* (Austin: Miner & Cruger, Printers, 1845; 1974).

25. Art. VI, Plan and Powers of the Provisional Government of Texas, November 13, 1835, in Vigness and Ward, eds., *Documents of Texas History,* 91-93; Art. IV, Sec. 13, The Texas Constitution of the Republic of Texas, 1836; Stuntz, *His, Hers, and Theirs,* 101-102.

26. Stuntz, *Hers, His, and Theirs,* 136-145, 168, 172.

27. Zagarri, "The Rights of Man and Woman in Post-Revolutionary America," 205, 220-221.

28. See Nancy Woloch, *Women and the American Experience,* 4th ed. (Boston: McGraw Hill, 2006), 81-84; Scheer, "Joys and Sorrows of Those Dear Old Times," in *Women and the Texas Revolution,* 89; William R. Hogan, *Texas Republic: A Social and Economic History* (Austin: University of Texas Press, 1969), 293.

29. Lack, *The Texas Revolutionary Experience,* 259; Hogan, *The Texas Republic,* vii, 190, 297-298.

30. Hogan, *The Texas Republic,* 190; *The Alamo* (1960).

31. Downs, "Texas Women: History at the Edges," 100-101.

CHAPTER 3

THE TEXAS RANGERS
IN MYTH AND MEMORY

By
Jody Edward Ginn

Editor's Note: One of the most iconic groups of Texans is the Texas Rangers. Formed during the Republic period as a volunteer mounted force to protect settlers on the frontier, they have played a key role in the development of modern Texas and especially in the construction of a Texas identity. As Jody Edward Ginn shows in this insightful essay, much of early Texas Ranger historiography was the collective product of myth and memory. Their image, as projected by early historians, the mass media, and individual Rangers, was one of an invincible fighting force charged with the advance of Anglo-American democracy and Manifest Destiny. Not surprisingly, such early traditional accounts tended to romanticize and mythologize the Rangers' place in Texas history. In the early nineteenth century, as the Texas Rangers evolved from a loosely organized militia to a professional investigative force in the twentieth century, revisionist writers began to challenge earlier notions of Anglo superiority and Ranger justice. Such works were just as rife with myths and stereotypes as the traditional accounts. Some recent Texas Rangers scholarship, however, has provided a more inclusive and balanced, less-romanticized or racially divided narrative, thereby pushing the discourse into a new era. Along with a basic understanding of the historical creation and purpose of the Texas Rangers, this essay exposes many of the myths and memories surrounding Texas Rangers history, showing how they have influenced academic historiography and public perception of their place in Texas history over time. In so doing, however, it does not seek to be comprehensive. Like the Alamo, the Rangers have a complexity in the story of Texas that precludes any single analysis from examining all of the nuances that speak to their place in myth and memory as enduring influences on identity.

Other than the Alamo defenders, no group of Texans has been more eulogized and mythologized than the Texas Rangers. They have played a key role in the development of the Texas identity, and many aspects of Texas Rangers history continue to evoke very strong emotions—both positive and negative. As historian Glen Sample Ely noted, "whoever controls Texas history also influences Texas identity," and the Texas Rangers have held a dominant place in the telling of the story of modern Texas since the days of the Republic. Their depiction in both the Anglo-centric traditionalist academic historiography and throughout popular media—as the prototypical pioneer-patriot archetype charged with leading the advance of Anglo-American democracy in fulfillment of Manifest Destiny in Texas—has positioned them as an inextricable component of Texan identity. While their overall significance in the creation of modern Texas is certainly substantial, this study will show that there are many perspectives on the value of and justification for the actions of the Rangers in many circumstances. It will also show that none of these perspectives is immune to mythmaking.[1]

The key element associated with the Texas Rangers in the collective myth and memory of many Anglo Texans is the perception that the Rangers have always been invincible, incorruptible, and indefatigable defenders of justice. This image was created by early historians and embedded into the national and international collective memory of the Texas Rangers by the news and popular media, since at least the US–Mexican War. But the extensive mass media attention they have received throughout their history has been a double-edged sword: they have been the beneficiary of some myths and the victims of others. In some quarters the Texas Rangers have been lionized as fearless, incorruptible demigods; in others, vilified as murderous tools of an oppressive and racially discriminatory establishment. As this study will reveal, the historical evidence evokes a far more nuanced view than either of those simplistic perceptions, and such viewpoints often depend in large part on the particular time, place, event, and specific participants involved. Myth and memory have often been intermixed with many of the available historical facts, along with both the remembering and forgetting of many aspects of Texas Rangers history.

Notwithstanding the different perspectives on aspects of their history, the Texas Rangers have long been recognized and feared around the world as a fierce and effective fighting force. As Charles H. Harris and Louis R. Sadler point out in their study, *The Texas Rangers and the Mexican Revolution,* "[They] are arguably the most celebrated lawmen in the world, their fame ranking with that of the Federal Bureau of Investigation, Scotland Yard, and the Royal Canadian Mounted Police." The comparison is all the more remarkable given that the others mentioned are national organizations with thousands of employees, while the Texas Rangers are a state-level entity with only a fraction of the personnel employed by these other organizations. The Rangers' international prominence, despite their limited size and regional area of operations, merits an examination of how this legacy was built.[2]

A basic understanding of the creation and purpose of the Texas Rangers is necessary in order to identify and assess the myths surrounding them. Officially founded in 1835 as a paramilitary mounted frontier force, the Texas Rangers were tasked primarily with defending settlements in the fledgling Republic of Texas against Indian raids and attacks. But Stephen F. Austin and his Anglo-American colonists did not step into a cultural, political, or military vacuum when they began settling in Mexican Texas in 1821. Since the end of the seventeenth century, units of mounted troopers known as *compañías volantes* (flying companies) had scoured the Indian trails and haunts across the northern frontier of New Spain, and later Mexico, in an attempt to pursue and destroy native bands that had resisted Spanish hegemony and frequently raided their frontier communities. By the time Anglo settlers began arriving in Texas, Tejanos and their forebears had been serving as specialized mounted frontier counter-insurgency troops for over one hundred and forty years. Upon their arrival, Austin's colonists were given detailed instructions in the formation and operation of traditional Tejano flying companies for purposes of local defense, by both Mexican authorities and their Tejano neighbors. Based on their Anglo-American frame of reference for non-traditional mobile military scouting units from life in the burgeoning United States of America, Austin and his colonists informally applied the familiar terms "ranging" and "rangers" to these duties, which was eventually codified by the Consultation once independence was declared and by the Congress of the Republic of Texas after independence had been achieved.[3]

The nomenclature "Texas Rangers" was merely an informal designation during the first 100 years of their history. Until the creation of the "Texas Rangers Division" of the Texas Department of Public Safety in 1935, the various units historically recognized as having rendered "ranging service" up until that time served under a wide variety of designations. In 1836 the new Texas Congress created the "Corps of Rangers" through an act encompassing units that had been performing such duties for more than a year previous to its passage. The units of "citizen soldiers" who served under that and subsequent Republic and early statehood-era legislation were known as "mounted rifles," "mounted spies," "mounted volunteers," "minutemen," and even "partisans." However, many of those who served in such units commonly referred to themselves informally as "Texas Rangers," as did many members of the general population.[4]

Figure 5. Texas Rangers on Horseback, 1921

Courtesy Briscoe Center for American History, University of Texas at Austin

In 1874 they gained permanent institutionalization as the administratively designated "Frontier Battalion" and "Frontier Force"—still a military unit intended to perform an identical role to their predecessors, only with hopes for more efficiency and effectiveness as a full-time, permanent, and mounted frontier fighting force. Shortly thereafter the frontier came to a close and the Rangers' slow and sometimes halting evolution into law enforcement began. This progress, however, would be impeded by events and assignments more suited to a military solution, particularly in the region of the Texas-Mexico international border. Shortly after the creation of the Frontier Battalion, the United States Army finally succeeded in relocating and subjugating even the most recalcitrant Comanches and other Plains Indians north of the Red River, leaving the Texas Rangers with little to occupy their time patrolling the frontier. As a result, the Rangers of that time slowly took up peace-keeping/ law enforcement duties, which, in the beginning, primarily involved tracking and arresting fugitives from justice. The Rangers undertook such assignments often on behalf of county and city officials, who did not have the manpower or range of jurisdiction to pursue outlaws who sought refuge from justice far out on the frontier. The Frontier Battalion Rangers received neither law enforcement training nor official authority in the beginning, but they were expected to adapt and serve as needed on the "violent, crime-ridden" frontier.[5]

Their role as lawmen was so nebulous at the time that legal issues finally arose over their involvement in such duties, leading to lawsuits and eventually to legislative action. This prompted an additional step forward in their evolution from paramilitary units to law enforcers. Additionally, during this period, a separate category known as "Special Rangers," and later the partisan "Loyalty Rangers," were created. These groups were not a part of the Texas Rangers organization, nor were they subject to that chain of command, despite the similarity in the designations and the fact that they possessed statewide law enforcement authority. Special Rangers were privately funded and served a wide variety of organizations, from railroad and oil companies to cattle associations, and there were typically far more Special Rangers at any given time than actual Texas Rangers. Loyalty Rangers were political partisans created and empowered under a special legislative act and specifically tasked with ferreting out alleged subversives across the state during World War I, as opposed to being general law enforcement officials. Like Special Rangers, there were far more Loyalty Rangers—three in each of Texas's 252 counties at the time, 756 total (approximately 38 times the average number of actual Texas Rangers during that period). The common use of the term "ranger" among those distinct and separately administered groups led to confusion among both contemporary citizens and some historians regarding who should be considered to have been a "real" Texas Ranger historically and, therefore, whether actual Texas Rangers were responsible for many of the acts that have long been attributed to them.[6]

In 1901 the Frontier Battalion was reorganized as the "Ranger Force," though they remained a subdivision of the Adjutant General's Department and were expected to continue to patrol and protect the border region and other sparsely settled areas. A mere three companies, often consisting of fewer than twenty men, were tasked with patrolling the entire state and maintaining order for millions of Texans. It proved an impossible job, and the men assigned to undertake it ranged from "highly capable to wholly unsuited," depending on both the available leadership and the political environment at any given time. In examining Ranger history, it is crucial to note that, until 1935 and due to the vague wording of the statute that had created the Ranger Force, Texas governors sought to increase their power in this traditionally "weak governor" state by exerting direct control over the appointment of all Texas Rangers, though their motivation was rarely seen to have been in the furtherance of good government.[7]

Beginning with Governor Oscar B. Colquitt, many of Texas' chief executives began to directly involve themselves in the selection not only of Ranger captains, but also of each and every Ranger on the force. More often than not, such selections were made based on the applicant's politics, rather than their law enforcement experience. The abuse of that process degenerated exponentially and to such a degree over the first three and a half decades of the twentieth century that it finally caused a complete overhaul of state law enforcement. The practice also coincided with many of the most criticized actions in the history of the Texas Rangers, their reputation suffering greatly among the population of the state at large during that period. The effects were so pronounced by the mid-1930s that a Texas journalist quipped, "A Ranger commission and a nickel will get you . . . a cup of coffee anywhere in Texas." (At the time, during the nadir

of the Great Depression, a cup of coffee only cost a nickel on average.)
The massive overhaul of state law enforcement in 1935 was specifically
undertaken as a result of the increasing politicization of the Texas Rangers
during the previous three decades. From that point forward, the Texas
Rangers Division of the Department of Public Safety evolved into an
elite unit of internationally respected criminal investigators, focusing
on major crimes such as murder and public corruption. Yet while the
Rangers themselves were modernizing, their emerging historiography
and the ever-expanding forms of popular media based on their tradition
remained mired in myths of the past.[8]

The breadth, depth, and longevity of the Texas Rangers mythology are
remarkable. But just who, exactly, is responsible for the creation of the
mystique, and the myths upon which it has been built? The answer is a
mixture of popular media, early historians, and sometimes even actual
Texas Rangers, whose generally uncoordinated yet often symbiotic tales
combined to form a seemingly intractable narrative in the minds of the
general public, separate from historical reality. A key problem is that the
first two generations of historiography dealing with the Texas Rangers
was founded and relied far too heavily on what scholars often refer to as
"oral traditions." Oral traditions do have a significant role in the context
of evaluating historical reality; but they are vulnerable to influence by
gossip, innuendo, and personal anecdotes, magnified across multiple
generations. Unfortunately, many scholars even today reference these
sources uncritically, accepting their conclusions without first examining
the validity of the information at the core of the matter or the credibility
and potential bias of the source.

Any discussion of the historiography of the Texas Rangers in myth
and memory must begin with historian Walter Prescott Webb and the
extraordinary scope of his influence on the topic. The history of the Texas
Rangers has long been a key component in the traditional Anglophone
historiography of the American West, which relied upon the Turner
Frontier Thesis to bolster Anglo-American notions of Manifest Destiny.

Published during the widely publicized Texas Centennial Celebrations, Webb immortalized the Rangers as righteous and invincible in his ethnocentric and sycophantic 1936 history, *The Texas Rangers: A Century of Frontier Defense*. While it was hardly the first book to document some aspect of Texas Rangers history, Webb's was the first scholarly publication and broad-reaching general history of the Rangers, a monumental treatise that remained unchallenged for nearly forty years. The comprehensive treatment by such an esteemed historian was accepted at the time to be beyond reproach. Furthermore, the book's influence on both academic and popular Texas Rangers historiography, and by extension the public consciousness, is objectively impressive: after almost eighty years it is still in print and, until recently, had sold more copies than any other book in the University of Texas Press catalog, several times over.[9]

This acknowledgement of Webb's influence is an indictment rather than an endorsement; his prominence and apparent authority led generations of scholars and authors to accept his purported facts, conclusions, and interpretations without question, thereby reproducing his errors and bias without critical examination for decades. This is particularly unfortunate in light of the fact that Webb himself had recognized the book's shortcomings, and was working on a heavily revised edition. Due to his untimely death, however, Webb never was able to publish that revised edition correcting his earlier errors. Since then, the University of Texas Press, which obtained the copyright and began reprinting the book in 1965, has continued to publish it in its original form, without the benefit of any prologue or other disclaimer. As a result many modern authors continue to cite Webb uncritically, thereby perpetuating a stilted and prejudiced view of the events and people involved. New generations of historical readers continue to be misled by reading this outdated and inherently flawed book, with no understanding that the author himself did not intend for it to continue to be published in that original version.[10]

Webb set the bar for Texas Rangers historiography disappointingly low, particularly where analysis and interpretation of racial dynamics were concerned. The intervening period (between the publication of Webb's Texas Rangers book and the eventual rise of works critical of Webb decades later) saw a litany of memoirs, biographies, pictorial histories, magazine articles, juvenile books (including one by Webb), and historical fiction publications flood the marketplace. Essentially all of those cited, affirmed, or were altogether based on Webb and followed his example. An unfortunate consequence of this trend was the resulting impression within the ranks of academic historians that any studies on the topic were unlikely to produce a scholarly and objective portrayal, and that only works critical of the Rangers were likely to have any merit. The perception of Texas Rangers' historiography as unsuited for scholarly attention still lingers among academic historians, even as numerous works taking Webb to task have appeared, due to the longevity and breadth of Webb's influence. The modern publication of narrative, non-academic works aimed at the commercial market that are primarily derivative and lacking in nuance and balance has only reinforced this notion. For that reason they contribute to the myth and memory of the Rangers, even today.

Some of the earliest myths regarding the Texas Rangers centered around the ethno-cultural centrism that was prevalent in the late nineteenth and early twentieth centuries in Texas, which espoused notions of the inherent superiority of Anglo-European Texans over the Indians and Latinos that they were seen to have either subjugated or displaced. The authors promoting this viewpoint insisted that Anglo-Texans were nobler and more honorable than their "foes," and that they possessed inherent military superiority as well. As the primary defenders of the frontier for the Anglo-dominated new Republic, the early Texas Rangers were glorified as an invincible and irreproachable mounted force. This was despite the fact that their record on the battlefield varied widely over time, and it was most dependent on the quality of leadership provided by the individual commanders, as well as the specialized combat experience and expertise of their chosen men.[11]

Two of the earliest chronicles of Texas history that influenced future works through romanticized accounts of Rangers exploits were *Indian Wars and Pioneers of Texas,* an ethnocentric compilation of brief biographies of people the author considered to be notable Texans of the nineteenth century, and *The History of Texas from 1685 to 1892,* a general history of Texas, as implied by the title. Both books were written by John Henry Brown, a journalist and soldier who served in numerous ranging companies during the Republic and early statehood period, and who was intimately involved in the process of removing Indians to reservations during his career. Brown's works are plagued by a lack of substance, an absence of documentation or source material, and a patently partisan perspective, which leads him to denigrate Indians as "savages," and assume all Mexicans to be acting in "bad faith," while romanticizing Anglos as universally honorable and valiant. Another example of the traditionalist narrative is James Thomas DeShields, whose writing career spanned from the 1880s until the 1940s, and who similarly eulogized Anglo historical actors as heroes while treating Indians and Tejanos as insignificant and inferior.[12]

Brown, DeShields, and several generations of Texas history authors who followed them conveniently highlighted any and all victories by the Rangers, while simultaneously ignoring any defeats and dishonorable episodes, often claiming victory and glory when the facts and circumstances suggested otherwise. Perhaps the most notable event involving the latter approach was that of the famous "battle" of Pease River, which involved a contingent of Texas Rangers under the legendary Lawrence Sullivan "Sul" Ross. Ross's fraudulent account of that event was carefully crafted and expanded in furtherance of his political career, which he capped with two terms as governor of Texas from 1887 to 1891. What has long captivated the public about an event that would otherwise have been considered a minor footnote in Rangers history is the connection to the saga of Cynthia Ann Parker and her son, Quanah—one of the last Comanche chiefs to resist the authority and western expansion of the United States. The combined involvement of the Parkers and Sul Ross "inspired an elaborate fabrication of [those] events," and turned what was an "indiscriminate slaughter" into a "decisive battle" that was proclaimed as having "shattered Comanche military power." Very little of Ross's account stands up to historical scrutiny, however, and it was the accounts of his own subordinate Rangers that often contradicted his claims.[13]

In *Myth, Memory, and Massacre: The Pease River Capture of Cynthia Ann Parker,* Paul H. Carlson and Tom Crum challenged many of the contemporary notions of Anglo racial superiority and reveal how such notions were propped up by highlighting Indian "atrocities" at every opportunity while simultaneously ignoring or even covering up similar acts of "brutality and barbarism" by Anglo Texans, including the massacre of mostly women and children at the "battle" of Pease River. As Carlson and Crum point out, there are many "sacred" mythical accounts and interpretations of events in Texas history that have shaped the modern Texas identity, but many originated from very problematic racial inter-pretations, unbeknownst to the members of the general public who cling to them. Nevertheless, early ethnocentric writers were not alone in the promulgation of pro-Ranger mythology. Sometimes actual Texas Rangers have engaged in such practices, to serve their own individual and professional ends.[14]

Despite the fact that they have and continue to receive such widespread media attention, most Texas Rangers have typically avoided public attention and scrutiny. However, there has always seemed to be at least one in each generation that craved the limelight. A few examples are Captain Bill McDonald of the late nineteenth and early twentieth century, Manuel "Lone Wolf" Gonzaullas of the mid-twentieth century, and Senior Captain Clint Peoples of the mid-to-late twentieth century. McDonald was perhaps best known for the motto, "No man in the wrong can stand up against a fellow that's in the right and keeps on acomin," and the mythical, "One Riot, One Ranger." Gonzaullas's biography erroneously identified him as the "first Hispanic Ranger captain," despite the fact that he had missed that distinction by more than a century. Peoples used his position and political contacts to situate himself as the preferred Ranger consultant for television and film in the 1960s and '70s. All three are regarded as having been effective Ranger commanders, though none were without flaw. In fact according to Robert Utley, author of *Lone Star Justice: The First Century of the Texas Rangers,* it was precisely Peoples's "mountainous ego" and questionable relationship with Hollywood that precipitated the end of his Ranger career, despite his strong political ties and relative success as a captain.[15]

Sometimes stories that appear to have originated with an actual Ranger eventually get exaggerated and take on a life all their own, eventually rising to the level of myth. Perhaps the best example of that phenomenon is a phrase that is often quoted as an unofficial Rangers motto (though not reflective of actual Rangers practices in the past or present). That is the seemingly ubiquitous idiom, "One Riot, One Ranger." The phrase appears to have originated with Ranger Captain Bill McDonald, though even his own authorized 1909 biography equivocates mightily when addressing this powerful meme of Texans' collective memory, and fails to offer pertinent historic details in its mere three-sentence account. Nevertheless, articles have appeared in books and newspapers around the country carrying versions of the story and purporting it to be true. The earliest publication found expounding a detailed version of the event is the book *Riding For Texas: The True Adventures of Captain Bill McDonald . . . As told by Colonel Edward M. House to Tyler Mason,* published in 1936. The Author's Notes in the book offer this equivocating disclaimer:

> This is not a biography—Albert Bigelow Paine's admirable "Life of Captain Bill McDonald" filled that need a quarter of a century ago—and the accuracy of an historical record is not to be sought in these pages. We have aimed at color and drama more moving than the rigid limitations of biographical exactitude would have permitted. The deeds performed by Captain Bill owe nothing to the imagination. Each story is founded on an actual true adventure; the subsidiary characters and background have been so combined as to throw the chief actor into sharp relief, but care has been

taken to avoid over-statement and false heroics. We have tried
to re-create a character whose life was the very stuff of which
fiction is made.

The account by Mason and House provides enough detail to recognize it
as related to historic events, but names are changed, details such as exact
locations and dates are omitted, and the interactions between McDonald
and the unnamed mayor of the unnamed town are not to be found in
any historical records or publications.[16]

The irony is that not only was McDonald not alone when Governor
Culberson sent the Rangers to stop a prize fight from happening in El Paso
in 1896 (the only such historical incident), but the entire Ranger force was
there with him. All four of the so-called "Great Captains" (Brooks, Rogers,
Hughes, and McDonald) and their companies were present, the only time
in history that this ever occurred. Walter Webb hedged on the issue,
saying that there was "some basis for the story," yet he also pointed out
its dubious nature, noting that McDonald's Ranger contemporaries would
laugh whenever they heard it. He also lamented that, "It seems to be the
only story that the public remembers about the Rangers." Robert Utley
referred to the alleged event as an "enduring legend" that originated from
McDonald's use of "theatrics," and the modern biography of McDonald—
published in 2009 by Harold Weiss—thoroughly and effectively commits
the story to its final resting place in the land of fables.[17]

An interesting gauge of the impact of this mythological creed spawned
by the fertile imaginations of Mason and House can be found in the
archives of the *Los Angeles Times*. There you will find that the "One Riot,
One Ranger" myth has become so engrained into the national psyche
that the Los Angeles Police Department has been chastised for not living
up to this fictional standard. An Op-Ed article in the *Los Angeles Times*
dated July 25, 1949, invoked the famous phrase and the perceived Texas
Rangers standard as a way to encourage the LAPD to eliminate two-man
patrol units to provide what the writer considered to be more judicious
use of police manpower. A December 31, 1932, *Los Angeles Times* article

also invokes the legendary "quote" while comparing the United States Marines to the venerated Texas organization, calling them "Uncle Sam's Rangers" (an ironic reference considering that the United States Army actually has always had a division officially designated as "Rangers" who, though famous in their own right, are still not as widely venerated as the Texas variety). Finally, an October 4, 1931 *Los Angeles Times* article issued a call for the "Texas Ranger Spirit" while trying to encourage local, state, and federal authorities not to shy away from their duty to bring dangerous organized crime figures (such as Al Capone) to justice. Incidentally, Texas Rangers of that era were known to brag about their relative success in limiting organized crime operations in the Lone Star State.[18]

Arguably, the most common method Rangers have used to perpetuate the myth surrounding them is simply ignoring or concealing the shortcomings or misdeeds of their predecessors and colleagues. That practice is most evident in regard to Texas Rangers in pursuit of Mexican bandits and revolutionaries from approximately 1910 to 1919. Rangers' actions during that period resulted in the deaths of hundreds of Latinos, some of whom may have been loyal Tejanos and likely innocent of any real malfeasance. The result of those alleged abuses on the Rangers' reputation in South Texas was aptly characterized by something that former Ranger Ray Martinez was told after being assigned there in the 1970s: "Every Texas Ranger has Mexican blood . . . on the tips of his boots." The motivations of later Rangers and media sources for such treatment cannot be entirely known, but some may have felt that the acknowledgement of shortcomings would undermine their effectiveness, while others may have sincerely believed the acts in question were justified.[19]

The comments and responses from numerous modern Rangers interviewed for the April 2007 *Texas Monthly* article "These Are Not Your Father's Texas Rangers" however, would seem to indicate that method of handling controversial subjects (among others) is no longer prevalent. Frank and critical commentary on Ranger actions during the 1967 Rio Grande Valley United Farm Workers Strike, made on camera by the late

Captain John Wood and other modern Rangers, also signifies that their approach to addressing the foibles of fellow Rangers has evolved. And while it is true that some Rangers and their adherents have, at times, propagated myths to their own benefit, it is also important to note that there are arguably as many anti-Ranger counter myths. Many of such myths are so prevalent and accepted in popular memory and by some academic historians that, as Robert M. Utley acknowledged in his preface to *Lone Star Lawmen*, he began his research expecting to find evidence of institutionalized racial bias among the Texas Rangers against Tejanos. It was a notion that, much to his surprise, was not borne out by the historical record and instead proved to be based on numerous historical fallacies.[20]

Regardless of justification or intent, there has been tension between many Tejanos from South Texas and the Texas Rangers for generations. But the historical record does not support simplistic "Anglo versus Hispanic" narratives in regard to these issues, and some Tejano/Latin American historians have fallen victim to the same stereotyping employed by many of the dueling traditionalist narratives. One of the issues driving conflict between South Texas Tejanos and the Rangers was the organization's diverse responsibilities during that period, most particularly defense of the United States–Mexico Border in Texas (a unique role for a state constabulary, and one that has recently been reinstated in the modern era). Historically such duties led to direct conflict with many Rio Grande Valley Tejanos, many of whom were often engaged in supporting Mexican exiles and filibustering activities after Mexico declared its independence from Spain, especially since opposition to the Porfirio Diaz regime began to build in the latter nineteenth century. Rangers interference in these illegal but locally popular activities often biased the South Texas perspective on the Rangers' efforts and actions.[21]

Furthermore, historian Robert M. Utley closely examined the relationship between Valley Tejanos and Rangers, thereby shining a scholarly light on the mythology of both groups. A primary example of what Utley refers to as the "stereotype[ing]" of Texas Rangers is how they have been accused of being willing conspirators and enforcers in the dispossession of Tejanos from their rightful lands, mainly in the region known as the Nueces Strip, which is situated along the border with Mexico. This perception appears to be a result of Texas Rangers involvement in the suppression of the "Cordova Rebellion" in 1838-1839, the "Cortina War" in the late nineteenth century, and their response to the threatened "Plan De San Diego" in early 1915. The story begins with Vincente Cordova of Nacogdoches, a Tejano leader in East Texas who had been an Anglo ally in the fight to restore the federalist Constitution of 1824, which Mexican President Antonio Lopez de Santa Anna declared invalid (despite having been elected on the federalist platform). Considering himself a loyal and patriotic Mexican citizen, Cordova would not support the eventual independence movement and thereafter acted as a filibuster in Texas on behalf of the Mexican Government. After Texas won its independence, Cordova led a revolt in 1838-1839 involving an attempted alliance with the Cherokees with the intention of returning Texas to Mexico. He was killed in the Battle of Salado Creek on September 18, 1842, though his descendants still live throughout the state.[22]

Following in Cordova's footsteps, Juan Nepomuceno Cortina fomented violence and rebellion under the guise of advocating for justice for displaced Tejanos. There is evidence, however, his actions were more likely motivated by the loss of the US–Mexican War, which served as a pretext for the commission of otherwise unrelated crimes. The 1915 Plan De San Diego "sought to reclaim territory taken by the United States from Mexico in 1848 [pursuant to the terms of the Treaty of Guadalupe Hidalgo] restore ancestral lands to indigenous people [it was unclear how conflicting Spanish/Mexican and Native claims would be dealt with] create an independent republic for Latinos, and kill every Anglo male over the age of sixteen." Despite having signed treaties relinquishing their claims to Texas after both the Texas revolt and the US–Mexican War, the Mexican Government was continually engaged in filibustering activities well into the twentieth century, thereby stoking intrigue and inflaming passions in the border region for close to a century after Texas first gained its independence from Mexico. It is arguable that such efforts contributed—more than any other single factor—to the conflicts between the Texas Rangers and South Texas Tejanos, at least some of whom maintained allegiance with their mother country and assisted its efforts at undermining Texas's sovereignty.[23]

As defenders of the Republic and later state of Texas, the Rangers had a lawful responsibility to respond to each of these perceived threats to Texas' sovereignty, regardless of the ethnicity of those involved. And while there are certain anecdotal historical incidents involving specific alleged bad acts by specific Texas Rangers—which have been repeated over and over by various historians and other critics—the historical record simply does not contain sufficient evidence to indicate that the Texas Rangers' actions overall, in furtherance of their lawful duties, were motivated by either racial hostility or a concerted plan to effect dispossession of Tejanos. Nor is there any evidence of the widespread displacement claimed or other adverse treatment by actual Texas Rangers. Examination of critical claims through the prism of the historical record reveals the inadequacy of simplistic "Anglo versus Hispanic" narratives in regard to these issues, or for the interpretation of Texas and US-Mexico border history, generally.[24]

In addition to such nuanced topics of historical debate, the Texas Rangers have also, at times, been blamed for acts that they simply did not commit. Perhaps the most notable example is that of the Gregorio Cortez episode. Cortez was the subject of a Mexican corrido, or folk song fable, which was made famous by the late folklorist and University of Texas professor of literature, Americo Paredes. Cortez was accused of killing a law enforcement officer and successfully evaded the sheriff's posses for months. According to contemporary news accounts and widespread public perception in South Texas, the Rangers killed Cortez. But in fact the Rangers joined the search for Cortez much later and captured him quickly and peacefully, then protected him from lynch mobs during his trials. Another example is that of Mexican Revolutionary General

Pascual Orozco, who was a federal fugitive indicted for violations of United States Neutrality laws. Contrary to a contemporary New York Times account claiming he had been "rangered," Cortez was actually killed in a shoot-out with a local civilian posse from El Paso, after he and his men allegedly opened fire on their pursuers. But the deaths of both men, in a persistent myth promulgated not only by some South Texas Tejanos but also by modern historians, are often still ascribed to the Rangers. Furthermore, Utley determined that evidence regarding specific "evaporations"—an historic regional colloquialism for alleged summary executions—might be considered sparse and ambiguous at best. The relative thinness of their ranks during this period also casts doubt on some of the claims of widespread misdeeds by actual Texas Rangers during this period, particularly since it has since been shown that numerous incidents originally attributed to the Rangers were in fact unconnected to actual Texas Rangers; many involved were instead either Special or Loyalty Rangers, as well as local and even federal lawmen in the region, if not others wholly unconnected to law enforcement, such as local ranch hands or private security agents.[25]

One reason for widespread errors of fact in this area is language misinterpretations. This has led some historians and others unfamiliar with the nuances of border region Tejano terminology to conflate allegations by Tejanos against Rangers with allegations against other lawmen who also operated in the Rio Grande Valley. As Utley noted, many different types of "Rangers" existed during that era, many created expressly for partisan purposes and operating independently of the formal institution's command structure. Furthermore, there were countless federal and local law enforcement officers working in the Rio Grande Valley, and the South Texas derogatory term "rinches" was a reference to *any* Anglo authority figure in the region on a horse, wearing a badge, hat, and gun. It is accurate to say that South Texas Tejanos often refer[red] to Rangers as "rinches," but the term did not apply to them exclusively, as so many modern scholars have asserted. As Americo Paredes pointed out, it was a term that—at a minimum—applied to all lawmen who operated in the

Rio Grande Valley, whether local, state, or federal, and possibly even without regard to their individual ethnicity.[26]

Recent research into sources originating out of northern Mexico indicates that the term may actually have originated as an amalgamation of "pinches rancheros" (Translation: damn ranchers), a fact that further vitiates any singular or exclusive connection to the Texas Rangers. According to that source, Mexican *tequileros* (smugglers), revolutionaries, and other Mexican nationals who sought to cross into the United States for unlawful purposes used the phrase to refer to the cowboys and ranch security personnel who frequently prevented their crossing private lands north of the Rio Grande in pursuit of their illicit activities. As a result of such linguistic confusion over time, and the accompanying uncritical assumptions on the topic made by many modern scholars, at times Rangers have likely been blamed for acts committed by entirely different law enforcement organizations, or perhaps even by non-law enforcement historical actors. Furthermore, few scholars or other Texas Rangers historians have studied that period thoroughly enough to understand the processes of their evolution from frontier defenders into law enforcement, or to fully evaluate the effect of politics on their quality and reputation. That oversight has often led critics of the Texas Rangers to apply unrealistic expectations to Rangers of this and even earlier periods, particularly when assessing their actions in accordance with standards of modern law enforcement officers. It is obviously unreasonable to analyze the actions of nineteenth-century citizen-soldiers or early twentieth-century political appointees based on professional law enforcement standards that first began to evolve in 1935.[27]

One of the most perplexing myths involving Tejanos and Texas Rangers, perpetuated by both traditionalists and early revisionists, is the notion that there were no Tejano Rangers until the latter twentieth century. In addition to Utley's two-volume institutional history of the Rangers, *Lone Star Justice* and *Lone Star Lawmen*, Stephen Moore's *Savage Frontier* series thoroughly documents that Tejanos (as well as American Indians) have served as Rangers and Ranger captains since the days of the legendary Captain Jack Hays. Two notable examples are Antonio Perez and Salvador Flores (the latter a brother-in-law to famous Texas patriot, Juan Seguin, whom both had served under in Mexican colonial-era flying squadrons). Additionally, it was an all-Tejano company under Captain Cesario Falcón that originally cultivated the Ranger's close, lasting, and often criticized relationship with the legendary King Ranch. Nevertheless, traditionalist Anglo-phone interpretations of Texas were often crafted to aid in the political oppression and disenfranchisement of Hispanic Texans from the late nineteenth to well into the twentieth century. In response, later twentieth century Chicano and other related revisionist interpretations reacted to the ethnocentrism of the Anglo narratives by simply arguing that it was their group that possessed the moral high ground, but otherwise relying on the same basic Anglo-Latino culture conflict interpretive model originally concocted by the Anglo traditionalists, which inevitably led the early revisionists also to ignore the service and contributions of Tejano Rangers. As a result both have unjustifiably denied Tejanos' agency in the creation and development of modern Texas, despite overwhelming historical evidence to the contrary.[28]

As Robert Utley's emphasis on the significance of the creation of the Texas Department of Public Safety in 1935 as a pivotal moment in their evolution from frontier fighters into modern lawmen demonstrated, an accurate evaluation of Ranger history requires a nuanced consideration of different times, places, administrations, commanders, individual Rangers, and other factors, which cannot be fully tested without a thorough examination of the second century of Texas Rangers history. To date few studies or biographies have been written on the Department of Public Safety Texas Rangers of the modern era, other than Utley's *Lone Star Lawmen*, thereby creating an unfortunate gap in the historiography that leaves even the most astute history aficionado with an outdated perspective on the still active and internationally renowned force.[29]

None of this is to say that all Texas Rangers throughout history were innocent of any particular charges of abuse by Tejanos, or by others for that matter. On the contrary, the point is simply that such allegations should be held up to the same scrutiny, as are the assertions of the Anglo-centric traditionalists like Webb and other apologists. And perhaps most importantly, even more care should be taken when using such anecdotal evidence in an attempt to extrapolate through interpretive analysis and apply such judgments to the entire force, and over time. Essentially, the leveling of sweeping indictments or sweeping endorsements to those who served as Texas Rangers across the state and over the past nearly two centuries is no more historically valid than any similar ethnic-based stereotype, be they based in Anglo notions of Manifest Destiny, or the counter-narratives of historically marginalized groups. Fortunately, many modern scholars now seek to promulgate a more inclusive interpretation of historical events, one that eschews stereotypes of any group across time and place, and which acknowledges the actions and involvement of all historical actors without regard to ethnicity or any other categorization. However, and despite such efforts on the part of academic historians, popular media has long perpetuated a simplistic characterization of Texas Rangers history in our collective memory. Unfortunately, such practices have not evolved in concert with that of the academic historical community. The result is that the majority of the population is still bombarded with a long outdated and one-sided view of that history which, in turn, reinforces ill feeling among many Tejanos of the Rio Grande Valley and also among Latin American historians.

While partisan perspectives have certainly contributed to the contin-uing dissemination of misinformation on the topic, the history of the Texas Rangers has been shrouded in myth and legend in the collec-tive consciousness almost since their origins in the Mexican colonial era, and popular news and entertainment media have been the most prolific propagators of that simplistic and narrowly tailored legend. Public perception has been shaped, for the most part, by deliberately manipulated interpretations orchestrated by a wide variety of popular media outlets. In each case, historical fact was often sacrificed in favor of varying degrees of fiction that served a variety of purposes, be they political agendas, personal vanity or, most commonly, the desire for one-dimensional, exciting entertainment. Long fascinated with the history of the Texas Rangers, popular media's effect on the collective memory of the populace has been exponentially more influential than that of all Texas Rangers historians combined. Since they came to international notice during the United States–Mexican War, every form of popular media has used a variety of sources to promulgate and propagate a hybrid pioneer-patriot archetype of the quintessential Texas Ranger. As evidenced by the proliferation of novels, newspaper and magazine articles, radio serials, silent films, television series, and modern feature films, Rangers lore has consistently found a solid following.

Historian Bill O'Neal's 2008 publication, *Reel Rangers,* documents the vastness of the genre in television, radio, and film:

> For nearly a century the world's most famous law enforcement body has inspired novelists, actors, and filmmakers. . . From *The Lone Ranger* to *Walker, Texas Ranger,* from Zane Grey's *The Lone Star Ranger* to Larry McMurtry's *Lonesome Dove,* Texas Rangers have been portrayed on the silver screen, network radio and television. John Wayne, Gary Cooper, Tom Mix, Clint Eastwood, Gene Autry, Roy Rogers, and a host of lesser Western stars each took his turn at depicting Texas Rangers . . . .

Hollywood's preoccupation with the Texas Rangers has not waned even in the slightest since O'Neal completed his study, as Texas Rangers stories, characters, and references continue to be found in even the most recent popular programming. A few examples are: the popular remake *Hawaii 5-O* featured a (ludicrous depiction of a) Texas Ranger in an 2013 episode; a short-lived ABC series—for which only the pilot ever aired—titled, *Killer Women,* featuring a modern female Ranger as the lead character; the *History Channel* has produced a fictional 2015 mini-series titled *Texas Rising,* which centers around the Texas Rangers of the Republic era from 1836 to 1846 and claims to tell "the story of how the Texas Rangers were created." This is an independent film written, produced and directed by Robert Duvall, and featuring his wife as a modern Texas Ranger in the lead role. Even a recent episode of *Justified*, a highly rated television series on the FX Channel now in its sixth season, referenced the mystique of Texas Rangers in its 2015 season premiere. In a scene between the lead character, a US Marshal, and a Mexican Federal Police Officer (Federales), the Federal scoffs when the Marshal displays his badge, telling him, "Look around you, *cabrón*, this is *México*, and that star you wear don't mean [expletive deleted] here! Now, a Ranger badge... that means something. They bang it out of a 1948 Mexican silver coin." And finally, former Texas Ranger Joaquin Jackson's two-volume memoir has eclipsed Webb's *Texas Rangers* as it has sold well over one hundred thousand copies, spawned numerous television and motion picture appearances, and built personal relationships for Jackson with some of modern Hollywood's biggest stars and directors. So, even after more than a century of motion picture productions and quantum leaps in the technology behind the industry, Hollywood's fascination with the mystique of the Texas Rangers is as fresh as ever. Unfortunately, that means we will likely continue to see the proliferation of a one-dimensional and prejudicial portrayal of the Texas Rangers to yet another generation of Americans and of the world.[30]

Bill O'Neal revealed in his book just how deeply the popular media image of the Texas Ranger is ingrained in the American psyche by explaining that virtually every day at the Texas Ranger Hall of Fame and Museum in Waco, museum staff members have to tell patrons that Walker, Texas Ranger (Chuck Norris), Gus McCrae (Robert Duvall), and Woodrow F. Call (Tommy Lee Jones) were fictional characters and not historic Rangers. No doubt they and similar institutions, including the *Texas Rangers Heritage Center* currently being developed in Fredericksburg, will soon be addressing similar issues in regard to the more recent Hollywood creations. In addition to this anecdotal evidence, a 2009 study done at Duke University found that people tend subconsciously to internalize information gleaned from television and movies far more quickly and intensely than from reading, making it difficult for them to separate fact from fiction—regardless of their exposure to more reliable written sources. This explains much about the creation of memory. Even those given forewarning that the book was the legitimate source and that the film was fictionalized not only provided the incorrect answers to the historical questions, but also argued that they were referencing the book when citing the erroneous information. This supports the argument that feature films and television programs have been the main drivers in establishing and shaping the public's decidedly inaccurate perception of the Texas Rangers.[31]

Figure 6. Cowboy Star Tom Mix (in white) with Texas Rangers at Capitol in Austin, ca. 1925

Courtesy Briscoe Center for American History, University of Texas at Austin

The proliferation of the Texas Rangers legend is not limited to the entertainment media, although the following examples are in all likelihood attempts to capitalize on the marketing prowess of the Texas Rangers international brand. Their legacy is invoked in the naming of professional sports teams (the professional baseball team, 2011 World Series contenders, the former professional polo team that swept every major title in England in 1939) and a litany of commercial products and businesses (Ford Ranger trucks, Ranger Boats, and the Texas Ranger Motel in Santa Anna, Texas, just to name a few). There is even a town in East Texas is named for them. Additionally, statues of Texas Rangers adorn sites throughout the state, from the "One Riot, One Ranger" bronze at Dallas's Love Field to the life-sized statue of Captain John C. Hays mounted on his horse on the courthouse square in his namesake county south of Austin. In sum the Texas Rangers' influence on popular culture is ubiquitous, and that culture has heavily influenced the collective memory of the Lone Star State, those interested in its history, and the Rangers themselves.

One key aspect of Ranger mystique is its sheer power and cultural reach. Sometimes this manifests as a desire to join the ranks of the Rangers. Most retired and current Rangers have stories about the first time they ever saw a Ranger and how the experience inspired them for the future. However, it is also common for men who never actually served as Rangers to claim that they had. Unfulfilled aspirations of Ranger service have been revealed in countless obituaries, like that of a Houston-area judge who claimed he was the legendary Captain Frank Hamer's driver when Hamer tracked down and killed Bonnie and Clyde. (Hamer never mentioned this man in his records and never had a "driver," and all those present at the ambush of Bonnie and Clyde were photographed and otherwise well-documented.) But this is not merely a Texas phenomenon.[32]

Self-declared Texas Rangers can be found nationwide, as evidenced by a *Los Angeles Times* article about a would-be pickpocket victim who slashed the hand of the suspect with a pocket knife in 1943; a 1938 *Los*

Angeles Times obituary for the judge who presided over the famous Owens Valley vs. Los Angeles water rights trial; and another *Los Angeles Times* obituary from 1933 for the county Chief Deputy Sheriff. In a 1920 article a Portland man named Jack London (not the author) was proclaimed a hero for saving several people from a building fire; and he also laid claim to previous service in the Texas Rangers. Official records at the Texas State Library and Archives in Austin do not back up any of those claims, but this did not dissuade such individuals from seeking to join the ranks of the Rangers at least in newsprint.[33]

The influence of Texas Rangers lore is not limited to North America, but rather it crosses both oceans and spans the globe. The misplaced fears of the Nazis and Vichy French in World War II demonstrate the Ranger mystique prevalence across Europe. News of an Allied raid at Dieppe that was reputed to include American "rangers" was the source of their fears because, according to the article, "to many Frenchmen there is only one type of Ranger—the Texas variety." Nazi Germany also experienced similar fears of Texas Ranger infiltration during the D-Day invasion. Their mystique has even traveled to Japan, where Texas Ranger books and a television show were staples in the childhood of Toyota executive T.J. Tashima. After being assigned to open the Toyota manufacturing plant in San Antonio, Texas, Tashima was able to fulfill his childhood dream of meeting real-life Texas Rangers. Japan's reverence for their ancient samurai culture, another mounted frontier defense force, may explain their affinity for the Texas Rangers. Such widespread attraction to the Texas Rangers' mystique is not merely a pop-culture phenomenon, however: it has practical implications for actual modern Rangers in the performance of their duties.[34]

As the Texas Rangers evolved from their origins as loosely organized mounted militia units in the early nineteenth century into a professional elite investigative force by the beginning of the twenty-first century, they have been helped and hindered by the myths surrounding their forebears, despite sharing little more in common than a name. The continuing myth surrounding their name actually assists modern Texas Rangers in their modern pursuit of law and order, and thus contributes to their success. In some situations myth and memory can convince both criminals and law-abiding citizens to offer a level of deference and cooperation to Texas Rangers that is often not extended to other law enforcement agencies. An example of this can be found in *One Ranger Returns*, Joaquin Jackson's second volume of his best-selling memoir of his time as a Ranger. Jackson relates an episode where a rancher refused to give a local sheriff access to his land but subsequently allowed Ranger Jackson access because of his mistaken belief that the Texas Ranger possessed more law enforcement authority than the sheriff. It was simply not the case legally, but the fact that the rancher believed it to be so directly influenced his decision to cooperate with the Ranger after having refused to do so with the sheriff.[35]

These anecdotes give rise to the question of whether aspects of the Texas Rangers myth are so entrenched that it has become a self-fulfilling prophecy, responsible at least in part for some of their most notable successes. Examples include bringing the 1997 Davis Mountains stand-off (by well-armed "Republic of Texas" anti-government separatists) to a non-violent conclusion, successfully investigating the 2007 Texas Youth Commission corruption and abuse cases after local officials failed to do so, and obtaining the surrender and confession of the infamous late 1990s "Railway Killer." One of the most notable is their negotiation of a peaceful surrender agreement with David Koresh, leader of the Branch Davidians—an arrangement unfortunately rejected by the FBI with disastrous and deadly consequences. In these situations the aspects of the mystique that cast Rangers as fair but relentless may have contributed to those outcomes.

Modern Rangers must also contend, however, with the other side of their myth and memory, which bears resentment based on past Rangers' misdeeds, both real and illusory. This is particularly true for a substantial segment of the Tejano population, especially in the South Texas border region, that perceives the Rangers as racially motivated oppressors serving the Anglo-dominated political establishment. The truth of the matter, as is so often the case with history and memory, lies somewhere in between the two extremes in the realm of myths.[36]

In closing it has been shown that while various individual Rangers have, at times, created and promulgated particular mythological anecdotes toward various personal or professional ends, such instances are exceptions and not the rule. Far more often, the myth and memory of the Texas Rangers has been perpetuated through the media, both popular and historical. Unfortunately, even the ostensibly historical treatments have often been lacking in depth, nuance, and, at times, basic factual accuracy. Furthermore, those myths are not relegated to esoteric academic debates, as modern Rangers both benefit from and suffer the ill effects of the myths in the performance of their official duties.

Fortunately, and thanks at least in part to Robert M. Utley's prompting, many scholars are now providing a more inclusive and balanced image of the Texas Rangers by moving beyond the romanticized and racially divisive rhetoric that has plagued much of Texas Rangers historiography, thereby pushing it into a new era. These historians are including an examination of the perspectives of people and communities among whom the Rangers have served and are beginning to delve into the second century of their existence, a long overdue necessity for providing a well-rounded understanding of the overall history of this nearly two-hundred-year-old institution. Unfortunately, and as the 2009 Duke study demonstrated, academic publications are only a small part of the equation. Unless and until popular media depictions of the Texas Rangers begin to reflect this approach, our collective memory and group identity will remain mired in the myths and legends of the past.

SELECTED BIBLIOGRAPHY

Carlson, Paul H., and Tom Crum. *Myth, Memory, and Massacre: The Pease River Capture of Cynthia Ann Parker.* Lubbock: Texas Tech Press, 2012.

Ely, Glen Sample. *Where The West Begins: Debating Texas Identity.* Lubbock: Texas Tech University Press, 2011.

Harris, Charles H. III, and Louis R. Sadler. *Texas Rangers and the Mexican Revolution: The Bloodiest Decade, 1910-1920.* Albuquerque: University of New Mexico Press, 2004.

Haynes, Sam W., and Cary D Wintz, eds. *Major Problems in Texas History.* New York: Houghton Mifflin, 2002.

Jackson, Joaquin, and James L. Haley. *One Ranger Returns.* Austin: University of Texas Press 2008.

McCaslin, Richard B. *Fighting Stock: John S. "Rip" Ford of Texas.* Fort Worth: Texas Christian University Press, 2011.

Moore, Stephen. *Savage Frontier: Volume I.* Denton: University of North Texas Press, 2002.

_____. *Savage Frontier: Volume II.* Denton: University of North Texas Press, 2006.

_____. *Savage Frontier: Volume III.* Denton: University of North Texas Press, 2007.

_____. *Savage Frontier: Volume IV.* Denton: University of North Texas Press, 2010.

O'Neal, Bill. *Reel Rangers: Texas Rangers in Movies, TV, Radio, and Other Forms of Popular Culture.* Austin: Eakin Press, 2008.

Utley, Robert M. *Lone Star Justice: The First Century of the Texas Rangers.* New York: Oxford University Press, 2002.

_____. *Lone Star Lawmen: The Second Century of the Texas Rangers.* New York: Oxford University Press, 2007.

Weiss, Harold J. Jr. *Yours to Command: The Life and Legend of Texas Ranger Captain Bill McDonald.* Denton: University of North Texas Press, 2009.

NOTES

1. Glen Sample Ely, *Where The West Begins: Debating Texas Identity* (Lubbock: Texas Tech University Press, 2011), 12.

2. Charles H. Harris III and Louis R. Sadler, *Texas Rangers and the Mexican Revolution: The Bloodiest Decade, 1910–1920* (Albuquerque: University of New Mexico Press, 2004), 1. Portions of this chapter were extracted, revised, and edited from a conference paper entitled "Texas Rangers in Myth and Memory" (presented at the 2010 Texas State Historical Association Conference in El Paso and the 2011 Windy City Graduate Student History Conference at the University of Illinois-Chicago). Additional material was derived from a graduate research paper completed in furtherance of the course work requirements fulfilling my Ph.D. in American History at the University of North Texas, entitled "Historiography of the Origins and Early Practices of the Texas Rangers" (completed in Fall 2009). The prologue of my 2014 dissertation contains a comprehensive analysis of Texas Rangers historiography. See Ginn: "Reckoning in the Redlands: The Texas Rangers' Clean-Up of San Augustine in 1935," Ph.D. Disseratation, University of North Texas, Fall 2014.

3. Andres A. Tijerina, *Tejanos and Texas under the Mexican Flag, 1821-1836* (College Station: Texas A&M University Press, 1994), 79-92; Stephen L. Hardin, "Efficient in the Cause," Gerald E. Poyo, ed., *Tejano Journey, 1750-1850* (Austin: University of Texas Press, 1996), 49-51; Dan E. Kilgore, *A Ranger Legacy: 150 Years of Service to Texas* (Austin: Madrona Press, 1973), 4-5, 21-26, 32.

4. Robert M. Utley, *Lone Star Justice: The First Century of the Texas Rangers* (New York: Oxford University Press, 2002), 15-16, 19, 145, 152, 287-294; Utley, *Lone Star Lawmen*, 2-7.

5. Utley, *Lone Star Justice*, x-xi, 271-73, 298-302.

6. Ibid., 228-29; Robert M. Utley, *Lone Star Lawmen: The Second Century of the Texas Rangers* (New York: Oxford University Press, 2007), 4-5, 10-11, 14, 57, 153, 172; Charles H. Harris III, Frances E. Harris, and Louis R. Sadler, *Texas Ranger Biographies: Those Who Served, 1910-1921* (Albuquerque: University of New Mexico Press, 2009), xi-xviii.

7. Ibid.; Utley, *Lone Star Lawmen*, 4-5.

8. Ben H. Procter, "Great Depression," *Handbook of Texas Online* (http://www.tshaonline.org/handbook/online/articles/npg01), accessed March

31, 2014. Uploaded on June 15, 2010. Published by the Texas State Historical Association.

9.   Walter L. Buenger and Robert A. Calvert, "The Shelf Life of Truth in Texas," *Major Problems in Texas History,* Sam W. Haynes and Cary D. Wintz, eds. (New York: Houghton Mifflin, 2002). 8-12; Webb was recently surpassed in this regard by the memoir of former Texas Ranger Joaquin Jackson, a late twentieth-century Ranger whose persona had already been used as the basis for a Hollywood film, *Extreme Prejudice,* released in 1987. http://www.imdb.com/title/tt0092997/?ref_=nv_sr_1 (accessed February 2, 2015).

10. Llerena B. Friend, "W. P. Webb's *Texas Rangers,*" *Southwestern Historical Quarterly,* vol. 74, no. 3 (January 1971): 293-323.

11. Utley, *Lone Star Justice,* 3-4.

12. Erma Baker, "Brown, John Henry," *Handbook of Texas Online* (http://www.tshaonline.org/handbook/online/articles/fbr94), accessed April 02, 2014. Uploaded on June 12, 2010. Published by the Texas State Historical Association; John Henry Brown, *Indian Wars and Pioneers of Texas* (Austin: L. E. Daniel, 1880); Brown, *The History of Texas from 1685 to 1892* (St. Louis: L. E. Daniel, 1892); Brown, *Indian Wars,* 5-8, 11. Wayne Gard, "DeShields, James Thomas," *Handbook of Texas Online* (http://www.tshaonline.org/handbook/online/articles/fde45), accessed April 03, 2014. Uploaded on June 12, 2010. Published by the Texas State Historical Association; James Thomas DeShields, *Border Wars of Texas* (Tioga: Herald Company, 1912).

13. Paul H. Carlson and Tom Crum, *Myth, Memory, and Massacre: The Pease River Capture of Cynthia Ann Parker* (Lubbock: Texas Tech Press, 2012), xiii-xix.

14. Ibid.

15. Brownson Malsch, *Lone Wolf: Captain M. T. Gonzaullas, the Only Texas Ranger Captain of Spanish Descent* (Austin: Shoal Creek Publishers, 1980); Utley, *Lone Star Justice,* 257-58.

16. Harris and Sadler, 1; Albert Bigelow Paine, *Captain Bill McDonald: Texas Ranger* (New York: J.J. Little & Ives Company, 1909), 220; "Bill McDonald, Evangelist: Captain of Texas Rangers Is Now Taking Shots at Sinners," *New York Times,* August 31, 1915; Tyler Mason, *Riding for Texas: As Told by Col. Edward M. House to Tyler Mason* (New York: Reynal & Hitchcock, 1936), xii, 101 – 116.

17. Utley, *Lone Star Justice...*, 257, 268–269; Walter Prescott Webb, *The Texas Rangers: A Century of Frontier Defense* (New York: Houghton Mifflin Company, 1935), 458.
18. V.W. Bennett, "One-Man Police Patrol Cars," *Los Angeles Times,* July 25, 1949; "Uncle Sam's Rangers," *Los Angeles Times,* December 31, 1932; D. Ramaley, "Texas Ranger Spirit Needed," *Los Angeles Times,* October 4, 1931; "Rangers Win Praise of San Augustine in Clean-up that Is High Spot in History of State Police Force," *Beaumont Journal,* May 9, 1936.
19. Pamela Colloff "These Are Not Your Father's Texas Rangers" *Texas Monthly,* April 2007 114–120, 208–224.
20. Utley, *Lone Star Lawmen...,* xii.
21. "Complaints of Texas Rangers: Gen. Nafarrate Says Their Acts Embitter Border Mexicans," *New York Times,* September 7, 1915; Harris and Sadler, 5, 7, 504.
22. Arnoldo Deleon and Robert A. Calvert, *The History of Texas,* 2nd ed. (Wheeling, Illinois: Harlan Davidson, 1996).
23. Jerry Thompson, *Cortina: Defending the Mexican Name in Texas* (College Station: Texas A&M University Press, 2007). 4-5.
24. "Complaints of Texas Rangers: Gen. Nafarrate Says Their Acts Imbitter Border Mexicans," *New York Times,* September 7, 1915; Harris and Sadler, 5.
25. "Mexican Raiders Killed: Five Shot By Rangers Near Texas Border— Orozco May Be One," *New York Times,* August 31, 1915; Utley, *Lone Star Lawmen,* 4-5, 52–53.
26. Harris and Sadler, 6; Americo Paredes, *With His Pistol in His Hand: A Border Ballad and Its Hero* (Austin: University of Texas Press, 1958).
27. *Yahoo Respuestas,* https://mx.answers.yahoo.com/question/index?qid=20081114104808AA0AbHm (accessed March 19, 2012); Utley, *Lone Star Justice,* 243-44.
28. Stephen Moore, *Savage Frontier: Volume III* (Denton: University of North Texas Press, 2007), x, 140, 181; Utley, *Lone Star Justice...,* 139–140.
29. Ben H. Procter, "Great Depression," *Handbook of Texas Online* (http://www.tshaonline.org/handbook/online/articles/npg01), accessed March 31, 2014. Uploaded on June 15, 2010. Published by the Texas State Historical Association.
30. "A'ale Ma'a Wau," *Hawaii 5-0, original air date October 4, 2013,* http://www.imdb.com/title/tt3074164/?ref_=ttep_ep15, (accessed February 2, 2015); "La Sicaria," *Killer Women,* original air date January 7, 2014, http://www.imdb.com/title/tt2925876/?ref_=ttep_ep1, (accessed

February 2, 2015); *Texas Rising, http://www.imdb.com/title/tt3598496/? ref_=nv_sr_1, (accessed February 2, 2015)*; Alice Howarth, "Why Robert Duvall Nearly Turned Down *The Judge," http://www.gq-magazine.co.uk/ entertainment/articles/2014-10/17/robert-duvall-the-judge-interview-the- godfather, accessed February 2, 2015;* "Fate's Right Hand," Season 6 Premiere, *Justified,* original air date January 20, 2015, FX Channel; Joaquin Jackson and James L. Haley, *One Ranger Returns* (Austin: University of Texas Press 2008).

31. Bill O'Neal, *Reel Rangers: Texas Rangers in Movies, TV, Radio, and Other Forms of Popular Culture* (Austin: Eakin Press, 2008), 1, 161; Jeremy Hsu, "Students Recall More Hollywood Than History," *LiveScience,* August 12, 2009, http://www.livescience.com/culture/090812-movie-memory.html (accessed August 18, 2009).

32. H. Gordon Frost and John H. Jenkins, *I'm Frank Hamer* (Austin, New York: The Pemberton Press, 1968), 178-248.

33. "Ex-Texas Ranger Foils Asserted Pickpocket Effort," *Los Angeles Times,* March 28, 1943; "News of the San Joaquin Valley, Water Rights Judge Expires: Jurist Who Heard Famed Cases Started as a Texas Ranger," *Los Angeles Times,* February 23, 1938; "Deputy Wright Dies in Office: Chief Officer Under Biscailuz Victim of Heart Attack, Fatally Stricken While He Talks With Colleague, Member of Texas Rangers in His Earlier Years," *Los Angeles Times,* August 11, 1933; "His Lariat Saves Five: Ex-Texas Ranger Hero at Fire," *Los Angeles Times,* August 8, 1920; Texas State Library and Archives Commission, Archives and Manuscripts, Adjutant General Service Records, http://www.tsl.state.tx.us/arc/service/index. php (accessed April 20 and May 4, 2008).

34. "Texas Rangers Excite Vichy: French Mistake Invaders for Famed Fighting Men of Lone Star State," *Los Angeles Times,* August 20, 1942; "HeartBrand Cattle Company Bridges the Gap Between Texas and Japan," *Straight Talk,* August 2005, 12; Texas Ranger Hall of Fame & Museum, Texas Ranger History, Special investigations http://www.texasranger.org/ history/Timespecial.htm (Accessed May 4, 2008).

35. Joaquin Jackson and James L. Haley, *One Ranger Returns* (Austin: University of Texas Press 2008).

36. Robert M. Utley, *Lone Star Lawmen: The Second Century of the Texas Rangers* (New York: Oxford University Press, 2007), 319-28, 304-14; Mike Cox, *Time of the Rangers: Texas Rangers From 1900 to the Present* (New York: Forge Books, 2009), 341-44, 453, fn9.

CHAPTER 4

ON BECOMING TEXANS

NINETEENTH-CENTURY JEWISH IMMIGRANTS CLAIM THEIR GERMAN IDENTITY

by
Kay Goldman

Editor's Note: In this essay Kay Goldman examines the activities of German-Jewish immigrants to Texas in the latter half of the nineteenth century and their successful forging of a little-known Texan identity. Unlike life in their homeland, Texas was "a welcoming place" where they could partake in German cultural institutions such as secular schools and social clubs. By holding fast to their cultural practices, while at the same time embracing their future as acculturated Texans, these immigrants forged a path of acceptance and equality with their non-Jewish neighbors. The author also shows how Jews so easily became Texans, thus countering the myth that German Jews were never accepted by the dominant Texas culture. Instead of the inequality and segregation prevalent in the German-speaking areas of Europe, they found true emancipation on Texas soil. In a land where they could be "culturally German, religiously Jewish, and politically Texan,"

German Jews "became Texans," thereby contributing to a more expansive definition of "what does it means to be Texan?"

Contemporary American historians who are mindful of the Jewish experience during the Nazi period in Germany frequently find it difficult to imagine that German-American Jews would ever proudly claim the same cultural heritage that produced such horrific crimes. Moreover, some scholars find unlikely that at one time American Jews from German-speaking areas of Europe emphasized their Germaneness or freely participated in and promoted German cultural activities. Likewise, some recent narratives describing nineteenth-century American Jewish life reflect how the writers *believe* Jewish life must have been, rather than how it actually was. For example some historians argue that American Jews who lived in southern states during the nineteenth century believed they were never fully welcomed or integrated into southern culture. Such statements suggest that in all southern states, from Virginia to Texas, Jews never felt completely accepted by the society and culture that surrounded them. However, historian and Judaic Studies authority Hasia Diner has challenged these assessments and called for a further evaluation of the lives of the German-Jewish immigrants who arrived prior to the end of the nineteenth century.[1]

Other misconceptions arise when historians knowingly or *unknowingly* include Jews, but do not identify them as such in their work even when they mention Catholics or Protestants. In an overwhelmingly Christian population, such portrayals lead to the assumption that all the individuals mentioned were Christian. Thus, when Jews are included, but not documented as Jews, they are assumed to be Christians. In an article about San Antonio in the 1850s, modern archivist and author Kent Keeth mentioned merchant Louis Zork, one of the founding members of San Antonio's Temple Beth El, while also discussing several Christian German immigrants. Keeth, however, did not identify Zork as Jewish, thus leading readers to assume that he was Christian. These omissions arise from the belief held by many Jews and Christians that Jews did not settle in early Texas or the West. Such assumptions contribute to the authorship of such books as *We Lived There Too* by Kenneth Libo and Irving Howe. Finally, some Jews were omitted even from Jewish histories because they were not documented in Jewish records, such as temple histories and membership lists, or because they married Christians and were buried in non-Jewish cemeteries.[2]

After they arrived, however, "German Jews in America [and Texas] sought to find equality with other Germans, one which they never knew or could aspire to in the fatherland." In nineteenth-century Europe, Jews were not considered citizens of the country or locality where they lived. They were instead considered second-class residents who had no inherent rights based on birth or residency, any rights they did have were granted to them by the sovereign of the territory. Thus, any prince or king could deny Jews rights to own land or file complaints against non-Jews or marry freely. In most instances they were taxed heavily, both as a group and as individuals, just for the privilege of residing where they were earning a living. Finally, even when the military conscripted Jewish men, they did not enjoy the rights of citizenship. Some of these limitations began to be lifted during the Napoleonic Wars, which ended in 1815, but most restrictions were reinstated after the failed revolutions during the late 1840s. These events contributed to the upsurge in immigration of Germans, including Jews.[3]

This essay examines the activities of German-Jewish immigrants who arrived in Texas shortly before and during the last half of the nineteenth century and argues that most Jews found Texas a welcoming place where they could support and participate in German cultural organizations such as German schools and social clubs. It further argues that the Jews who settled in Texas easily became Texans, partly because they shared the German identity and culture, which grew to be an integral part of Texas society. Today such affiliations might seem unfathomable because these immigrants were embracing a culture that had denied them equality and had, in fact, imposed severe social and political restrictions on them. In Texas, however, these Jews were embraced as equals, thereby becoming Texans. The fact that these Jews participated in overtly German cultural activities runs contrary to assumptions held by most Eastern European Jewish immigrants and their descendants who arrived in the United States late in the nineteenth century and early in the twentieth century. Furthermore because the number of Eastern European Jewish immigrants vastly outnumbered the Jews who had become established in the United States when they arrived, the new immigrants transformed the collective memory of American Jews. Moreover, the new immigrants had never experienced the hope of equality that western European Jews had experienced during the failed revolutions of the 1840s. Although the Jews from the western areas of Europe had suffered political and personal hardships they did not experience the pogroms, organized government supported riots, physical abuses, and massacres, which were common in Eastern Europe and Russian held territories. Finally, and more importantly, even after arriving in the United States many Eastern European immigrants never sought full integration into the surrounding culture and thus never formed a historical memory of such tolerance or acceptance. Instead, they preferred to remain in primarily Jewish communities and associate with other Jews of similar background. Thus, they never sought the kind of assimilated life that the German Jews had and as the two groups intermarried their numbers overwhelmed the ethos of the assimilated German Jews.[4]

German immigration to Texas began early in the history of the territory. By 1850, five percent of the Texas population was born in culturally German areas of Europe, and by 1860 over twenty thousand German-speaking immigrants had settled in Texas. These immigrants included Jewish settlers who originated from the same areas of Europe. Both groups were seeking a better life in a new country, an opportunity to move up in society and to prosper. Because Jews arrived at about the same time as the non-Jewish Germans and because they both had similar aspirations, they joined together in seeking a new life in Texas while preserving some of the culture they left behind. More specifically, during the nineteenth century German-Jewish Texans, like their non-Jewish German neighbors, found true political emancipation in Texas. In Texas Jews experienced freedom of religion, political equality, and comradeship in the large German and non-German population thriving in Texas. Moreover, German-Jewish settlers did not forsake their Jewish religion and believed that they could be culturally German, religiously Jewish, and politically Texan.[5]

German immigrants to Texas could express German culture both publicly and privately, and each path reinforced their German identity. The traditional myth and memory of Texas is populated with Anglo European men; however, more current Texas histories accept a pluralistic description of the population of Texas and recognizes that various immigrant groups not only shape current Texas but also contributed to early Texas settlement and culture. Today anthropologists, sociologists, and historians find evidence that these cultures flourished and influenced the formation of Texas. These cultures appear in foods, events, architecture, and, most importantly, in the individuals who settled in Texas willingly or unwillingly.

Language and culture proved to be powerful influences on the arriving Jewish population in their propensity to identify with other German immigrants. Furthermore, it was a unifying force within the German immigrant community—Jew and Christian. Many Jewish settlers spoke German at home and preferred to eat German food. For instance, Joseph Landa, an immigrant from Kempen, Germany, who had settled in the bustling city of San Antonio in 1844, departed San Antonio for the small German town of New Braunfels where he spoke German both at home and with his friends and neighbors. In Dallas and Waco, the Sanger brothers, who immigrated from Obernbreit, Bavaria, employed German nannies who spoke German to their children. Furthermore, forty years after he emigrated, Alex Sanger still requested that his German housekeeper prepare the German food that he fondly remembered from his youth.[6]

Like Alex Sanger, forty years after leaving Poland and settling in Texas, Harris Kempner expressed a desire for his son, Ike, to study the German language and to be immersed in German culture. Kempner wrote to his son who was attending school on the East Coast: "It is my wish and desire that you should . . . go to Germany and remain there until you have learned to speak German fluently." Kempner planned for his son to live in Europe for at least two years before returning to Galveston to join his business. Unfortunately, Kempner died shortly after writing these words. Ike left law school without graduating and returned to Galveston. Several years later, however, when Ike's younger brother Dan neared his twenty-first birthday, Ike shared his father's wishes with Dan, and sent him to Germany. Thus, these immigrants retained German culture at home and taught it to their children, passing it down from the immigrant generation to the first American-born generation. These actions emphasized the important place Europe and Germany played in the memory of the Jews who settled in Texas.[7]

Some Jewish immigrants from German-speaking areas in Europe also maintained ties with business associates and relatives by traveling back to Germany or by seeking German brides. Samuel Maas, for example, traveled to Europe to court the woman who became his bride, Isabella Offenbach. Others, such as M. L. Oppenheimer, who took both his wife and daughter on vacation to Germany, sought the familiarity of the country of his birth. Finally, in public most German immigrants, including Jews, demonstrated their affinity for German culture by joining German associations such as Casino Clubs, Saengerbunds, and Vereins, and by financially supporting these organizations and German day schools.[8]

Although a few Jewish immigrants settled in Texas as early as the 1820s and 1830s, many of those left during the Texas Revolution during late 1835 and early 1836, along with the politically unstable years that followed the revolution. But the number of Jewish settlers increased after Texas joined the union in 1845. The majority of these settlers were European-born immigrants who arrived in Texas after fleeing oppression in Europe. But despite having fled persecution in their native homelands, once these immigrants arrived in Texas, they demonstrated a strong desire to retain their German identity and to participate in German cultural activities, which flourished in their new home.[9]

In Europe most Jewish boys attended yeshivas, or schools which taught Jewish boys to read, write, and understanding Hebrew Scriptures. They also learned to debate various interpretations of Jewish writings. Furthermore boys were taught some math, science, and even astronomy so that they could work out the Jewish calendar, thus being able to predict when Jewish holidays would occur. After arriving in Texas Jewish families quickly accepted the idea that secular education was superior to religious education. This change in perspective thrust the German Jews into the sphere of enlightened citizens that they found in the United States and in Texas. Such an education prepared their children for the open society the Jewish immigrants found in America and which helped build a tolerant citizenry. Since Texas had not yet developed a public school system—and education was left to private citizens—Jews and other progressive citizens strove to educate their children, males and females alike. For instance, because Joseph Landa, who lived a few miles from New Braunfels, wanted his children to be educated, he built a schoolhouse on his property, hired a teacher, and even provided housing for the teacher. German-speaking Landa recognized the importance of knowing all the local languages. Accordingly, he hired teachers who not only were able to teach math, history, and social studies, but also German and Spanish, the latter being a language Landa considered essential in South Texas. Landa opened his school to children from nearby farms—providing education and shared experiences for his children, as well as his non-Jewish neighbors' children.[10]

Because most cities in Texas were slow to establish public schools, citizens founded private schools or academies. Even the Freemasons founded schools for children in some areas of the state. But in an attempt to maintain bonds with the German homeland and instill German culture to their children, many German settlers, Christians and Jews, established German/English day schools where they could educate their children in the German style. Thus, the students who attended these schools learned not only the German language, but also German culture, which strengthened their German-American identity. One of the most well-known and enduring German English academies was the San Antonio German English Day School, which began holding classes in 1859; by the next year, the school had registered 187 students. From the beginning, this school provided a comprehensive education for both boys and girls. The board of directors created a seven-year curriculum, which included history, English, geography, natural philosophy, arithmetic, German, Spanish, and poetry. After the Civil War, the school's directors expanded the curriculum to include classes in singing and gymnastics—subjects that prepared the students to participate in overtly German cultural activities such as Vereins and Saengerbunds.[11]

The San Antonio German English Day School accepted students from various religious backgrounds: Protestant, Jewish, and most likely even Catholics, since some Hispanic children attended the academy. Furthermore, the charter allowed students from impoverished families to matriculate into the school without paying tuition—thus broadening the socioeconomic structure of the academy.[12]

From its inception, Jewish men not only patronized the school by enrolling their children, but also contributed financially to the establishment, growth, and maintenance of the school. Before the Civil War Henry Mayer,, his father-in-law Sigmund Feinberg, Benito Schwarz, Louis Zork, and Marcus Koenigheim made significant cash contributions to the organizational fund drive. Other donations were made in kind because H. Mayer and Co. contributed stationery used by the school and clothing items for needy students.[13]

In 1861 three of Louis Zork's daughters and several of Henry Mayer's children were included on the enrolment list. Two years later the rosters included four more of Zork's children, along with Emil Levy and Marie

Wulff. Jewish support, however, decreased during the Civil War because Henry Mayer and Marcus Koenigheim left San Antonio during the conflict, and Feinberg's widow left the city after he died in a gunfight.[14]

Jewish enrollment rebounded after the war and, by the end of the school's first decade, over 250 students regularly attended the academy. During that time both Louis Zork and Benito Schwarz served on the board of directors. Furthermore, after the Civil War more Jewish men arrived in San Antonio, joining the Jewish citizens already actively supporting the school. During the 1870s, Louis Zork, A. B. Frank, L. Moke, and the firm of Halff & Levy made financial contributions to support the general fund that maintained the school. About the same time the school initiated a building fund drive so the school could acquire a structure to permanently house the school. The firm of Halff & Levy, along with Abe and L. Zork, A. B. Frank, Simon Frank, and A. Goldfrank, contributed to the building fund. By 1875 the list of Jewish students had lengthened and included children from about a dozen families, including Albert Levyson from Gonzales, Texas, who was living with his aunt and uncle in San Antonio. Not all the students belonged to families who could pay the tuition, therefore the directors supported exceptional students from poor families. Thus, the school not only accepted a religiously diverse population of students, but also enrolled students who were not from San Antonio's socially prominent families. By accepting students from various religious and social classes, the school founders displayed strong progressive ideas. For three decades Jewish families remained enthusiastic supporters of the German English Day School both with their money and by enrolling their children in the academy. [15]

German schools also opened in other towns with strong German and German- Jewish populations. For example in 1867 members of Houston's Congregation Beth Israel voted to establish the "Hebrew and German English School" and to allow it to use rooms within Beth Israel's building. Additionally, the congregation specified it would not charge for the use of the building, but in turn the school must admit "indigent children" free of charge. As the building neared completion, preparations were made to admit about sixty children—including non-Jews.[16]

Houston's German academy was not the only German English School associated with a Jewish congregation. In the smaller town of Waco, not only did the German Jewish and German non-Jewish settlers support the German academy, but their Rabbi, A. Suhler, also ran it. Rabbi Suhler, who arrived in Waco in 1883 to serve Congregation Rodef Sholom as its spiritual leader, received his education in Germany and had even taught German language and literature in Mainz, Germany. While previously serving as a rabbi in Dallas, he established Congregation Emanu-El's school teaching German, English, and Hebrew to its students. Although he served as Waco's rabbi for only a few months, he remained in the town and continued to run "A. Suhler's Select English and German School," which was housed in the synagogue. According to Rabbi Mordecai Podet's history of Waco's early Jewish families, Suhler's school enrolled about forty students and conducted classes from nine a.m. to three p.m. The length of the school day suggests that the curriculum not only included English and German, but other classes needed for a broad secular education.[17]

Suhler frequently advertised his academy in the Waco *Examiner* and one advertisement announced that Dr. Suhler would continue offering classes through the summer months without a vacation because the basement of the synagogue (where he taught) remained cool. Furthermore, Suhler reminded Waco citizens that his academy offered students a chance to learn German from a German native. Since Suhler advertised in the local paper and ran the school as a commercial enterprise, it is clear that he welcomed non-Jewish pupils. He also promoted German culture throughout the entire German-speaking community by publishing Waco's German language newspaper *The Echo*.[18]

After the Civil War itinerant Rabbi A. Rosenspitz opened a German-English school in Galveston. His association with the Galveston Jewish community offered Galveston's Jews and Christians an opportunity to mingle together at social events. One rather unique event took place in May of 1870, when Temple B'nai Israel's Sunday school students and their families joined Professor Rosenspitz's "select school" of German and English in celebrating the approaching end of the school year. The large celebration commemorated both the end of school and May Day, 1870. The event was so large that a local military band entertained the group. This celebration represented not just a shared social gathering, but was also an opportunity for the German-Jewish students and their parents to mingle with non-Jewish-German students and their parents, indicating that there was no social separation between the two groups.[19]

As settlements in Texas spread inland and westward from the coast, Jews settled in many cities simultaneously with other German-speaking immigrants, and these two groups socialized together. Furthermore, these urban or club Germans tended to be less parochial and church-oriented and more politically liberal than German immigrants who settled in rural areas or on farms. Thus, German Jews discarded many Jewish customs so that they could assimilate into American culture, and the more educated and religiously liberal German Christians who lived in cities and towns formed a strong sense of comradeship because they no longer maintained religious taboos against such association.[20]

Beginning in the 1850s both German Jews and non-Jewish Germans socialized together at German Casino Clubs, which began to be chartered across the state. For example, in 1859 Texas pioneer Sam Maas from the town of Meinbeim, territory of Baden, in Germany, and his friend, Moritz Kopperl, joined other German immigrants in chartering the Casino Club of Galveston. Although Jews joined German Clubs in other places in the United States, at this time in Europe Jews were generally excluded from such social organizations. Maas had arrived in Texas about 1836. Kopperl, however, who was born in Moravia and educated in Vienna, had just arrived two years before the Casino Club was chartered. [21]

About this same time other Germans chartered similar clubs in Victoria and San Antonio. These clubs also welcomed Jews as members. The San

Antonio Casino Club served mainly as a gentleman's club, but at least once a month it offered activities for the entire family. Nevertheless, Casino Club rules required members to speak German while attending club events, thus excluding all those who were not fluent in the language. Because women often attended club events, the Casino Club provided a more refined atmosphere than that found in settings such as taverns or fraternal organizations. In this venue German Jews and non-Jews, men and women, all socialized together, indicating that there were no barriers to socializing outside of one's own religious affiliation.[22]

The San Antonio Casino Club began operating around 1855, and by 1856 its members began planning to purchase land for a building. Louis Zork, one of the first Jews to settle in San Antonio, along with four other members signed a promissory note guaranteeing payment for the cost of the lot. The club quickly drew up plans for a building that included a theatre with a seating capacity of 400. This large room would accommodate traveling musicals, lectures, plays, and other cultural events that would be open to the entire San Antonio population. The club, which opened daily, provided a place where men could drink, relax, play games, and discuss politics. In November of 1857 the club filed incorporation papers with the State of Texas, listing Zork as treasurer. About this time Emanuel Moke and Henry Mayer also became active club members. Zork and Moke were long-time residents of San Antonio, but German-born Mayer had just arrived in the city after living in Mexico. Seeking to strengthen the German culture of San Antonio, Mayer's business, H. Mayer Company, pledged $2,000 to support the Casino Club.[23]

During the next twenty years many of the Jewish merchants who lived in San Antonio or the surrounding area maintained a membership in the club. The list included Louis and Abraham Zork, Henry Mayer, A. B. Frank, Alexander and Marcus Koenigheim, Henry Berg, A. Levy, brothers Anton and Dan Oppenheimer, their cousins Barney and M. L. Oppenheimer, Solomon Halff; L. Halff, Eli Hertzberg, M. Goldfrank, M. Moke, J. Rosenberg, and Y. Epstein. Such an extensive list included many of the Jewish merchants in town and indicates that no Jewish quota existed. More than likely, any Jew who could afford to be a member and pay the assessments could remain a member.[24]

Even newcomers to San Antonio joined San Antonio's Casino Club. In fact M. L. Oppenheimer, who emigrated from Germany to the United States after the Civil War, settled in Texas in 1867 to be near his cousins Julius, Dan, and Anton. Shortly after arriving, Oppenheimer joined both the Verein and the Casino Association. In his autobiography published in 1927, M. L. Oppenheimer described his participation in the activities of these San Antonio clubs. "We had picnics and dances twice a week in different places: [additionally] I rolled nine-pins at the Casino . . . The Casino gave theatrical performances for its members every other Sunday and its New Year's balls were looked for by everybody with keen anxiety." This event was special, not just because it was held on New Year's Eve, but also because it was the night when Jewish and Christian "fathers introduced their daughters to society."[25]

Ultimately, in 1882 when M. L. Oppenheimer decided that he should marry, he traveled from Eagle Pass, where he was living, to San Antonio to attend the social activities planned during the holiday season—including the Casino Club's New Year's Eve ball. Oppenheimer speculated that the dance would offer a chance to meet single Jewish women, and his speculation proved to be true. He met Rachel Gans at the event, and after returning to Eagle Pass, he proposed. Selecting the San Antonio Casino Club as a place to find a bride virtually ensured that Oppenheimer would find a German-Jewish bride. Although Rachel Gans was born in Texas, both her parents were German immigrants.[26]

Jews were still actively participating in San Antonio's Casino Club during the last two decades of the nineteenth century. For example, Dan Oppenheimer's name appeared in one German document dated 1879, and he and his brother and business partner, Anton, demonstrated their support by purchasing $500 of Casino Association bonds.[27]

Other anecdotes further illustrate the easy relationship Jewish Germans and non-Jewish Germans enjoyed in Texas. New Braunfels native Harry Landa, the son of Joseph Landa mentioned earlier, had traveled to Berlin, Germany, for medical treatment, and while in a German hospital, Landa befriended Friedrich Herman Von Blucher. Von Blucher's father asked Landa to bring Friedrich back to Texas with him, and during his stay the two visited the Casino Club. Landa later wrote that members "made a great deal of him [Von Blucher] as he was a German nobleman and a member of the great Blucher family." These records reveal that Jewish men and their families socialized freely with other German immigrants, and that a Jewish Texan could host a non-Jewish man, even a German nobleman, as his guest. By the last decades of the century, the leadership of the Casino Association shifted to a younger generation, but this change did not affect Jewish participation, and Jews maintained an active role in the organization until the end of the century.[28]

German-English schools and Casino Clubs offered opportunities for German immigrants—Christians and Jews—to share German education, language, and social events with other German immigrants and their friends in an open environment. German immigrants also participated in several other German cultural organizations such as Texas Saengerbunds, Texas Vereins, or similar organizations. These organizations had roots in Germany and the early German immigrants brought the seeds of these organizations with them when they settled in Texas. Nevertheless, the schools or Casino Clubs were not the same kinds of organizations as the Saengerbunds and Turner Societies. Although each type of organization originated in Europe, the former had more benign origins while the Saengerbunds and Turner Societies had begun to promote political activities and strengthen the overtly German nationalistic movements of the early nineteenth century. In Europe, many of these organizations were closed to Jews, or if memberships were available, the clubs were organized by religious professions of faith so that members were segregated by religion.[29]

Figure 7. Rabbi Jacob Voorsanger

Courtesy Bancroft Library, University of California, Berkeley

Nonetheless, once established in Texas, Turner Societies, Vereins, and Saengerbunds left their origins behind to sponsor non-politicized activities such as schools, volunteer fire brigades, and German social events in addition to the usual choral associations and gymnastics training. The first German singing club in Texas was organized in New Braunfels about 1850, and within a few years such societies had spread throughout German areas of the state. These clubs were extensions of European singing associations that promoted nationalistic music and German identity, and many of these Texas clubs held regional gatherings intermittently during the next few years. [30]

The Houston Saengerbund was officially founded in 1883; however, there had been German singing groups in Houston earlier because the city sent representatives to a Galveston Saengerfest held in May of 1881. For that performance the Galveston planners built bleachers on the beach to hold 5,000 visitors. In addition to the open-air performances, organizers scheduled two indoor events. A triple quartet represented Houston, and at least four of the twelve members were Jewish: E. Raphael, John Reichman, Louis Peine, and Jacob Voorsanger. Raphael and Reichman remained active in the Houston Jewish community throughout their lives. Voorsanger, who was serving Congregation Beth Israel as its rabbi, had lived in Houston for three years. Five years later he left Houston to serve as rabbi in San Francisco. During his tenure there he became nationally recognized as a Jewish activist and speaker.[31]

A few years later Houston supported two Saengerbunds, and together they sponsored a state Saengerfest. John Reichman, Houston's city secretary and trustee for Temple Beth Israel, organized and managed the event and continued to participate in the Saengerbund until his death in 1898. Shortly before Reichman's death, Houston hosted another Saengerfest and city councilman Julius Hirsch served on the planning committee, which engaged Miss Clara Landsberg as soloist.[32]

At the turn of the century, Joseph Loewenstein, A. Weinbaum, Julius Blumenthal, and Sid Westheimer were members of Houston's Saengerbund. Not much is known about the first three men, but Sid Westheimer emigrated from Baden and arrived in Houston after the Civil War. He joined his brother M. L. Westheimer and other relatives in Houston. Westheimer continued to participate in the Saengerbund until about 1912. [33]

Saengerbunds and similar organizations flourished during the second half of the century in those cities with sizable German populations such as Dallas and in German areas of the state such as Fayette County, Comal County, and the Texas Hill Country. German immigrants in Dallas established the *Frohsinn* in 1877. This choral society was opened only to men. Five years later, *The Dallas Weekly Herald* ran an article under the heading "The Saengerfest." The article announced that Dallas would host the next statewide Saengerfest, and it listed many leading Texas citizens who were expected to contribute to the event. Although the list primarily included only the names of men, it did include a few couples. Among them were prominent Dallas merchants, Philip and Alex Sanger, who were included with their wives, Cornelia and Fannie Sanger. Furthermore, it also included men who were well known throughout the state, such as bankers Dan and Anton Oppenheimer from San Antonio. [34]

One decade later Dallas dignitaries planned to host the nineteenth Grand Saengerfest. The city leaders obtained a charter for the event and sold shares in the "Jubilee Saengerfest and Musical Festival Association of Dallas." A year-long subscription cost $10 and entitled the purchaser to two season tickets. A. Harris, who had left Houston and settled in Dallas, served as vice president of the association. Harris, along with Alex Sanger, R. Lebman, and W. H. Abrams served on the board of directors for this venture. The planners hired Theresa Goldberg, who had just returned to Texas from Vienna, Austria, as the pianist. At the time the article was written, San Antonio, New Braunfels, La Grange, and Victoria had already agreed to participate in the event. [35]

Henry Hirshfield, who supported Austin's Texas German and English Academy, also participated in that city's Saengerbund. Posen-born

Hirshfield, who settled in Austin around 1859, became a prosperous Austin businessman and active member of the Jewish community. He also served as the first president of Temple Beth Israel after its founding in 1876.[36]

As German immigrants become more financially secure in Texas, their communities stabilized. Small crossroad villages became settled cities and German immigrants grew more self-confident in their new surroundings, and they had the stability to found social organizations. Between the early 1850s and the end of the Civil War, German associations proliferated. In larger cities, Vereins or German athletic clubs sponsored cultural events, gymnastic instruction, firearms trainings, bowling, skating, choral performances, and lectures. The first Verein in Texas was founded in Galveston about 1851. By mid-decade Galveston also boasted a German reading room, which employed a full time librarian and occupied two floors of a building on the Strand. Within a few years Vereins could be found in twenty-one Texas cities. As an extension of their promotion of physical fitness activities, some Vereins organized volunteer fire brigades to protect their cities. In Houston the strength of the German community was illustrated when six different German organizations, including Schutzen Verein, Gwerbe Verein, Turn Verein, and Germania Club, assembled in Houston to honor the thirty-nine-year-old president of the Schutzen Verein who had died unexpectedly. The gathering passed a resolution of mourning, which was signed by a representative from each club. In this action A. Harris, who later became a prominent Dallas Jewish merchant, represented one of the Vereins.[37]

During the height of the Verein movement, these organizations also sponsored German Days, or Volksfests, which entertained the entire community. One of the earliest Volksfests took place in Houston and was held on June 7, 1869. The Houston German club sponsored the event. Festivities began with a parade starting at the courthouse. The marshals led the parade, followed by a band and then marchers brandishing flags. Dignitaries from various German organizations followed in carriages.

S. Fox served as one marshal and Adolph Harris, riding in one of the carriages, represented the Volks Association.

Two years later Houston German citizens hosted their third German Festival. Bunting adorned the buildings along the parade route. Because this event had grown in size, this parade began at eight o'clock a.m. The newspaper declared that the entire city was "Germanized." Everyone ate pretzels and drank Bock beer and Rhine wine. The fire department marched along with their trucks, and other participants dressed as German folk heroes. One carriage held Ignatz Veith, a Hungarian-born Jew, who was decked out in the costume of Gambrinus, the legendary hero of brewers. In 1890 Dallas Germans also held a May fest at Turner's Hall, and then in 1898 Mrs. Alex (Fannie) Sanger spearheaded a *Jahrmacht*, or German festival, to raise money for Temple Emanu-El's building fund. German-Jewish Texans were accepted into these groups, not only as members, but also as leaders or parade marshals. Furthermore, Veith was comfortable portraying a German folk hero, and German-born Fannie Sanger perceived no problem with utilizing a German cultural festival to support a Jewish religious institution.[38]

Although the Houston Turnverein began holding gatherings in January of 1854, it was not incorporated until December of 1871. The corporate documents named ten men, including Ignatz Veith, as board members. At that time Veith had been in Texas for over twenty-five years. Veith died two years later and was buried in Houston's Glenwood Cemetery, a non-Jewish cemetery.[39]

In 1904 the Houston Turnverein celebrated its golden jubilee. Its president, Dr. Max Urwitz, oversaw this significant event, but he died less than two years later. Rabbi Henry Barnston conducted the memorial services for Dr. Urwitz in Turner Hall. Urwitz, like Veith, was not buried in a Jewish cemetery and was instead taken to his wife's family burial plot located in Cuero, Texas. [40]

Figure 8. San Antonio Turner Hall, late nineteenth century

From the collection of the author

Even the smaller organizations such as the Houston Schutzen Verein, which was organized only to hold hunting trips or shooting matches, had a few Jewish members. Simon Roos, who arrived in Texas after the Civil War, became an active member about the time the organization was chartered and he served as an officer on-and-off throughout the last quarter of the nineteenth century. His name appeared on letters of condolences and club announcements. Jacob Keller applied for membership in 1887 at about the same time that Charles Grumbach and Henry Freund were also active members of the Houston Schutzen Verein. Other names, such as J. J. Weiss and A. or H. Kamin, who were included on the membership rosters might have been Jewish since men with similar names were buried in Houston Jewish cemeteries.[41]

German citizens in smaller towns such as Austin, Victoria, and El Paso also organized German clubs. For example, German citizens of El Paso built a Turner Hall, which served as a meeting place for several German organizations. And in 1870, Austin citizens chartered a Verein society, which was recognized as one of the most prominent organizations in the city. In October of that year Max Maas was elected secretary, and Louis Maas was named Turnwart. Over the next several decades, Jewish men—especially those who had arrived prior to about 1870—continued to be active in these German organizations. And most of them publicly maintained a pride in German culture and their own German background; however, by the end of the century, fewer Jewish names appeared in organizational records.[42]

The Jews' participation in these organizations exemplifies the nexus between German-Jewish immigrants to Texas and their non-Jewish German neighbors, and it illustrates that Jewish immigrants, from rabbis to struggling businessmen who arrived in Texas from German-speaking territories of Europe, actively participated in the promotion of German culture. Such activities gave the German-speaking Jews a place where they could feel a connection, although not religious, to their previous lives. Significantly, these activities connected Jews to a culture in which they were rarely welcomed prior to their emigration. In the German organizations mentioned here, German Jews in Texas spoke the language of their childhood, ate the food of their youth, and felt a kinship with other German immigrants. Finally, the melding of German culture into Texas culture provided a path into mainstream Texas society. As historian Harold Hyman noted when he described Galveston: "Few '5 o'clock curtains' separated prominent. . . Hebrews from Gentiles." The records indicate that Hyman's description also represented Jewish and non-Jewish citizens across the state.[43]

In Texas during the last half of the nineteenth century, German Jews and German non-Jews lived and socialized together in an open society; they also educated their children in the same schools. On one important question, that of slavery, they differed. Most Texas Jews did not speak out against slavery, and many fought for the South or, as they believed, for their new home, Texas. For example, when Harris Kempner was questioned about his service in the Confederate Forces, he stated that he "came to America to be an American," and he continued, "I was young and the right to participate in all phases of American life—political, social, economic, and even military—was wonderful to me so that I could not keep from joining the army." For similar reasons, many Jewish Texans supported the Southern cause.[44]

Although the desire to claim a German heritage and identity existed when the German Jews arrived in Texas, within a generation or two it waned. By the beginning of the twentieth century, several changes contributed to the decline in this impetus. As their numbers increased, some Jews, especially those in larger cities, established their own social organizations such as B'nai Brith, which chartered chapters in Texas as early as the 1890s, and the National Council of Jewish Women, which was founded in 1893. Moreover, many of the Jews who had belonged to German organizations and promoted German education retired from active participation in those organizations or died before the end of the century. For example, Joseph Landa, who arrived in Texas in 1844, died in New Braunfels in 1896. Harris Kempner, who arrived prior to the Civil War, died in 1894. Adolph Harris, who participated in German organizations in both Houston and Dallas, died in 1912, the same year that Leon Zork died in San Antonio. These men left behind children who were thoroughly assimilated, had no living memory of life in Germany, and no longer needed German culture to join the surrounding Texas society. Furthermore, the character of the Jewish population itself began to change as the existing population of culturally German Jews was overwhelmed by the onslaught of Eastern European Jews who never sought assimilation. Furthermore, by 1890 many rabbis were advocating the elimination of the German language in the synagogue, especially German sermons. Finally, many Jews of German descent, even those residing in the United States, felt ill at ease with the increasingly anti-Jewish rhetoric they heard from German politicians. In fact Rabbi Jacob Voorsanger, who had joined the Houston Saengerbund and delivered German sermons, questioned his affinity for German culture because it had become the language of anti-Semitism. But despite these changes, for over fifty years in the nineteenth century many German Jews in Texas, from small town merchants to well-known rabbis, joined and supported an array of German cultural organizations. By participating in Casino Clubs or Saengerbunds, and by educating their children in German day schools, these Jewish immigrants could hold fast to aspects of their previous life while also embracing their future as acculturated American Texans.[45]

The lives and activities of these men and their families run contrary to the myths that existed until recently about Jews in Texas. First they prove as a fallacy the idea held by many that there were no Jews in Texas prior to the turn of the twentieth century or later. Furthermore, they illustrate the strong affinity these immigrants had for the culture of their homelands, a culture in which they were unable to fully participate while still living in Europe. And finally because German culture strongly influenced Texas culture, it proves that these Jewish immigrants assimilated as equals into Texas and even helped create the Texas identity developing in the state during the nineteenth century. They claimed their German identity while living in Texas and became Americans while also creating Texas society.[46]

SELECTED BIBLIOGRAPHY

Barkai, Abraham. *Branching Out: German-Jewish Immigration to the United States, 1820-1914.* New York: Holmes & Meier Publishers Inc., 1994.

Cohen, Gary B. "Jews in German Liberal Politics: Prague, 1880-1914." *Jewish History,* vol. 1, no. 1 (Spring, 1986): 55-74.

Cristol, Gerry. *A Light in the Prairie: Temple Emanu-El of Dallas 1872-1997.* Fort Worth: Texas Christian University Press, 1998.

Feingold, Harold, ed. *The Jewish People in America.* 5 vols. Baltimore: Johns Hopkins University Press, 1992.

Hyman, Harold M. *Oleander Odyssey: The Kempners of Galveston, Texas 1854-1980.* College Station: Texas A&M University Press, 1990.

Jaehn, Tomas. *Germans in the Southwest, 1850-1920.* Albuquerque: University of New Mexico Press, 2005.

Katz, Jacob. *Out of the Ghetto: The Social Background of Jewish Emancipation 1770-1870.* Cambridge: Harvard University Press, 1973; republished New York, Schocken Books, 1978.

Merrill, Ellen. *Germans of Louisiana.* Gretna, Louisiana: Pelican Publishing Company, 2005.

Rosenberg, Leon Joseph. *Sangers': Pioneer Texas Merchants.* Austin: Texas State Historical Association, 1978.

Schmier, Louis, ed. *Reflections of Southern Jewry: The Letters of Charles Wessolowsky 1878-79.* n.p.: Mercer University Press, 1982.

Stone, Bryan. *The Chosen Folks: Jews on the Frontiers of Texas.* Austin: University of Texas Press, 2010.

Tal, Uriel. "Liberal Protestantism and the Jews in the Second Reich 1870-1919." *Jewish Social Studies,* vol. 26, no. 1 (Jan. 1964): 23-41.

Tiling, Moritz P. G. *History of the German Element in Texas from 1820-1850: And Historical Sketches of the German Texas Singers' League and Houston Turnverein from 1853-1913.* Houston: Moritz Tiling, 1913; reproduction from public domain.

Tobias, Henry J. *A History of the Jews in New Mexico.* Albuquerque: University of New Mexico Press, 1990.

Weiner, Hollace Ava, and Kenneth D. Roseman, eds. *Lone Stars of David: The Jews of Texas.* Waltham, MA: Brandeis University Press, 2007.

Winegarten, Ruthe, and Cathy Schechter. *Deep in the Heart: The Lives and Legends of Texas Jews.* Austin: Eakin Press, 1990.

NOTES

1. References to German immigrants denote immigrants from any German-speaking areas of Europe and in this essay, no distinction is made between Jews from the eastern or western German speaking areas. Thus, it includes all Jews who at one time or another claimed German heritage. Furthermore, the argument that some posit that Eastern European Jews who spoke German claimed German heritage to gain admittance into what was considered a superior culture is left for others to debate. Additionally, the men mentioned in this essay are recognized as Jewish because their names were identified by comparing names found in other works, archives, genealogical manuscripts and newspaper articles to Jewish burial records and to information in the Texas Jewish Historical Society's Collection housed at the Dolph Briscoe Center for American History at The University of Texas at Austin. Some names have been previously identified as Jewish in the author's dissertation or research. Two of the men in this work, I, Veith and Max Urwitz, were proved to be Jewish by researching other documents. Men such as Rabbi Voorsanger, Rabbi Henry Barnstone, or Alex Sanger are recognizable as Jews because of their prominence or fame. It is possible that additional Jews were active in these organizations; however, because of the similarity of Jewish and non-Jewish German names, it is impossible to identify others with certainty. Gerhard Grytz, "'Triple Identity:' The Evolution of a German Jewish Arizonan Ethnic Identity in Arizona Territory," *Journal of Ethnic History*, vol. 26, no. 1 (Fall 2006): 20. Hasia R. Diner, *The Jewish People in America, A Time for Gathering: The Second Migration 1820-1880* (Baltimore: Johns Hopkins University Press, 1992), 2. Gregg Cantrell, and Elizabeth Hayes Turner, ed., *Lone Star Pasts: Memory and History in Texas*, (College Station: Texas A&M University Press; 2007), 41. The Texas Jewish Historical Society published *Texas Jewish Burials*, which lists most Jewish burials found in Jewish cemeteries or in Jewish sections of community cemeteries. This work is a great asset when trying to identify Jews in Texas.
2. Mark K. Bauman, "On German American and American Jewish History," *Journal of American Ethnic History* (fall, 2009): 67-68; Kent Keeth, "Sankit Antonius: Germans in the Alamo City in the 1850's," *The Southwestern Historical Quarterly* (October 1972), 185.

3. William M. Kramer and Norton B. Stern, "The Turnverein: A German Experience for Western Jews," *Western States Jewish Historical Quarterly* 16, 3 (April 1984): 227-229. Jacob Katz, *Out of the Ghetto: The Social Background of Jewish Emancipation, 1770-1870* (Cambridge: Harvard University Press, 1973; 1978).

4. Prior to modern times, the lives of Jews in Europe were rigorously controlled. Jews were compelled to live in confined sections of a city and forced to follow a strict dress code that identified them as Jews. Regulations limited the number of Jewish households that could exist in each town and these regulations prevented Jews from moving from one city to another without permission. Moreover, the number of Jewish marriages was restricted, thus limiting population growth. Finally, when some restrictions were eased, the changes were implemented as leverage to encourage Jews to convert to Christianity, rather than as a step toward offering emancipation or true equality to Jews. For more information about these restrictions see Katz, *Out of the Ghetto: The Social Background of Jewish Emancipation 1770-1870*; Gary B. Cohen, "Jews in German Liberal Politics: Prague, 1880-1914," *Jewish History* (Spring, 1986) 55-74; and Tal Uriel, "Liberal Protestantism and the Jews in the Second Reich 1870-1919," *Jewish Social Studies* (Jan. 1964): 23-41.

5. The fact that these Jews could be part of Texas society and remain Jewish was part of what attracted Jewish Germans to the United States and to Texas, since this was not true in Europe. Gerhard Greitz quoted Rabbi Bernhard Felseenthal who stated "racially I am a Jew...politically I am an American...spiritually I'm a German." This quote from Grytz, "Triple Identity," 21. Handbook of Texas History online accessed August 1, 2015, https://tshaonline.org/handbook/online/articles/png02.

6. According to Alex Sanger's great-nephew, Sanger maintained a bond with other German immigrants throughout his life. Even Texas-born Harry Landa wrote that he preferred to be served German food at home. Harry Landa, *As I Remember . . .* (San Antonio: Carleton Printing Co., 1945); Dannehl Maureen Twomey, "The Influence of Alex Sanger on the Development of Dallas, Texas," M.A. thesis, University of Oklahoma, 1987, 88.

7. Donald Day, "The Americanism of Harris Kempner," *Southwest Review* (Winter 1945) 125-128.

8. Saengerbunds and Vereins were German organizations that originated in Europe during the early nineteenth century. Saengerbunds were choral groups that presented traditional German music, music that pro-

moted German identity. Vereins were clubs that primarily focused on physical activities. In the literature, these organizations were variously referred to simply as verein, Turn-varein, Turnvereins, Schutzen Verein or other variations of the terms, which might identify the type of physical activity they sponsored. However, the kinds of activities practiced in various Vereins overlapped. Some promoted health, physical conditioning and gymnastics, while others sponsored shooting activities or bowling leagues. And some offered combinations of these. Schutzen vereins usually focused primarily on military activities and marksmanship. Often Vereins organized volunteer fire brigades, which required physical strength and demonstrated the ability of men to work together. Different authors and newspapers used varying forms of these words. Henceforth, in this essay, these organizations will be referred to as Vereins. M. L. Oppenheimer, *Some Leaves from the Book of My Life* (nc: np, 1927).

9. In Texas, as in other southern places, many German Jews accepted their neighbors' convictions about states' rights and "were critical of radical Northern abolitionists" because they believed that abolitionists were "destroying the Union." Marilyn Kay Goldman, "Jewish Fringes, Texas Fabric: Nineteenth Century Jewish Merchants Living Texas Reality and Myth," Ph.D. dissertation, Texas A&M University, 2003. Quote in note 9 from Patricia Herminghouse, "The German Secrets of New Orleans," *German Studies Review*, vol. 27, 10. Rabbi and historian Jacob Rader Marcus estimated that about 1,000 Jews had settled in Texas in 1859. However, this is only an estimate. Furthermore, this author believes that the number was higher since many Jewish men settled in small communities or traveled around the state as merchants or peddlers. Finally, counting Jews forces one to contemplate who was a Jew and this question must be left for another time. Jacob Rader Marcus, *To Count a People: American Jewish Population Data, 1585-1984* (Lanham, Md. 1990).

10. Only the poorest boys did not study at a yeshiva, but even they learned to read and write. Landa, *As I Remember. . .*25-26.

11. It is difficult to determine exactly what percentage of the students were Jewish because no notation of religion is made in the records. It is possible, however, that 10 percent of the students or more were Jewish. Keeth, "Sankit Antonius," 198.

12. German English Day School Records, Box 2, DRT Library at the Alamo, San Antonio, Texas. Unpublished manuscript presented at the Social Science History Association meeting October 1996, Washington D.C. by Walter Kamphoefner on nineteenth-century bilingual education in San

Antonio. Charter held in the Secretary of State Office, Austin, Texas. Incorporation documents found in the office of Secretary of State for Texas also found in volume 1 of the German English School record book in the Dolph Briscoe Center for American History, Austin Texas. Walter Kamphoefner analyzed the ethnicity and economic background of the students who attended the school in 1879 and noted that during the year eight students attended without paying tuition.

13. Henry Mayer was born in Ober Ingelheim, Germany, and immigrated to the United States in 1834. He and his wife Rebecca Cohen traveled the Santa Fe Trail in 1852 and settled in Mexico. Due to unrest in Mexico they moved to San Antonio, Texas, a few years later.

14. This author has made a compilation of names found in various records and other articles. According to Peter-Bodo Gawenda's dissertation, German had become the language of education, science, and even commerce in 1860 San Antonio. Peter Bodo Gawenda, "The Use of the German Language in the Schools of San Antonio," Ed.P. Thesis University of Houston, 1986. German English Day School Records, Box 1-3, DRT Library at the Alamo, San Antonio, Texas.

15. Albert Levyson's parents lived in Gonzales, Texas, but he resided with his aunt and uncle, Marcus and Eliza Levyson Koenigheim, while he attended school. The Halff family was one of the Alsatian families who vacillated between claiming French or German heritage. German English Day School Records, Box 4, DRT Library at the Alamo, San Antonio, Texas.

16. Anne Nathan Cohen, *The Centenary History of Congregation Beth Israel of Houston, Texas 1854-1954* (Houston: Congregation Beth Israel, Houston, 1954), 5-16.

17. Mordecai Podet, *Pioneer Jews of Waco* (Waco, Texas, Self-published: 1986), 26.

18. German language schools also opened in other small towns such as Victoria and Austin. The Austin German Free School Association was originally chartered in 1858 but that charter expired in 1879. A renewal was granted in 1884, but the school did not survive long after the charter was renewed. Like other German English Schools, the school admitted non-paying students; however, in Austin those students were supported by the state. Because early Austin grew as a center of government rather than a commercial hub, few Jewish men found it economically desirable to settle there. Hirshfield Papers, Austin History Center, Austin Public Library Archives, Austin, Texas; "School to Continue," *Waco Examiner,*

May 32, 1883; Podet, *Pioneer Jews of Waco*, 25; Charles F. Kalteyer, "GERMAN FREE SCHOOL ASSOCIATION OF AUSTIN," *Handbook of Texas Online* (http://www.tshaonline.org/handbook/online/articles/kbg0 7), accessed April 15, 2014. Uploaded on June 15, 2010. Published by the Texas State Historical Association.

19. This probably was Reverend (Rabbi) Alexander Rosenspitz who served as a traveling rabbi around the south and was in Galveston at that time. "Hebrew Pic-Nic," *Galveston News*, April 29, 1870.

20. Frederick C. Luebke, *Germans in the New World: Essays in the History of Immigration* (Urbana and Chicago: University of Illinois Press, 1990), *170-171*.

21. Mark Greenberg pointed out that by the mid-1870s in some areas of the United States Jews were denied membership in and access to the best clubs and hotels; however, he wrote that this was not taking place in the South. He also argues that in several very distinct ways southern Jews differed from their northern co-religionists. The most notable distinction was that southern Jews socialized with their Christian neighbors. For example, he observed that Jews in Savannah joined the "most prestigious clubs, literary societies and socialized with elite families." What Greenberg noted in Georgia was also true in Texas; however, in Texas Jews not only joined these clubs but in many instances they served as founding members. For more information about the interaction on Jews and Christians in Texas see Goldman, "Jewish Fringes, Texas Fabric." Constitution of Galveston Casino Club, 1859, Casino Club file, Rosenberg Library, Galveston, Texas. Mark I. Greenberg, "Becoming Southern: The Jews of Savannah, Georgia, 1830-1870," *American Jewish History*, 86 (1998): 5559.

22. Keeth, "Sankit Antonius," 195-202; M. L. Oppenheimer, *Some Leaves from the Book of My Life*, 48, 22.

23. Keeth wrote that the Casino Club was the only respectable social club in town. Casino Club Deed, Casino Association Collection, University of Texas at San Antonio, Special Collections. Incorporation statement filed with the State of Texas December 7, 1857. Keeth, "Sankit Antonius," 196.

24. Zork was born in Prussia, Koenigheim was from West Phalia, and the Oppenheimer brothers and their cousins were from Bavaria. Incorporation statement filed with the State of Texas December 7, 1857 and found in the Secretary of State's Office Austin, Texas.

25. The New Year's Eve ball would be equivalent to a debutante ball. Since both Jews and non-Jewish Germans attended together, San Antonio's

German society was not segregated by religion. First quote Oppenheimer, *Some Leaves from the Book of My Life*, 48, 22. Second quote Keeth,
"Sankit Antonius," 197.

26. See consecutive census from 1860-1880 for Simon Gans in Houston and
San Antonio, Texas. Oppenheimer, *Some Leaves from the Book of My Life*,
22.

27. Dan and Anton Oppenheimer were distinguished bankers and active in
the Jewish community. Casino Club Incorporation statement filed with
the State of Texas December 7, 1857.

28. Landa became one of the first industrialists in Texas. Landa, *As I Remember. . .*53.

29. For charter dates of these organizations see *The New Handbook of Texas*
online under each organization. Email, Anton Hike to author, March 28,
2014.

30. Moritz Philip Tiling, *History of the German Element in Texas from
1820-1850* (reprint; Houston: n.p., 1913).

31. Tiling, *History of the German Element in Texas from 1820-1850*, 153. Ruthe
Winegarten and Cathy Schechter, *Deep in the Heart: The Lives and Legends of Texas Jews, a Photographic History* (Austin: Eakin Press,1990), 56,
63 and 65.

32. Although this author is unable to prove that Clara Landsberg was Jewish,
three Landsbergs are buried in a Houston Jewish cemetery.

33. Ledger Books 3-5, Saengerbund Collection, M. D. Anderson Library University of Houston, Houston, Texas; Winegarten and Schechter, *Deep in
the Heart*, 34.

34. History of Dallas *Frohsinn* accessed on May 7, 2014. http://www.
dallasfrohsinn.org/.*Dallas Weekly Herald,* January 26, 1882.

35. Although this author is unable to document that either Abrams or Goldberg were Jewish, similar names are found in Texas Jewish cemeteries.
Dallas Morning News, November 29, 1891.

36. Hirshfield Papers, Austin History Center, Austin Public Library
Archives, Austin, Texas. Twomey, "The Influence of Alex Sanger on the
Development of Dallas"; Winegarten and Schechter, *Deep in the Heart*,
20.

37. Mary Lou LeCompte, "Turnverein Movement," *The New Handbook of
Texas* Online (http:www.tshonline.org/handbook/online/articles/vnt02),
accessed December 2, 2013, published by the Texas State Historical Association; Earl Wesley Fornell, *The Galveston Era: The Texas Crescent on the
Eve of Secession* (Austin: University of Texas Press, 1976), 134. LeCompte,

"Turnverein Movement"; "Tribute of Respect," *Union*, Houston, Texas, September 18, 1869.

38. Zachariah Emmich, who arrived in Texas in 1859 to serve as the first rabbi of Temple Beth Israel and to also be the *chazzan* or cantor and ritual slaughterer, served as the president of the Volksfest in 1869. By this time Emmich had left the rabbinate but was still serving as a mohel or ordained circumciser. The event raised $11,000. Tiling, *History of the German Element in Texas from 1820-1850*, 72. Winegarten and Schechter, *Deep in the Heart*, 51. "Mrs. Alex Sanger's Death," *Dallas Morning News*, November 2, 1898.

39. I. Veith is not included in *Texas Jewish Burials* because he married a non-Jewish woman and was buried in Houston Glenwood Cemetery. "German Colonists and Their Descendants in Houston," compiled by Dorothy Justman, 1974 document, in the possession of author. Tiling, *History of the German Element in Texas*, 172.

40. There is a discrepancy between Moritz Tiling's spelling of Barnstein and the spelling on Henry Barnston as it appears in the list of Jewish burials and in Winegarten and Schechter, *Deep in the Heart*; Tiling, *History of the German Element in Texas from 1820-1850*, 172.

41. Minutes of the Houston Schutzen verein were originally written in German; however, on July 25, 1886, a note in the book indicated that the organization was writing a new constitution and would begin recording the minutes in English. Several of the Jewish men who joined the Schutzen Verein were less financially secure. One was a baker and another ran a stable. Schutzen Verein minute book, in possession of Barbara Rosenberg, Sugarland, Texas, viewed by the author on November 4, 2014.

42. Buck's Directory, 1902, El Paso, accessed September 14, 2014, http://digitalcommons.utep.edu/city_direct/15/. *Flake's Bulletin*, Galveston, Texas, October 19, 1870.

43. This term refers to the act of closing the curtains in the home after dusk, and the statement indicates that there was no social separation between Jews and Gentiles after business hours. Jews and non-Jews socialized together even in their respective homes, not just in business settings. Harold Hyman, *Oleander Odyssey: The Kempners of Galveston, Texas, 1854-1880s* (College Station: Texas A&M University Press, 1990), 68.

44. Henry Mayer and Marcus Koenigheim both left San Antonio during the Civil War. Joseph Landa, who departed San Antonio for the more German town of New Braunfels, owned slaves, but freed them during the

war. However, in Texas more Jewish men joined the Confederate forces than took a stand against slavery. Other Jews agreed with Kempner and believed that in Texas they had found a place where they felt equal to other citizens and where they were able to join the social system that developed in the state. For information about Civil War service see Goldman, "Jewish Fringes Texas Fabric." Donald Day, "The Americanism of Harris Kempner," *Southwest Review* (Winter 1945): 125-128.

45. The publication American Jewish Year Book estimated that the Jewish population of Texas reached about 15,000 in 1900 and 17,500 in 1905. The 1905 estimate for Dallas was about 1,200 and for Houston it was around 2,500. Jacob Rader Marcus, *To Count a People: American Jewish Population Data, 1585-1984* (Lanham, Md.); Alan Silverstein, *Alternatives to Assimilation: The Response of Reform Judaism to American Culture, 1840-1930* (Hanover, New Hampshire: Brandeis University Press, 1994), 114, 150. In an unpublished statistical comparison of second generation Jewish-Germans and non-Jewish Germans from early twentieth-century Texas census records done by this author, a striking difference was noticed in native language. Second generation Jews overwhelmingly declared that they spoke English as a native language, whereas the non-Jews declared that they spoke German as a native language. This difference was noted especially in German areas such as New Braunfels and Schulenburg.

46. Geographer D. W. Meinig argued that Jewish visibility in such cities as Victoria, San Antonio, and Galveston-Houston belied their numbers. This author believes that because they settled in cities and towns and were active in fraternal societies, civic organizations, and cultural groups such as those mentioned in this work, the Jewish population appeared to be a larger percentage of the total population than they actually were. They were more visible than a minority who might live almost exclusively in rural areas of the state. D. W. Meinig, *Imperial Texas: An Interpretive Essay in Cultural Geography* (Austin: University of Texas Press, 1969, 1993).

CHAPTER 5

ETHEL TUNSTALL DROUGHT

SAN ANTONIO CLUB WOMAN AND ART PATRON

by
Light Townsend Cummins

Editor's Note: There are places in the United States today that exist in the popular mind as centers for the visual arts. Few people would disagree that New York City is one of them with its museums, art galleries, and neighborhoods such as Greenwich Village, the home to generations of artists and art patrons. In Gotham's case, it can be noted the myth and public memory identified with neighborhoods such as Greenwich Village in our national culture would include a heavy emphasis on art and artistic development. Such is not to be the case for Texas. The world of art and its recognition does not comprehend even a fleeting part of the Texas identity, nor does it play a role in defining the context of myth and memory in the Lone Star State. This lack of inclusion, in fact, constitutes a fallacy in terms of the important role art has played for well over a century in the development of Texas. Although every Texan knows about the great cattle drives, how many of them know of the artist Frank Reaugh who earned a reputation as the painter of Longhorns? The fundamental myth and memory at work in bolstering Texas identities has been masculine in basic nature. It may be the lacuna of art found in the Texas identity is in part explained by the historical reality that women have played a significant role as artists and artistic promoters in the state from the mid-nineteenth century to the present day. A recognition of both art and the role of women in its development, however, is changing, something Light Cummins notes in this essay. Determined women all across Texas, including Ethel T. Drought in San Antonio, worked diligently and with great success in bringing recognition of art to Texas starting in the decades following the Civil War. They founded art associations, galleries, and museums in their efforts to promote art, while they served as patrons to Texas artists. Identities, of course, change across time, as do the myths and memories that bolster them. As Texas continues to become more urban, and with the attendant growth of art and art institutions in the state, the work of women such as Ethel Drought may eventually enter the mainstream of Texas myth and memory.

Women as a group have not been much a part of the myth and memory of Texas, except in two categories. First, they exist there as helpmates to men who inhabit the popular stories of Texas and its historical panoply. They are the wives, mothers, sisters, and daughters of men who can be found in the mainstream of myth and memory. Second, a relatively small number of women have indeed found a place for themselves therein because they made the same sorts of historical contributions as men, doing the sorts of things in history associated with male activities. These women have found a place in Texas myth and memory because they were public servants, elected officials, professionals, and leaders of business, industry, and commerce. It is almost impossible to encounter women as part of the myth and memory of the Lone Star State who followed the feminine conventions of their era. Discovering and writing about such women, however, is what academic historians have been doing for much of the last generation of scholarship. Since at least the late 1970s, Texas historians who write about the story of this state from an academic perspective have studied a wide variety of individual women and female groups with historical parameters unrelated to the traditional criteria embodied in myth and memory. Many of these academic studies have refocused their standards for determining significance onto feminine concerns of home, family, civic association, and work in the public sector that fall outside the earlier definitions with which historians once categorized historical significance. This essay follows in that vein as it considers the role women played in the promotion of the visual arts in late nineteenth and early twentieth century Texas.[1]

Accordingly, this essay also comments on an additional, second area of historical development that is largely absent from the myth and memory of Texas: the visual arts. Esse Forrester O'Brien contended in her 1935 book *Art and Artists of Texas* that the state was historically deficient in the production of art, as well as in the public's appreciation of the visual arts, during the late nineteenth and early twentieth centuries. She believed this to have been the case because Texas lagged behind other states due to its long and extended frontier heritage. "Art is especially slow," O'Brien wrote somewhat metaphorically "when scalping is in fashion." Many others have echoed this viewpoint in the years since publication of O'Brien's book. Given this, it can be said that the visual arts, as such, are not much a part of the myth and memory of Texas, certainly during the late nineteenth and early twentieth centuries. Nevertheless, academic historians do write about them as part of the state's cultural history. Historians know about this area of history because this period of early Texas art witnessed a considerable amount of activity in the state as its sculptors, painters, and watercolorists entered the mainstream of American art. A group of successful Texas artists established a strong tradition of doing art during the very years that Esse O'Brien disparaged. For example, William Henry Huddle and his wife Nannie, Henry A. McArdle, Elisabet Ney, Frank Reaugh, and Robert Onderdonk, among many others, emerged starting in the decades after the Civil War as active and important Texas artists. Their careers occurred during the very years of frontier expansion that included the ending of Native-American resistance, coupled to the rise of open range cattle-raising, both component parts of a Texas myth and public memory more familiar to Texans than the establishment of an artistic tradition in the Lone Star State.[2]

This essay thus exists at the juncture of history about Texas women and of the development of the visual arts in the state. The creation of a Texas artistic tradition by women during the late nineteenth and early twentieth centuries constitutes for the average historically informed person a generally unknown story of cultural development. This absence of women and the visual arts from our historical memory exists in large part because, at least as the twentieth century began, the state lacked mechanisms for the promotion of the arts as a civic enterprise and as an important means of intellectual commentary. And, at the same time, since many women led the way in these activities, their participation is equally obscured. At the time no one much noticed it outside established artistic circles, so the general public knew little about the growth of the visual arts in the state. As the nineteenth century ended and a new one began, the state lacked museums, galleries open to the public, and other places where exhibitions of art could take place. This situation began to change as the twentieth century rolled forward as the promotion of the visual arts in Texas accelerated tremendously, starting especially in the decade prior to World War I. Such promotion continued and became a major undertaking of the 1920s. For the most part Texas women predominated in these initial efforts to promote the visual arts. Indeed, they were the first to advance the visual arts in the state, thus bringing it eventually a measure of recognition and appreciation. Women's club members, female art critics, and other women created art clubs, sponsored public exhibitions, and founded public art museums that eventually highlighted the importance of the visual arts in Texas.

In particular, civically active women played significant roles as founders and trustees of art museums in El Paso, Abilene, San Antonio, Austin, Houston, Fort Worth, and Dallas during the early decades of the twentieth century. An historical examination of Dallas women from 1843 to 1920 by academic historian Elizabeth York Enstam, for example, substantiates the reality that female residents of the city "assumed community leadership in perpetuating the traditions, learning, fine arts, and customs of the larger culture." This specifically proved true regarding the role of women's groups promoting the visual arts. Texas art expert William E. Reaves, Jr. has especially noted that members of two organizations, the Texas Federation of Women's Clubs (1897) and the Texas Fine Arts Association (1911), "were instrumental in founding a series of local art leagues and associations." Ethel Tunstall Drought of San Antonio was one of these women. As such, her successful activities in support of the visual arts deserve a place in the historical memory of the state.[3]

This essay will therefore examine the career of Ethel Tunstall Drought as a case study to highlight the role women played in the promotion of the visual arts in Texas starting at the close of the nineteenth century, thus calling into question the mythic image and popular memory of the state as a raw frontier where "art was slow." In so doing, it will highlight Drought as a representative of women across the state who advanced the visual arts starting in the late nineteenth century. Ethel Drought stood at the vanguard of promoting the visual arts in Texas even though scalping was fresh in the memory of many Texans at the time she began her career as a promoter of the fine arts. It is somewhat ironic that, as Steven Hardin notes earlier in this volume, Drought's home city of San Antonio is the location of the Alamo with its centrality to the myth and memory of Texas. The wife of a wealthy and influential attorney in San Antonio, Drought was an active member of the San Antonio Woman's Club, an organization that diligently promoted art and artists. In 1911 she helped create the Texas Fine Arts Association. Drought founded the San Antonio Art League the following year. She was also one of the significant forces in establishing the Witte Museum, serving on its board of directors for many years and directed the famous Texas Wildflower Competitions of the late 1920s.

All of this was possible because Drought had emerged during the final decades of the nineteenth century as one of the most active and committed clubwomen in Texas. Born in December of 1864 in San Antonio, Ethel Tunstall's grandfather was a Presbyterian minister who had personally known Andrew Jackson. She descended from a prominent family that traced its origins back to colonial Virginia while her husband, Henry P. Drought, was an Irish immigrant who had become one of the most successful attorneys in San Antonio. He founded his own law firm in the early 1880s, which became one of the most important in South Texas. Although raised as a Protestant, Ethel Tunstall converted to the Roman Catholic Church when she married Drought and became a staunch supporter of its civic causes. For example, she underwrote one of the early restorations of the chapel at Mission San Jose and was also elected President of the Catholic Women's Association. In her secular activities Drought had a burning commitment to civic betterment throughout her life. She was involved in the burgeoning women's study club movement from its earliest beginnings in the Alamo City. In 1892, for example, she helped found a reading club for women. They met several times a month to discuss works of literature and history. She played a significant role in founding San Antonio's Carnegie Public Library and served as a charter member of its board of directors. In 1898 Drought organized a free soup kitchen that eventually grew into a health clinic that, in turn, became San Antonio's public charity hospital.[4]

In 1901 the Drought family moved into a palatial and elegant home located a short distance northeast of downtown in what was then the most fashionable residential district of the city. Legend held that the location of the Drought home was the spot where Ben Milam had rallied Texian followers for his historic December 5, 1835, attack on the Mexican army in San Antonio. Ethel made this substantial residence into one of the social centers for the elite society of the city. She enjoyed entertaining and presided over a continuing round of dinners, receptions, and parties that made her one of the most prominent hostesses and social arbiters in the Alamo City. For many years she invited a revolving array of friends and acquaintances to a formal "at home" salon held each Sunday evening. This recurring weekly event first began when she decided to entertain soldiers from a local army post and continued it thereafter for decades, reoriented toward inviting members of the city's social elite. Invitations to her Sunday salon proved to be among the most prestigious and sought-after in the highest echelons of San Antonio society. These evenings always featured distinctive table settings complete with delicious elaborate hors d'oeuvres, exquisite canapés, and rich pastries, all accompanied by musical entertainments. Drought made special efforts to invite visiting luminaries to these Sunday evenings when they passed through San Antonio. Over the years these special guests included classical musicians Rosa Ponselle, Jascha Heifetz, and Tito Schipa; artists Gutzon Borglum and Bernhard Wall; composer Percy Grainger; anthropologist Albert Spaulding; architect Josef Hoffman; and Lady Randolph Churchill, Sir Winston's mother. These evenings also regularly attracted many of the city's business and educational leaders and were the occasions at "which the most prominent of San Antonio's art community routinely came together to assay the local art scene and advance the cause of art within the city."[5]

Ethel Drought also entertained friends with more extended getaways to her rural estate, built in 1908 specifically for entertaining and located north of San Antonio in the rolling, scenic Hill Country area twelve miles south of Comfort, Texas. Drought and her husband named this country home "Droughtfels." It was of almost baronial proportions. A family member from a later generation recalled, "it had an enormous living room, dining room, and eleven bedrooms, each with a marble sink in the corner." All of the downstairs rooms had floor-to-ceiling windows without draperies in order to provide full views of the nearby Guadalupe River. The Droughts maintained a full domestic staff at Droughtfels including a cook, maids, and a chauffeur. Ethel often spent much of each summer there, during which time the house usually contained guests who came to stay for weekends or sometimes longer periods of time. [6]

As a person of economic means, Ethel Drought greatly enjoyed collecting art, something she began doing in the 1890s. Her interests ranged widely across all time periods and styles. As a young woman she had studied art and drawing as a student of Robert Onderdonk and, although she never pursued a career as an artist in her own right, Ethel never wavered in her support for advancing artistic causes. She was an inveterate traveler who enjoyed taking trips abroad, something she did regularly over the decades. She went to Europe on many occasions, always visiting art museums and galleries. Drought also toured Japan, China, and the Malayan Peninsula, making the latter trip in the company of Asia expert and radio commentator Upton Close. She stayed with her friends Generalissimo and Madame Chiang Kai-Shek when she visited China. She frequently collected art on her travels. Her art collection eventually grew to impressive proportions. The Drought home in San Antonio eventually included a specially designed gallery for her art.

Drought's interest in promoting the visual arts beyond her personal collection expanded when Drought became a stalwart of the San Antonio Woman's Club, founded by her friends Eleanor Brackenridge and Marin B. Fenwick in 1898. It adopted as its credo the "mutual improvement and cooperation in all that pertains to the greater good of humanity," and took as its official motto, "Not For Self, But for All." A department club, it fostered a wide variety of activities and causes that ranged from encouraging Mother's Clubs in the schools, supporting the local orphans' home, promoting the establishment of juvenile courts, and engaging in other kinds of civic activism including strong support for women's suffrage during the early years of the century. In 1905 Drought regularly served on the club's board of directors and later as first vice president. The Woman's Club particularly worked to encourage the visual arts in San Antonio and this became the special domain of Ethel Drought, who was uniquely suited to the task as a knowledgeable collector of art herself. Under her leadership, the Fine Arts Department of the club regularly hosted an annual arts exhibition that featured local artists. Many of its monthly programs introduced members to the general outlines of art history.[7]

In addition to her work with the San Antonio Woman's club, Ethel Drought also joined the first state-wide arts organization, the Texas Fine Arts Association (TFAA), founded in 1911 by her friend Ella Dibrell of Seguin. She was the wife of state Senator Joseph E. Dibrell, both friends of the Droughts. The Texas Fine Arts Association had several purposes: it would operate Formosa, the late sculptor Elizabet Ney's Austin studio, as an art gallery; it would promote the visual arts throughout the state; and it would serve as a group to encourage the creation of other groups promoting the visual arts. Drought took an active role in the affairs of this association, quickly joining its board of directors. She also served on a variety of its committees, including one to consider giving awards to artists for their work. Drought continued as a member of the TFAA for many years, regularly travelling to Austin for its meetings. In addition, she also attended its annual conventions while she encouraged other San Antonio women to join the organization. [8]

Responding to the suggestion of the Texas Fine Arts Association that local groups promoting the visual arts ought to be established in major Texas cities, Drought took the lead in doing so for San Antonio. She served as the main catalyst for the founding of the San Antonio Art League in 1912, which drew support in large part from the membership of the San Antonio Woman's Club. Along with her former art teacher Robert Onderdonk and civic leader William Herff, Drought called a meeting held at the Carnegie Library on March 13, 1912, to found an organization for promoting the visual arts in the city. "Its purpose," the newspaper reported, "is to obtain for San Antonio a permanent collection of paintings by the best American artists, and to conduct, from time to time, exhibitions of art works, as well as to bring to the city, once a year, a collection of works of the best painters of the country." Although some men joined the organization, most of its members were female and clubwomen constituted the main membership base. William Herff became its first president and Ethel Drought was elected first vice president. The League boldly announced at the first meeting that "works of art will be collected as rapidly as possible to form a nucleus for what is expected to be eventually one of the leading free art galleries of the Southwest." Although such an exalted status would not come for many years, at its first meeting the League included working artists as members, along with individuals who supported the arts but did not create works of art. [9]

Within months after its founding, the League's membership met twice to discuss purchasing its first painting. The members voted to appoint a special fund-raising committee to begin seeking donations for this purpose. Ethel Drought was one of the first people to contribute, pledging twenty-five dollars. She also agreed to serve on the committee charged with securing additional donations. Robert Onderdonk suggested the oil *Sun and Mist* by Charlotte B. Corman. He reported that it could be purchased for the sum of $400. The league followed his advice and bought the painting as its first acquisition. As purchasing of additional paintings went forward, the Art League under Drought's leadership quickly committed itself to exhibiting the work of "recognized artists," thus giving special attention to advancing the public recognition "of local artists thru exhibitions of their work" while "fostering the development of school children of artistic ability."[10]

The League also attracted favorable attention within a few months of its founding by sponsoring an exhibit of Julian Onderdonk's work at San Antonio's Carnegie Public Library, an institution Drought had helped to found. During the spring of 1913 the Art League as well hosted a travelling exhibition from the American Federation of Arts and sponsored several "free days" at the Carnegie Library where members of the public would not have to pay the admission fees. The League celebrated the opening of this exhibit with several special events, the first being an "Art and Musical Evening" at the library hosted by Elizabeth diBarbieri Coppini, wife of the San Antonio sculptor Pompeo Coppini, and a League member along with Ethel Drought. Festivities included a musical program by the conductor of the San Antonio Symphony with several of its musicians, a talk by Pompeo Coppini and additional remarks by painter Julian Onderdonk in which he discussed his views about art and an appeal for additional League members. In that regard, the League hoped that it might eventually have as many as 2,000 members.[11]

The following day, the Art League sponsored a second event hosted by Ethel Drought in celebration of the exhibit during which Congressman James L. Slayden delivered a talk to the membership about plans for a proposed Art Commission then being considered by the federal government. The Art League also encouraged members of the various Mother's Clubs in each of the San Antonio Public Schools to attend the exhibition as chaperones for the youngsters. Monitors at the exhibit kept track of the number of mothers and children who visited the show because the group having the highest attendance would receive a painting donated by Julian Onderdonk to its respective school. By the close of this exhibition, William Herff as League president could proclaim: "We have certainly had a most successful exhibit. Crowds have attended every day and much interest has been shown by the school children. The members of the league are much gratified with the interest shown as it speaks well for the future of art in this city." The two-week run of the show, in fact, proved so popular that the Art League held it over for an additional day before packing it for shipment to its next destination. [12]

San Antonio artists quickly joined the League. Rolla S. Taylor, an established artist in the city, was one of the first to note his membership. This was because the San Antonio Art League made special efforts to highlight the work of local artists. Within a year of its founding, it had adopted the strategy of sponsoring three art exhibitions each year, two of which would highlight the work of artists from San Antonio and the South Texas region. Julian and Robert Onderdonk, Jose Arpa, Roll Taylor, Lucy Maverick, Agnes Schasse, and Ernst Rabba were among the first local artists featured with the implementation of this policy in 1913.

Figure 9. Drought at the Art League Gallery

Courtesy Alamo Research Center, San Antonio, Texas

The San Antonio Art League continued to prosper when Ethel Drought assumed its presidency in 1914 after William L. Herff decided to step down from that post. She continued to supervise, hosting the annual travelling exhibition sent around the country by the American Federation of the Arts, always taking care to ensure that the school children and Mother's Clubs of the city would have easy access to the show. Drought at times combined the activities of the Art League with those of the Woman's Club. For example, she hosted card parties at her home for members of the Woman's Club as fundraising events for the Art League.[13]

Drought brought determination and vigor to serving as president of the Art League, a post she would hold until 1938. She worked hard during her first year as president to arrange a public art exhibition held in the assembly room of the Carnegie Library. This would be a major show highlighting both the works of art already purchased by the League, as well as paintings loaned to the exhibit, including several by members of the Onderdonk family. Drought enlisted various members of the club to serve as docents during the exhibitions, assigning each of them times to be present in order to answer questions from those attending. She willingly took her turn as one of these volunteers. Initially, the Art League had planned to charge a small admission fee to the show, but instead decided to dispense with admission tickets and make it free to the public. Drought also consulted with the Mother's Clubs in each of the San Antonio Schools about sponsoring a student art contest that would take place concurrently with the exhibition. Drought's hard work and organizing efforts proved successful to the extent that favorable public response convinced the League to keep the show open for several weeks after its anticipated closing date. This 1914 show became the first of many that Drought would thereafter organize during the years the Art League held its meeting at the Carnegie Library.[14]

During World War I the League moved this annual art exhibition to the premises of the Y.M.C.A and extended its run to three weeks in an effort to attract soldiers from the local military posts, a strategy that proved successful. These shows quickly became prized exhibition venues for South Texas artists and received much support from the community. Drought also oversaw the steady acquisition of artwork for the organization, both by purchase with League funds and from donation by patrons. This art would become the core collection of a permanent, public art gallery operated by the League, a key part of its original mission. In addition to acquiring works of art and sponsoring art exhibitions, the League also began to sponsor a regular series of lectures for its members starting in the early 1920s. For example, in June of 1922, Stella Shurtleff of Houston spoke to the group. Shurtleff was establishing a reputation around the Lone Star State as a popular lecturer on art history topics and her presentation to the Art League was no exception. She spoke before the art league on many occasions. [15]

A permanent, dedicated gallery became reality for Drought and the Art League in the summer of 1923 when banker T. C. Frost, Jr. made exhibition space available to the organization. The Frost National Bank, one of San Antonio's premier banking institutions, had constructed a state-of-the-art building on Main Plaza in 1922. This twelve-story building featured a grand interior lobby faced with Italian marble and graced by lighting fixtures from the Tiffany Company, while the exterior decorations made striking use of *terra cotta* ornamentation. Offices on the upper floors constituted the most modern found in the city at that time. Centrally located, it stood next to the historic San Fernando Cathedral and across the plaza from the Bexar County Courthouse. Frost, the bank's president, made three large rooms on the second floor available to the Art League, a space that had easy access from the mezzanine of the main lobby. Members of the League spent the late spring of 1923 outfitting these rooms as an art gallery and sorted through the organization's collection for works to display. Max Krueger, a San Antonio art collector, loaned ten of his paintings to the project while Ethel Drought prepared to inaugurate the gallery in June of that year. The League proposed to open the space to the public on Mondays, Wednesdays, and Saturdays, with members serving as docents. In addition, the League planned to host at least one art lecture each month in the new gallery. The list of paintings selected for exhibition included four works by Julian Onderdonk with others by E. Richardson Cherry, Jose Arpa, Charlotte B. Coman, M. Jean McLane, Collin Campbell Cooper, and the ten loaned by Max Krueger.[16]

In addition to opening the new gallery under Drought's leadership, the Art League also began a successful education program in partnership with the San Antonio public schools. Aline Rather, supervisor of art for the school district, created a master class for selected students who had evidenced marked artistic talent. Junior and senior level students from each of the city's high schools received invitations to participate in this class, which would provide them specialized instructions in painting and drawing. Drought and the Art League underwrote this class, providing it space in the Art League rooms each Saturday afternoon. The League also paid the salary of local artist Xavier Gonzalez as its instructor while the school district provided the needed supplies. This program, which became known as the Rather-Gonzalez Art Class, proved very popular, providing significant training to several students who later had important careers in Texas art, including Julius E. Woeltz.[17]

The success of the Art League's opening exhibit occurred at the same time another group of San Antonio residents were also working towards founding a museum, in this case one that would highlight natural history, flora, and fauna. In the early 1920s, Ellen D. Schultz, a local high school science teacher, learned that a Houston naturalist, A. P. Attwater, desired to sell his personal natural history collection. Attwater had amassed a very large collection of items that numbered in the thousands including nuts, bird nests, taxidermy wildlife, and various other examples of flora and fauna. In early 1923 Schultz and several other women, most all of them local clubwomen, created a new group, the San Antonio Museum Association. The expressed purpose of the museum association would be to raise funds to buy the Attwater Collection. Once that was accomplished, the group announced that it would turn its attention to building a permanent museum facility in which to display it.[18]

The new museum group found a powerful ally in the person of San Antonio mayor John Tobin, who enlisted the assistance of Parks Commissioner Ray Lambert as the two men brought a proposal for public funding of the new natural history museum to the San Antonio City Council. The City Council considered this proposal in early June, 1925, with the result that it appropriated $25,000 for construction of the new building for the proposed natural history museum. The architectural firm of Ayres and Ayres agreed to donate its services in designing the new facility. It would be built as a one-story building, but so engineered that a second floor could be added at some point in the future.[19]

It was at this juncture that Ethel Drought and the San Antonio Art League became involved in the proposal for the natural history museum. Drought had long wanted the Art League to secure its own premises. In 1921, for example, she had attempted to raise funds for the League to purchase the Old Market House, a well-known downtown structure that was being moved because of a street-widening project. Drought hoped the League could acquire the building, move it to a new location, and install its galleries in it. However, the costs associated with the project proved to be too expensive. She remained very interested in having a public museum for an art gallery although the League was enjoying the exhibit space located in the Frost Bank building. Drought and the Art League decided to join together with Schultz and the new museum association. Drought suggested that the anticipated second floor should be immediately added to the Ayres design of the new museum for the purpose of housing a public art gallery under the control of the Art League. Schultz and Drought came to a quick agreement on this change in plans for the museum. They made several trips to lobby Mayor Tobin for an additional $25,000 to make this expansion, but he proved reluctant. Although leaving for a long-planned European vacation, Drought delayed her departure until such time as the mayor would approve the art gallery plan. "I won't leave until you sign the contract," she told Tobin. To help influence the mayor to support Drought's plan for the art gallery, Schultz and Drought enlisted one hundred civic leaders and organizations to send postcards or letters supporting Drought's proposed expansion of the museum. These letters, and Drought's persistence, convinced the mayor to allocate an additional $25,000 for a second floor art gallery. As this went forward, a third group composed mostly of women, the San Antonio Conservation Society, joined the proposal so that the new museum would have three different orientations: natural history, art, and history, each with its own dedicated space. [20]

Plans for the new museum moved ahead very quickly in September of 1925 with the unexpected death of San Antonio businessman Alfred G. Witte. He was a long-time resident who had enjoyed great success in his business ventures. He left the City of San Antonio a bequest in the amount of $85,000 for a museum to be named in honor of his parents. In particular, he bequeathed $75,000 for construction of its building with an additional $10,000 to purchase art and paintings for the museum, providing that no picture cost more than one hundred dollars. Witte's will directed the museum be constructed in Brackenridge Park, then located on the far northern edge of the city on River Avenue, a street now known as Broadway. Mayor Tobin announced a month after Witte's death that the "museum shall be maintained for the display of objects of art, science, and natural history." The City Council formally accepted these changes, saving itself money in the process since San Antonio would now pay only the original $25,000 requested for the museum. The Witte estate would pay another $75,000, thus making a total building fund of $100,000. Most everyone in the city approved of the new museum's location at Brackenridge Park. A local newspaper editorial pointed out: "Such a site invites visitors on Sunday, when people have leisure to devote to the study of art, historical relics, and scientific specimens."[21]

By the late summer of 1926 work had progressed on the new building to the point that Drought supervised moving the League's art collection to the second floor galleries from the Frost Bank Building. By agreement with the museum association, the Art League led by Ethel Drought would have complete charge of the galleries on the second floor. The Witte

Museum formally opened to the public on October 8, 1926, during a day of special festivities and gala receptions. An estimated three thousand visitors passed through the Witte on the first Sunday the new museum was open to the public. The only paintings on display that first day were those already owned by the League and which had come from the bank building downtown. Drought wanted to add more works of art to the collection, especially since the Alfred Witte bequest contained $10,000 for the purchase of additional art, although as stated above it stipulated that no single work could cost more than one hundred dollars. Drought, who felt this limited the acquisition of important pieces, found a way around this restriction; namely, the museum would not touch any of the principal in the Witte fund. Instead, only the accrued interest would be spent for artwork since the one hundred dollar limit, she decreed, applied only to the principal balance. The board therefore created the "picture account" and steadily acquired new purchases over the ensuring years only with funds coming from interest accumulation in amounts far larger than one hundred dollars. Between 1928 and 1933 works by Theodore Morgan, Charles Curran, Jean Despujols, and Bessie Porter Vonnah joined the permanent collection. The Art League also began a series of shows featuring the work of individual artists while it also mounted exhibitions of Texas artists. Within a few years, it began to host the Texas General Exhibition, a travelling exhibit of artists that also went to Dallas and Houston. "The obvious purpose," Ellen Schulz later wrote of these activities by the Art League, "was to educate the public in art appreciation, and to give many of the participating artists an opportunity to increase their standing in the art world."[22]

During the first few months of the Witte Museum's operation, the League had secured the services of Sybil Browne, a San Antonio teacher, to be part-time art curator at city expense, but Ethel Drought believed that a full-time person was needed at the Witte to curate the art gallery. Accordingly, she convinced Mayor Tobin to add a full-time position to the roster of city employees and to assign that person as a member of the museum staff. Ellen Schultz later noted of her ally from the Art League:

"If Mrs. Drought wants it, we'll have it." Drought hired as the first curator in 1927 a woman she knew very well and with whom she would have much contact: Eleanor Rogers Onderdonk, the daughter of San Antonio art pioneer Robert J. Onderdonk and the sister of the late artist Julian who had passed away several years earlier. Eleanor Onderdonk became one of the Southwest's most influential art curators. "Eleanor and Mrs. Drought made a very competent and well-matched team," Onderdonk's friend and biographer Cecilia Steinfeldt recalled. "Their personalities, their tastes, and the devotion to the cause of art in San Antonio art were not only compatible but also complementary."[23]

Drought and Eleanor Onderdonk soon became involved in a major exhibition that spanned a three-year period just as the new curator joined the museum staff. Ethel Drought enlisted the collaboration of Onderdonk to coordinate and manage a 1927 competition that would award prizes for the best paintings of Texas wildflowers. This wildflower show and competition would reoccur again in 1928 and 1929. It was the idea of Texas oil baron Edgar B. Davis, who had long admired the natural beauty of the state's flora. Davis, a native of Massachusetts, had earlier come to Texas during an oil boom in the southern part of the state and amassed a fortune by developing the Darst Field approximately sixty miles east of San Antonio near the small town of Luling. A person of notable beneficence, he eventually endowed a number of charitable enterprises in South Texas and provided money to causes of which he approved, doing so with a fervor that some people of that era found a bit unorthodox. This became the case for the art competition, a contest for artists who painted Texas wildflowers and other natural scenes indigenous to that part of Texas. Davis had become enamored of the beauty seen each spring across the areas where the many colorful wildflowers of that region bloomed. He determined that talented artists should paint these flowers in an attempt to capture on canvass the resulting riot of natural color because, as art historian William E. Reaves Jr. has observed, Davis "was worldly and sophisticated, imbued with a deep appreciation of the fine arts and with a special affection for Texas wildflowers." Davis accordingly approached Ethel Drought about having the San Antonio Art League sponsor a national competition that would attract the best artists possible to this purpose. "Bolstered by record-setting cash purchase prizes, generous publicity, and national exhibitions," Reaves has noted, "the Davis competitions, as they became popularly known, proved to be among the most significant cultural events in Texas during the formative years of the twentieth century."[24]

Davis ceded to his friend Ethel Drought and the San Antonio Art League all aspects of organizing and operating this competition at the Witte Museum. He confined himself to paying its expenses and providing the lavish cash prizes. As Onderdonk recalled, "not feeling competent to launch the project himself, Mr. Davis entrusted management to the Art League due to his friendship and admiration of Mrs. Drought." This proved to be a landmark undertaking that went a great distance towards calling public attention to the Witte Museum while it also constituted a watershed event in the history of Texas art. Ethel Drought solicited artists from all over the nation to participate in this competition. The amount of the cash prizes Davis offered were among the largest ever seen in the history of American art. They attracted artists from across the United States. The first year of the contest's criteria in 1927 required artists to paint flowers only, but in the subsequent two years the competition existed, acceptable subjects expanded to include indigenous scenes of cotton farming and ranching. Although it did not survive the Stock Market Crash of 1929, the three years of this annual competition helped to legitimize Texas art in the eyes of the national art community and encouraged the development of a southwestern regional school of painting in the decades following. Although all of this reflected Drought's work, she gave Davis a great deal of credit for underwriting these competitions, noting "that appropriate evidence be given Mr. Davis in recognition of his splendid generosity in offering prizes for paintings exhibited by the Art League, and for his stimulating of the development of art in the State of Texas." Davis reciprocated by telling Drought: "Please accept my thanks for the splendid leadership you have shown in furthering the cause of art in Texas."[25]

Soon after the closing of the 1928 Davis Wildflower Competitions, Drought secured an important place for the Witte Museum and the Art League in the regional art world when she invited the Southern States Art League to hold its annual meeting in San Antonio. As an October, 1928, press release from that organization stated: "Drought has been appointed chairman of the executive committee which has charge of preparations, and will be assisted by local committees on entertainment, arrangements, etc., as well as by officers of the League, and the jury and the hanging committee for the exhibition." Meeting during the first week of April, the Southern States Art League attracted over 600 of its members to the Alamo City. Drought formally opened its proceedings in a convocation held in the city's newly constructed Municipal Auditorium, during which noted sculptor Gutzon Borglum of later Mount Rushmore fame delivered a formal address of welcome. Mayor C. M. Chambers, noted artist Dawson Dawson-Watson, and Ellsworth Woodward of Tulane University, Southern States Art League president, also participated in these ceremonies. After a gala luncheon at the Menger Hotel, delegates attended sessions at the Witte Museum and visited its galleries where several hundred works by its members had been displayed. In what must have been a considerable social undertaking Drought hosted a reception at her home for all 600 people attending the conference. The next day the San Antonio Art League sponsored a luncheon for the delegates at a popular local restaurant specializing in Mexican food. In keeping with Ethel Drought's interest in native flora "the tables were exquisitely decorated in the brilliant wild flower blossoms of the fields and prairies. Blue bonnets, yellow daisies, wild poppies, huisache blossoms, and verbenas were used to fill baskets of Mexican pottery bowls and jugs."[26]

Drought continued her work in support of the visual arts all through the 1930s. As that decade began she took time out from her civic and art activities to make an around-the-world trip that lasted for eight months. On her return to San Antonio, friends and associates hosted a gala welcome home dinner at the Menger Hotel. "Interspersed with the musical numbers on the program," the city's newspaper reported, "were messages of love and appreciation to Mrs. Drought from many friends all over the country." Dean H. T. Parlin of the University of Texas expressed on behalf of that institution "a sincere appreciation for the part Mrs. Drought has played in advancing an appreciation and love for art in San Antonio and in Texas." J. Frank Davis took the podium to laud her "untiring work with and for the San Antonio Art League" in the face of discouragements and scant enthusiasm by many in the city. Over a dozen individuals who were unable to attend instead sent telegrams specifically noting Drought's importance to advancing art in Texas. The year following this gala banquet, the Art League commissioned a formal portrait of Ethel Drought by Rosamond Nile to be hung in the art rooms of the museum. It was unveiled at a special tea in October of that year commemorating the upcoming twentieth anniversary of the Art League's founding and the fifth anniversary of the Witte Museum's opening.[27]

These honors, however, did not diminish Drought's hard work in promoting the visual arts. During most of the Depression decade, she continued to sponsor art exhibitions, invite speakers to meetings of the Art League, and never missed an opportunity to advance the visual arts. This certainly proved the case during the Centennial of 1936, a statewide celebration that noted the one hundred year anniversary of the Texas Revolution. Under Drought's leadership, for example, the Art Department of the Woman's Club hosted a gala celebration that featured a special exhibition of artists along with a talk by a representative of the Witte Museum. Ethel Drought invited her friend Mrs. James V. Allred, wife of the Governor of Texas, to attend as guest of honor. Sadness, however, came into Drought's life shortly after the conclusion of this event when her son, Frederick Gerald Drought, lost his life in an auto accident. His untimely passing, coupled with her advancing age, slowed the pace of Ethel's many activities in the months thereafter. She stopped holding her Sunday night "at homes" in the wake of his death. Two years later, she gave up the presidency of the San Antonio Art League, although she still continued to attend many of its meetings. She did, however, participate whenever possible in the meetings of the Ethel Drought Art Club, a local group that had been named for her. By the early 1940s, however, chronic illness significantly plagued her. She died on August 6, 1943. [28]

By the time of her passing, Ethel Drought had become one of the best-known and most respected women in San Antonio. A second floor art gallery at the Witte Museum bore her name, presided over by the grand portrait of her. The art club named in her honor continued for many years. As well, for decades thereafter, several of her family members, including daughters-in-law Kathleen and Anne Drought, continued her activities in their own right as leaders of civic causes and art associations in the city, doing so well into the 1960s. Since then the Drought family has remained in the city across four subsequent generations. Some of them today are attorneys who still practice in the law firm founded by Ethel's husband in 1881, one of the oldest in the state. Others of them have distinguished themselves in the business community of the Alamo City, especially in civil engineering and real estate. In spite of her considerable legacy and that of her descendants in promoting the visual arts, however, Ethel Tunstall Drought's name has faded into obscurity with the passing decades. The art gallery named for her at the Witte was remodeled out of existence many years ago. The San Antonio Art League disaffiliated from the museum in the 1960s, since that time maintaining its own galleries elsewhere in the city. At one point, in fact, Anne Drought had to rescue her mother-in-law's portrait from obscurity in the storage attic of the Witte Museum. It today hangs on the main staircase of the Art League's headquarters located in the historic King William district of San Antonio. The palatial Drought home, once the scene of so many significant social events in the city, still stands at present, but it bears the name of a modern donor who underwrote its restoration as the campus center for a Catholic High School in San Antonio. Nonetheless, Ethel Drought's legacy endures for those who know where to look for it. It belies the myth of late nineteenth and early twentieth Texas as an uncultured, raw frontier where the visual arts failed to flourish. Her accomplishments substantiate absolutely the role that dedicated, hard-working, and civic-minded Texas women played in the urban development of the state generally, and of the visual arts specifically. They did so at a time when the Southwest was indeed making the transition from an era "when scalping" had recently been in fashion to an urban sophistication that today is the hallmark of many Texas cities including San Antonio. In his study of Texas art and the Bryan Museum Collection, Michael W. Duty highlights a recent television advertisement aired in Houston advancing tourism to the that city. "Jim Parsons," Duty writes, "the star of the popular series *The Big Bang Theory* and a Houston native, tells viewers that he has lived in both New York City and Houston and has seen more horses in New York and more art in Houston." Parsons can say that today because of what a number of Texas women did across the state in the early twentieth century, including Ethel T. Drought for San Antonio. Her promotion of the visual arts constitutes her enduring contribution to the state, along with similar activities of other women who did the same during her era in other places including Houston. Their story deserves a place in the historical memory of Texas. [29]

Figure 10. 1930 Portrait of Ethel T. Drought by Rosamund Niles

Courtesy San Antonio Art League

SELECTED BIBLIOGRAPHY

Cummins, Victoria, and Light Townsend Cummins. "Frances Battaile Fisk: Clubwoman and Promoter of the Visual Arts in Texas," in *Texas Women: Their History, Their Lives,* edited by Elizabeth Hayes Turner, Stephanie Cole, and Rebecca Sharpless. Athens: University of Georgia Press, 2015.

Edwards, Jacqueline. *A Century of Art and Community: The History of the San Antonio Art League and Its Permanent Collections.* San Antonio: HPN Books, 2012.

O'Brien, Esse Forrester. *Art and Artists of Texas.* Dallas: Tardy Publishing Company, 1935.

Reaves, William E., Jr. *Texas Art and a Wildcatter's Dream: Edgar B. Davis and the San Antonio Art League.* College Station: Texas A&M University Press, 1998.

Steinfeldt, Cecilia. *The Onderdonks: A Family of Texas Painters.* San Antonio: Trinity University Press, 1976.

Woolford, Bess, and Ellen S. Quillin. *The Story of the Witte Memorial Museum, 1922 to 1960.* San Antonio: Witte Museum, 1960.

NOTES

1. For a recent discussion of this literature, see: Rebecca Sharpless, "Texas Women," in *Discovering Texas History*, ed. by Bruce Glasrud, Light Townsend Cummins, and Cary D. Wintz (Norman: University of Oklahoma Press, 2015), 76-93.

2. Esse Forrester O'Brien, *Art and Artists of Texas* (Dallas: Tardy Publishing Company, 1935), 4. Victoria H. and Light Townsend Cummins, "Literature, the Visual Arts, and Music in Texas," in *Discovering Texas History*, edited by Bruce Glasrud, et al. (Norman: University of Oklahoma Press, 2014), 114-20; Michael Grauer, "Wider Than the Limits of Our State, Texas Art in the Twentieth Century," in *Twentieth Century Texas: A Social and Cultural History*, ed. John W. Storey and Mary L. Kelley (Denton: University of North Texas Press, 2008), 267-299; Sam DeShong Ratcliffe, *Painting in Texas to 1900* (Austin: University of Texas Press, 1992); Pauline Pinckney, *Painting in Texas: The Nineteenth Century* (Austin: University of Texas Press, 1976); Michael R. Grauer, *Texas Impressionism: Branding with Brushstroke and Color, 1885-1933* (Canyon, Tex.: Panhandle Plains Historical Museum, 2012). Victoria Cummins and Light Townsend Cummins, "Frances Battaile Fisk: Clubwoman and Promoter of the Visual Arts in Texas," in *Texas Women: Their History, Their Lives*, edited by Elizabeth Hayes Turner, Stephanie Cole, and Rebecca Sharpless (Athens: University of Georgia Press, 2015), 281-301; Susan Landauer and Becky Duval Reese, "Lone Star Spirits," in *Independent Spirits: Women Painters of the American West, 1890-1945*, edited by Patricia Trenton (Berkeley: University of California Press, 1995), 183; Kristen Swinth, *Painting Professionals: Women Artists and the Development of Modern American Art, 1870-1930* (Chapel Hill: University of North Carolina Press, 2001).

3. Elizabeth York Enstam, *Women and the Creation of Urban Life in Dallas, 1843-1920* (College Station: Texas A&M University Press, 1998), 4. William E. Reaves, Jr., *Texas Art and a Wildcatter's Dream: Edgar B. Davis and the San Antonio Art League* (College Station: Texas A&M University Press, 1998), 7.

4. "Ethel Tunstall Drought Obituary," San Antonio *Express*, July 31, 1943. Thomas S. Bremer, *Blessed with Tourists: The Borderlands of Religion and Tourism in San Antonio* (Chapel Hill: University of North Carolina Press,

2004), 74. In 1903, for example, Drought's book club read the entire works of historian John Fiske. "Oral History Interview with Kathleen Drought," Oral History Collection, Archives and Special Collections, University of Texas at San Antonio, San Antonio, Texas.

5.   The Drought house still stands at this writing as the Student Center of Providence High School, a school for girls operated on its former grounds by the Catholic Archdiocese of San Antonio. Carol Baass Sowa, "Providence's Drought House—Reconnecting the Past with the Future," *Today's Catholic*, May 9, 2008. Reaves, *Texas Art and a Wildcatter's Dream*, 35; Ethel Tunstall Drought Obituary, San Antonio *Express*, July 31, 1943.

6.   Juanita Herff Drought Chipman, *The Passing of Gifts* (Bloomington, Ind.: Xlibris, 2011), 279-80.

7.   "The Woman's Club of San Antonio: A History by Mrs. T. J. Womack," typescript, Box 1, Woman's Club of San Antonio Collection, Archives, University of Texas at San Antonio (Hereafter referred to as Woman's Club Collection, UTSA); San Antonio *Gazette*, April 6, 1905. Yearbooks of the San Antonio Woman's Club, 1912 through 1928, Box RG1, Woman's Club Collection, UTSA.

8.   "Articles of Incorporation, Texas Fine Arts Association," May, 18, 1929, and "Minute Book, 1911-1914," Box 2325/G217, Texas Fine Arts Association Papers, Briscoe Center for American History, University of Texas at Austin; "History of the Texas Fine Arts Association," Typescript, Box 4, TFAA Papers, Austin History Center, Austin, Texas; Mrs. Thomas P. Taylor, "A Short History of the Texas Fine Arts Association," typescript, Box 2R205, Bride Nell Taylor Papers, Briscoe Center for American History.

9.   "Minutes of the San Antonio Art League," March 13, 1912, Archives, San Antonio Art League, San Antonio, Texas (Hereafter referred to as Archives, SAAL). In 2012, the Art League commissioned the writing of a short history. See: Jacqueline Edwards, *A Century of Art and Community: The History of the San Antonio Art League and Its Permanent Collections* (San Antonio: HPN Books, 2012); "Recent Nature Portrayals of Julian Onderdonk Will Be Shown," San Antonio *Light*, June 9, 1912; "Want Free Art Gallery," Galveston *Daily News*, March 15, 1912.

10. "Minutes of the Art League," April 2 and May 2, 1912, Archives, SAAL; "The San Antonio Art League, 1926-27," typescript, Ibid.

11. "Special Program Is Arranged at Exhibit," San Antonio *Light*, March 27, 1913.

12. Although a Federal Art Commission never came to pass, Slayden supported such an agency. Ethel Drought, along with several other members of the league, hosted a reception for the Congressman. The other hostesses included Elizabeth Houston, Eleanor Onderdonk, Manetta Thomas, and Freda Koerner. San Antonio *Light*, March 29, 1913; Mother's Clubs were the forerunners of the modern Parent Teacher Associations. "Mother's Congress to Attend Exhibit," San Antonio *Daily Light*, April 4, 1913; "Art League Exhibit Will End Tomorrow," San Antonio *Light*, April 6, 1913.

13. Catalog of the Art Exhibition at the State Fair of Texas, October 18–November 2, 1913, Organized by the Art Department and Archives, Dallas Museum of Art, Dallas, Texas; "Art League Exhibit Will Close Today," San Antonio *Light*, May 25, 1913; "Minutes of the Woman's Club," 1923-27, Minute Books, Woman's Club Collection, Archives, UTSA.

14. "Minutes of the Art League," February 2, March 2, March 30, 1914, Archives, SAAL.

15. "Minutes of the Art League," June 2, 1922. Archives, SAAL.

16. This imposing edifice served as headquarters of the Frost National Bank from 1922 until 1973, whereupon a Luby's Cafeteria occupied the large lobby space and the building's management leased the private offices on the upper floors. The City of San Antonio purchased the building in 1989 for use as city offices. The grand lobby was retrofitted in 1992 to become the City Council Chamber, a usage that it still has at this writing. "The Municipal Plaza Building"; http://www.sanantonio.gov/clerk/Archives/CityCouncilChambers.pdf, accessed December 27, 2012; "Art League Opens Gallery in Frost Building, June 14," San Antonio *Light*, June 10, 1923.

17. "The San Antonio Art League: VI. Relation to the Schools," 1926-27. Archives, SAAL.

18. J. Stuart Pierce was elected president of the Museum Association, clubwoman Mrs. J. K. Beretta became vice president, and Schultz along with Lena McAllister served on the board of directors. Emma Gutzeit served as the group's publicity chair. The roster of attendees represented a listing of the city's most influential and elite family names including Gross, Kampmann, Holmgreen, McAllister, de Zavala, Herff, Napier, Dietmann, Carvajal, Taylor, and Drought, the latter represented in the new group by Ethel Tunstall Drought. "New Museum Association Will Start Fund Drive: Organization Formed Wednesday Will Purchase Attwater Science Collection," San Antonio *Express*, February 8, 1923.

19. Bess Woolford and Ellen S. Quillin, *The Story of the Witte Memorial Museum, 1922 to 1960* (San Antonio: Witte Museum, 1960), 35; "City Fathers to Discuss Museum," San Antonio *Light,* June 1, 1925.

20. "Minutes of the Art League," February 8 and 23, 1921, Archives, SAAL; Woolford and Quillin, *The Story of the Witte Memorial Museum,* 39.

21. "Alfred G. Witte, 63, Dies at His Home," San Antonio *Light,* September 25, 1925; "City to Accept Witte $85,000 Bequest for Museum, Says Tobin," San Antonio *Express,* October 15, 1925; "Splendid Gift to Public Education," San Antonio *Express,* October 16, 1925.

22. Woolford and Quillin, *The Story of the Witte Memorial Museum,* 141.

23. Ibid., 149; Cecilia Steinfeldt, *The Onderdonks: A Family of Texas Painters* (San Antonio: Trinity University Press, 1976), 179.

24. Riley Froh, *Edgar B. Davis: Wildcatter Extraordinary* (Luling, Tex.: The Luling Foundation, 1984), 62-63, 70-73; Reaves, *Texas Art and a Wildcatter's Dream,* 3.

25. Eleanor Onderdonk, "The San Antonio Competitive Exhibitions, 1927-1928-1929," Archives, SAAL; "Resolution of the Art League," February 1927, Archives, SAAL; Minutes of the Art League, March 6, 1930, Ibid.

26. Southern States Art League, vol. 3, no. 7, October 1928, typescript, Ibid. Southern States Art League Clipping File, Ibid.

27. "League Gives Luncheon for Mrs. Drought," Newspaper clipping, January 10, 1930, Ibid.; "Minutes of the Art League," October 1, 1931, Ibid.

28. "Art Department of the Woman's Club, Report of Chairman, Mrs. J. R. McCaldin, 1935-36," Box RG1, Woman's Collection, SAAL; San Antonio *Light,* November 6, 1936; Laredo *Times,* November 6, 1936; Port Arthur *Times,* November 8, 1936; Ardmore (OK) *Daily Armorite,* November 6, 1936.

29. Michael D. Duty, ed. *Deep in the Art of Texas: A Century of Paintings and Drawings* (Fort Worth: TCU Press, 2015), 23.

CHAPTER 6

W. W. JONES OF SOUTH TEXAS

PIONEER RANCHER AND CAPITALIST

by
Patrick Cox

Editor's Note: The geographical area south of San Antonio, including the brush country known as El Monte and running south to the lower Rio Grande River, has always been one of the most rural parts of the state. Sometimes known as the "Wild Horse Desert," this area has been the traditional home of some of the largest ranches in Texas, including those founded by Captain Richard King and Mifflin Kenedy. As well, the region has enjoyed a long and rich Hispanic history, with areas along the river having been part of the Spanish province of Nueva Santander, an eighteenth century jurisdiction separate from colonial Texas. The early years of the twentieth century witnessed an immigration into this area from the rest of Texas and the United States as railroads opened the region to new settlers. The lower Rio Grande valley became an area of citrus farming while some towns in the area began to grow in population for the first time in their respective histories. Corpus Christi quickly became the largest and most important of these, in large part due to civic and business development encouraged by large ranching families led by individuals such as W. W. Jones. This essay by Patrick Cox concentrates on the work Jones undertook to develop Corpus Christi to the exclusion of his prominent role as a South Texas rancher. This essay does not attempt to assess Jones's career as a rancher or present a full picture of his personality, considerations that go beyond the scope of its focus centered on town building. The strong and determined effort that Jones brought to all of his endeavors does, however, show through in examining his role as an urban developer. The myth of the Texas rancher usually does not include popular images of civic and business development as important activities usually identified with individuals who encouraged urban growth. However, as historian Jacqueline Moore notes in a volume cited in the introduction to this book, cattlemen were primarily capitalists whom she equates with the captains of American industry. Moore observes that the Texas myths surrounding the great Texas cattle barons and ranch owners largely ignore their important roles as influential capitalists in the business development of the state. The essay that follows agrees with Moore's conclusions and provides a powerful corrective to the fallacy of myth and memory, which emphasizes individuals such as Charles Goodnight, Samuel "Burk" Burnett, W. T. Waggoner, and W. W. Jones as rural agrarians who concentrated on developing an economic wealth based solely on land and cattle.

Most people have a very distinct image of the historic Texas rancher —a rugged male tied to the soil and his ranch, braving the elements, strongly independent and always prepared to overcome any challenge or adversity the range presented. Much of the historical literature dealing with the cattle industry in Texas considers the great ranchers of the state in isolation from other kinds of economic development that occurred in urban areas of the state during their lifetimes. From the nineteenth century to the mid-twentieth century, the owners of large ranches represented the dominant economic, political, and social force in Texas. Waggoners, Klebergs, Harrells, Burnets, Adairs, and other stereotypical ranchers are mostly remembered today for their contributions in creating the Texas cattle kingdom. This somewhat restricted view of cattlemen solely as individuals of the land is part and parcel of both the myth and historical memory of Texas that constitutes a fallacy.

In reality many important ranchers across the state were much broader based in their economic interests with their activities centered on the burgeoning cities of Texas. They were as much urban developers as ranchers. Such was true for the Waggoner and Burnett families in Fort Worth. This was also the case for the activities of South Texas rancher William Whitby (W. W.) Jones, whose life story constitutes a little-known chapter in the creation of an urban Texas. He became a successful cattleman and landowner in South Texas in the early 1900s. But his wealth and influence came not just from his ability to acquire property and survive in the cattle business. Jones also became a businessman and leading figure in developing the port city of Corpus Christi. This essay provides a case study of W. W. Jones as a corrective to the restricted view of the great Texas ranchers as rural figures focused on the cattle industry. In so doing, this assessment of Jones focuses entirely on his activities as an urban developer to the exclusion of his career as a rancher. Jones, although worthy of a full biography, has never attracted the attention of a scholar who had told the full story of his life, which would of course include detailed discussions of his ranching business and his role as a cattleman beyond the matters addressed in this essay.

While W. W. Jones became known throughout the state and nation as an innovative and wealthy rancher, he was also a banker and invested in a number of businesses. He played a role in the development of Corpus Christi as a major port and financial center during the first four decades of the twentieth century. He built a major office building in the city, encouraged business development in the port, and owned the Nueces Hotel—the premier hotel in the city for much of the early twentieth century. He served on several bank boards in Corpus Christi and other South Texas communities. Jones was a longtime director of the Nueces County Navigation District Commission. As one of the commissioners on the navigation district, he worked with many community leaders and officials to fund and operate the Port of Corpus Christi. He and other community leaders worked together to rebuild their city after the destructive hurricane of 1919.

Reflecting his standing in the community, Jones became known as "the Anchor Post" in Corpus Christi. Jones thus fashioned a career as a civic leader and urban developer that provides a counter to the myth of the "typical" rancher in late nineteenth and early twentieth century Texas. From the day in 1905 when he moved with his family to Corpus Christi, Texas, until his death in that city in 1943, W. W. Jones became a leader in business, political, and civic affairs. His involvement in banking, hotels, oil and gas, shipping and port activities, along with his service on many volunteer organizations made him the prototype of the modern Texas capitalist. When W. W. Jones rode on horseback across the brush-covered prairies known as the "Wild Horse Desert" of South Texas in the 1890s, he embarked on a lifelong pursuit to acquire and build one of the most historic ranches in Texas. His initiatives in acquiring and managing the extensive ranches he came to own, combined with the development of oil and gas resources, served as a model for modern ranching operations. In addition, Jones's contributions to the economic diversification of Corpus Christi along with the larger region of South Texas as a major trade and financial center, make him an important figure in Texas history beyond the history of cattle-raising.

Before W. W. Jones began building his ranching and business operations in the 1890s, the economy and communities of South Texas lagged far behind other areas of the state and nation. In the nineteenth to the mid-twentieth century, the owners of large ranches represented the dominant economic, political, and social force in South Texas. Thanks to W. W. Jones and others, the role of cities and a diversified economy slowly evolved in the region during the twentieth century. While Jones became known throughout the state and nation as an innovative rancher, banker, and investor, he played an important role in the development of Corpus Christi, Texas, as a major port and financial center in the twentieth century. Surviving and prospering as a rancher and businessman through decades of storms, droughts, revolution, political instability, economic depressions, unpredictable markets, and the inherent risks of managing an extensive ranch in this area of the country was a difficult achievement for any person in south Texas engaged in raising cattle.

The history of the W. W. Jones Ranch is the typical narrative of a family and a culture that contributed to one of the overlooked stories of our state and nation. At the dawn of the twentieth century, more than four out of five Texans lived in rural areas of the state. But the state was also in transition to an urban one. San Antonio was the largest city with more than 53,000 inhabitants followed by Houston, Dallas, Galveston, and Fort Worth. Corpus Christi, a port city on the Nueces Bay with a population of 4,700, became more attractive as a commercial and shipping center for South Texas at the turn of the century. The demand for beef after the Civil War played a large role in the growth of Corpus Christi in the late nineteenth century and into the twentieth century. Oil and gas would not gain prominence until later discoveries in South Texas in the 1920s. The increased trade resulting from improving port facilities permitted larger steamships to serve the city. The Corpus Christi, San Diego, and Rio Grande Narrow Gauge Railroad linked the city to other inland destinations. In 1881 the line was extended to Laredo as the Texas Mexican Railway. When the line became a standard-gauge railroad in 1902, uninterrupted rail transit from Mexico City through Laredo and Corpus Christi to the major commercial centers throughout the US became a reality.[1]

In 1890 New York investors announced plans to build a deep-water seaport that would make Corpus Christi a "Chicago of the Southwest" and a "Long Branch of the South." The national depression and the extreme drought of the early 1890s ended this plan. However, this vision and its scenic location on Corpus Christi Bay attracted others. By 1900 the city had three banks, a customhouse, railroad machine shops, an ice factory, carriage factories, several hotels, Episcopal, Presbyterian, Methodist,

Catholic, and Baptist churches, and two newspapers, the *Caller* and the *Critic.*[2] The emerging community of Corpus Christi captured the attention of South Texas rancher William Whitby Jones. Spending most of his early life in Goliad County managing his ranching operations there, Jones saw personal opportunity in the business and civic life in Corpus Christi. W. W. Jones was born in Nacogdoches County on September 6, 1855, the first son of Captain Allen Carter (A. C.) Jones and his wife Margaret Whitby Jones. A few years later the family moved to the historic community of Goliad, Texas. His mother Margaret Jones passed away when he was only three years old so his maternal grandparents raised him in Goliad —one of the largest cattle-producing communities in Texas at the time. Before the Civil War, his father had served as Goliad County sheriff. A. C. Jones remarried to Caroline Jane Fields and moved his family farther south to Beeville, Texas. During the Civil War, Captain Jones fought for the Confederate Army in South Texas and later he became known in the community for his leadership in business and civic affairs. For example, he led a group of Beeville merchants and ranchers to bring the first railroad to the community in 1886. A. C. Jones was also one of the founders of the First National Bank of Beeville, president of the Beeville Oil Mill, the first mayor of Beeville, and donated the land for the community's public school. He soon became known as the "Father of Beeville" for his accomplishments and standing in the community.[3]

A. C. Jones wanted his son W. W. Jones to become well-educated and involved in business. Young Jones attended Roanoke College in Salem, Virginia, where he graduated with honors. While at Roanoke, he adopted one of his lifelong mottos: *Labor omnia vincit*: work overcomes all. After attending Poughkeepsie Business College in New York, in 1875 W. W. Jones returned to Beeville at the age of twenty. Although his father apparently wanted his son to enter business or banking, Jones maintained an interest in the cattle business. He went on his first cattle drive from Texas to Kansas with some well-known cattlemen of the era, including Bill Kuykendall and Shanghai Pierce. According to an interview that he provided to author Marion Knight, Jones said that on that drive they "had close to three thousand head—brands from seven or eight different ranches—and were to drive the cattle to Kansas City." For the next few years Jones drove cattle to Kansas while working as a merchant and banker in some of his father's businesses.[4]

In 1880 W. W. Jones married Lou Ella Marsden. She was from Wisconsin and the couple settled initially in Beeville. The couple had four children: one son, Allen Carter (A. C. or Dick); and three daughters, Lorine, Alice, and Kathleen. A.C. Jones married Anna Gertrude Russell. Lorine married Marshall Spoonts, who died in 1923. She then married Frank Morton Lewis. Kathleen married Lee Blanchette who passed away in 1921. Her second husband, Clarence Hocker, died in 1937. Her third husband was Donald Alexander. Alice married Benjamin Eshleman, Sr. These family members would form six generations of the Jones ranching dynasty in South Texas.

In the late 1880s Jones leased his first ranch in nearby Live Oak County. With his father's assistance, he purchased several thousand cattle for his first venture. However, his timing for the investment was unfortunate. The drought of the early 1890s combined with the national economic depression drove many ranchers out of business. W. W. Jones confessed that by 1893 "I was broke." After he realized that his investment had not worked to his expectations, he made an important decision. While he still owned 8,000 cattle in Kansas, he decided to approach his friend and cattle broker George Barse of Kansas City for a loan, using his Kansas cattle as collateral. With the funds from the Barse loan, Jones made several life-changing decisions. "I went home with my mind made up: to get out of debt, to get out of Live Oak County, and to buy me a range in Starr County." These choices led to his initial purchase in 1895 of the Mesteña land grants in what was then eastern Starr County. In his first years of assembling the ranch and buying cattle prior to 1900, he also borrowed funds from his father. Thus, over the next thirty years he began and accomplished his quest to build one of the largest cattle ranches in Texas.

He also learned a valuable lesson on the role of capital and the need for credit to expand in business ventures.[5]

The Jones Family Ranches are historically significant properties that have been owned and operated by W.W. Jones and his wife Lou Ella Marsden Jones and their descendants since the 1890s. The family to this day maintains ownership and continues a working commercial cattle operation on the vast ranch. The historic ranch includes acreage in what are now Jim Hogg, Brooks, Starr, and Hidalgo Counties, and remains one of the largest in Texas. It contains the original headquarters at *Alta Vista*, located about 115 miles southwest of Corpus Christi in Jim Hogg County. Ranching in this region dates to the Spanish colonial era of the eighteenth century. The vast majority of acreage in the present-day ranch can be traced back to Spanish land grants and their original owners. The early Spanish settlers established *ranchos* on the northern *frontera* of Mexico. They capitalized on the millions of wild cattle and horses that populated the lands between the Rio Grande and Nueces rivers.

The early Spanish land grants on the Jones Ranch included *Las Mesteña, Las Mesteñas, La Mesteña y Gonzalena, Palo Blanco, Diego Ynojosa, Marcelo Ynojosa, Las Animas, Agua Nueva de Arriba* and *Agua Nueva de Abajo*, and *La Rucia*. Based on information and maps from the Texas General Land Office, the current holdings of the Jones Family Ranches include all or portions of seventeen land grants originally issued by the Spanish or Mexican governments largely between 1800 and 1836. Many of these Spanish names and more survive on the Jones Family Ranches as pastures, divisions, and other distinguished features on the property.

The history of the Jones family ranches reveals a complex story of cattle ranching in South Texas—from the introduction of livestock by the early Spanish and Mexican settlers to the acquisition of the ranches by W. W. Jones, followed by the implementation of modern ranching methods and livestock. The ranch's integrity is unique: W. W. Jones assembled the entire acreage from 1895 to 1925 in more than one hundred different transactions—most of which involved cash payments to the property owners. In the one hundred-plus purchases that Jones made to build his ranch, 98 percent of these were cash transactions for both Tejano and Anglo sellers. Title records showed that Jones purchased several properties from Anglo sellers who acquired their property through sheriff's sales.

The struggle to incorporate people of diverse backgrounds, nationalities, and religious beliefs into American society is not unique to South Texas. Lawlessness, border disturbances before and during the 1910 Mexican Revolution, business booms and depressions, local political strife, and rivalries all influenced the history of the Jones Family Ranches and the region. Jones utilized his credit and his skills in managing and marketing cattle to acquire acreage during these years and to finance his operations. He also benefited from an expanding economy in the early twentieth century and a growing demand for beef. Jones also utilized the technology of the new industrial age to improve the ranch.

The success of the ranch as part of an industrialized society and marketplace in the twentieth century is illustrated through the introduction of windmills and mechanized wells, fencing, electricity, motorized vehicles, deeper water wells, larger storage facilities, access to railroads and paved highways, and newer breeds of disease resistant cattle better suited for the marketplace. Jones incorporated all of these activities and improvements into his ranch operations as he expanded through the early twentieth century.

W. W. Jones worked during a changing and sometimes tumultuous environment from the late nineteenth century to the mid-twentieth century. Those who lived in South Texas during this period witnessed not just the beginning of modernization and the industrial era, but also the rise of Anglo American political and financial influence. This was most recognizable in South Texas through the transfer of land from many original Tejano owners to Anglo-American owners such as Jones. Third and fourth generation Tejano ranching families struggled with a different government and culture along with natural disasters such as the severe drought of the 1890s. The physical boundaries of the ranch remain essentially as they were when Jones died in 1942; the land use patterns and property layout remain largely unchanged from the early 1900s when the ranch came under the Jones family management. Many contributing resources and cultural attributes from the Spanish/Mexican colonial era and the early twentieth-century Anglo-American ranching period also remain, and the descendants of W. W. Jones still own and operate the ranches, which are now in their sixth generation.

Many structures and improvements dating to the eighteenth and nineteenth centuries are located throughout the ranch. These include buildings, barns, camp houses, loading chutes, fences, corrals, wells, watering systems, windmills, storage tanks, and dipping vats. Numerous improvements predate the acquisition of the ranch by the Jones family and date to the Spanish/Mexican colonial era, as well as the formative Texas statehood period. From a broader context, this heritage influences the social, economic, and political structure of this region that remains unique within the state and nation. The ranching culture combined with its Spanish legacy and Anglo-American influences also make the ranches a distinctive property important to national and borderlands history.

Within the 300,000-plus acres are four clusters that contain historic features from the Spanish/Mexican colonial era through 1940 with the establishment and incorporation of the ranches under the ownership of W. W. Jones. These divisions of the property include: (1) the original Alta Vista/San Javier ranch with numerous Spanish colonial-era *norias* (water wells) and the San Javier Casa Mayor; the early 1900 headquarters at Alta Vista constructed by W. W. Jones, with his home, agricultural buildings and pens of this era; (2) the Alto Colorado/La Rucia ranch divisions with their Spanish/Mexican era structures, *norias,* wells, tanks, water features, pens, and the historic Alto Colorado ranch headquarters; (3) the historic ranch headquarters of Agua Nueva/Borregos with their Spanish/Mexican era structures, *norias,* wells, tanks, pens, and collection of auxiliary buildings; (4) and the Balduras Ranch headquarters located adjacent to the historic Texas Mexican Railroad and with *norias,* wells, tanks, and pens from the Spanish/Mexican colonial period and the later settlement period.

From the day he moved his wife Lou Ella and his four children to Corpus Christi in 1905 until his death in 1942, W. W. Jones maintained an active presence in that community. He owned several residences at his ranch headquarters, but could usually be found in Corpus Christi. He ventured into many areas of business and finance from his adopted city. While W. W. Jones and Lou Ella maintained the early ranch headquarters at Alta Vista, the couple built a home at 511 South Broadway and attended the First Methodist Church. In 1915 he invested in and eventually acquired the 300-room Nueces Hotel and made it the center of the growing city's commercial and tourist business. Instead of having an office, he operated from a chair in the center of the open lobby of his Nueces Hotel. As Marion Knight noted in her 1941 interview with Jones, he was at home either on the rustic Alta Vista Ranch or at the Nueces Hotel. "He is utterly unaware that the hosts of young and old men, who gather to pay him court, accept his words of wisdom and kindly advice as from a great Sage," Knight surmised.[6] During his early years in Corpus Christi, Jones expanded his investments in the Nueces Hotel and other commercial structures. The ten-story Jones Building, located across the street from the Nueces Hotel, was the city's first major office building. In 1935 the Jones family donated their home at 511 South Broadway to the city of Corpus Christi. The two-story Georgian style home with its broad porches and balconies later became the La Retama Public Library.

By 1915 four railroads formed a transportation network for Corpus Christi that provided a stimulus to the city's commercial and financial growth. These included the Texas Mexican, the San Antonio and Aransas Pass; the St. Louis, Brownsville and Mexico; and the San Antonio, Uvalde and Gulf. The railroads provided an essential link that made Corpus Christi an attractive commercial and tourist destination. They also aggressively promoted the city and its coastline through inexpensive fares. Rail agents touted Corpus Christi to the emerging market for tourists, billing the city as a resort "where the weary can come to rest, the invalid can come for health, and the gay devotee come for pleasure." Many people immigrated to the city, resulting in a construction boom for hotels, cottages, and boardinghouses. [7]

Jones rotated his time between his ranches and his family in Corpus Christi. Although he traveled by rail between Corpus Christi and Hebbronville (the closest rail connection to the Jones Ranches), he still traversed the Trans Nueces by horseback. Maude Gillian, a local writer on the history of Rincon, said that their remote ranch had very few visitors during the year. But one of their friends who made his way to the ranch was W. W. Jones. "When he paid us a visit he came straight through the country from his ranch driving a pair of mules to a two wheel cart," she wrote. With very few improved roads in the region, cattlemen used carts with broad rimmed wheels to keep from getting stuck in areas with deep sands. "In crossing through the pastures he took down the fences here and there but always told Papa just where so the fence riders could go out and repair after his visits," Gillian recalled.[8] She noted that although W. W. Jones was wealthy and influential, he was also known for his "frugal ways." At the same time he enjoyed the good things of life. Gillian provided a description of the "unusual walking stick" that Jones kept with him. When he accidentally left it one day at the ranch, Gillian said she examined the cane at close range. "Carved at the top was a steer's head. Set in the eye sockets were two sparkling rubies," she stated.[9]

Hurricanes have been and still are frequent unwelcome visitors to the Texas coast. People who reside and work near the shores of the Gulf of Mexico know that the annual hurricane season can deliver one hundred-mile-per-hour winds (or greater), storm surges, flooding from torrential rains, and extensive damage to lives and property. The 1919 Hurricane that struck Corpus Christi was one of those historic storms that ultimately shaped the modern port city. It was a catastrophic hurricane that devastated the Texas coast and killed over 1,100 people in Corpus

Christi. The Nueces Hotel served as a safe harbor for many residents from the storm. Observers and eyewitnesses left horrific stories of the event. "It was not just the wind and the water and the rain. Those barrier isles, Mustang and San José, that were to have protected the city, had been scoured by the hurricane on its way inland. Bombarding the seas holding Teddy's float were huge barrels of oil swept from Port Aransas docks, telephone poles ripped from the dunes, and bulls, heifers, and near-grown calves already drowned in fourteen-foot high waves that had enveloped the islands." City officials converted the Nueces County Courthouse into a morgue and Governor William P. Hobby placed the city under martial law. All able-bodied citizens were instructed to work on cleanup and rescue efforts.[10] The storm destroyed many commercial buildings and hotels, which hampered rescue efforts. It leveled the popular Pavilion Hotel and Pier. Jones's landmark hotel survived but suffered extensive damage. The family saved the hotel and immediately began restoration of the building to its pre-hurricane grandeur. Daughter Lorine Jones Lewis planted three palms in the patio of the Nueces Hotel, representing W. W. and Lou Ella's three daughters, but also representing faith, hope, and charity.[11]

The gesture was symbolic not only for the Jones family, but for the City of Corpus Christi. In an effort to resuscitate the city (and save it from the fate of Indianola, Texas, which became a ghost town after a catastrophic hurricane in 1875), city leaders looked to the federal government to help rebuild their city. In the late nineteenth century Corpus Christi received federal aid to construct jetties and improve the harbor. Once John Nance Garner became Congressman after 1902, the city began to receive more attention and federal appropriations for improvements. Garner passed legislation and funding in 1907 for the Intracoastal Canal. Subsequent federal funds enlarged the harbor and deepened the channels. But the 1919 hurricane devastated Harbor Island and other areas of the Corpus Christi Bay. As a consequence the disaster led to a new citizens' committee, the Corpus Christi Deep Water Committee, to persuade federal officials to locate the new deep water port facility at the Corpus

Christi bay front. W. W. Jones joined this influential group, consisting of the region's bankers, ranchers, businessmen, and elected officials. The organization pledged land, wharves, and terminals at a value estimated at the time to be $3 million.[12]

In 1922 the voters of Nueces County created the Nueces County Navigation District Number 1 to oversee the operation of the port facilities. The Corpus Christi City Council and the Nueces County Commissioners Court appointed a three-member board: Robert Driscoll, Chairman; John W. Kellam of Robstown; and W. W. Jones, who served from 1925 until his death in 1942, making him one of the longest serving members on the commission. Following voter approval of the district, in 1923 the U.S. Congress authorized the Army Corps of Engineers to construct a channel twenty-five feet in depth with a 200-foot bottom width, from the Gulf of Mexico through the jetties at Port Aransas to a point on the shoreline of Corpus Christi Bay. Channel dredging began in 1925 and was completed in January 1926. On September 15, 1926, an official "statewide" celebration took place at the Marine Room of Jones's Nueces Hotel, marking this historic achievement.[13]

Physically, W. W. Jones resembled the outward appearance of the stereotypical Texas rancher; he was 6-feet 4-inches tall and "always wore a big Stetson hat." Yet, when he stayed in Corpus Christi, he "always had on a necktie, never wore boots, and never went to town without his coat." At the same time Jones was also a great conversationalist with a quick wit. "He could quote Shakespeare and the Bible more accurately than almost anyone I knew," daughter Kathleen remembered. She also recalled that he was "extremely fond of children. He was the one who always wanted us to have parties when we were children." Kathleen added that her mother "had a great influence over all of us. First of all, she had a very high code of ethics," she stated. "My mother never raised her voice."[14]

Figure 11. W. W. Jones at his roll top desk

Courtesy Jones Family Archives, Corpus Christi, Texas

In 1907 W. W. Jones wrote some fatherly advice in a letter to his daughter Lorine shortly after her marriage to Marshall Spoonts. He also revealed some of his own life history. "Your mother and I were married 27 years ago last February & everything we had at that time was not worth as much as yours and Marshall's wedding presents. During hard times we had a lot of reverses and our expenses had been very heavy. Many a man with less energy and ambitions would have become despondent & given up but I was not built that way," he wrote. Further, "I did not allow myself to be baffled or sent off by obstacles that came in my way but I handed these to one side & kept pursuing a large wish & embracing energy & ambition," he declared.[15]

Jones also paid credit to his wife Lou Ella for her commitment during the good and the difficult times the couple faced. "I have reached that point where my credit is good if not better than any other man in this country & our mother shares the credit equally with me. For if she had not have assisted me by staying at home and taken care of things as she did I never could have accomplished with I have," he stated. He offered insight about his father and how he planned to help his own children. W. W. Jones wrote, "It is true my father signed my notes when I needed help but I paid every note that he ever signed for me & will do just as much & more for you & Marshall. When you all make & save ten thousand dollars I will give you ten thousand dollars but you must make that much first yourselves. So get busy."[16]

Throughout their lives Lou Ella and W. W. Jones extended support to many organizations in Corpus Christi and in Texas. They provided financial contributions to the First Methodist Church, the Methodist Home, and the Texas and Southwest Cattle Raisers Association. The couple bestowed financial assistance and monetary contributions to many individuals and organizations throughout South Texas. During the Great Depression of the 1930s, when banks around the nation failed, W. W. Jones reportedly saved the Alice State Bank and Trust from closing. "He went down there and told the people that he was leaving his money in there, and that the bank was all right, they left their money there," Kathleen recalled. A similar situation took place in Beeville at the bank his father helped organize. "He saved that bank, because people saw that he was behind it," Kathleen affirmed.[17]

In one of his personal achievements in which he took great pride, W. W. Jones hosted the 1931 Texas and Southwest Cattle Raisers Association annual meeting at his Nueces Hotel in Corpus Christi. At the time, W. W. Jones was one of the last original members of his generation of South Texas cattle raisers. Richard King, Mifflin Kenedy, Al McFaddin, Ed C. Lasater, and many of Jones's contemporaries had passed away. At this meeting Jones delivered one of his few recorded public speeches at the event. With the state and the nation in the throes of the Great Depression, Jones provided encouragement and perseverance. He told the audience: "We know the most substantial thing about any business is not in the value of the investment, but lies in the energy and the spirit of the men." He then said: "Keep your courage—the Star of hope is still shining. In time you will realize the cattle business is one of the greatest; for its products are among the great necessities of life."[18]

Lou Ella Jones suffered from a number of illnesses in the final years of her life. Kathleen stated that her mother "was an invalid for at least thirty-five years before she died." She described her as suffering from tic douloureux—a form of neuropathic pain associated with nerve injury or nerve lesion, which results in a sudden burning or facial pain. The intensity of pain from this condition can be physically and mentally incapacitating. "She had several operations for that which didn't really relieve it entirely. She always had a slight headache, and the last operation left one side of her face absolutely numb," Kathleen stated. In spite of the debilitating attacks, Lou Ella remained active in the church and her Monday Club, a reading organization in Corpus Christi. "She had all sorts of books that she could put her hands on," Kathleen stated. "She was always writing papers for somebody in the club." [19]

Lou Ella Jones died on November 30, 1932, at the couple's home. Many friends and associates mourned her loss and praised her unselfish contributions. The *Corpus Christi Times* reported on December 1, 1932, that she was "a member of one of the most widely-known and prominent families in South Texas." Abundant letters in the Corpus Christi newspapers spoke of her devotion to family, community, and the Methodist Church. Mrs. Frank A. Thompkins wrote: "she not only sought to make conditions better but to make life richer and stronger for those around her. She was recognized as a leader in social circles, a leader in church affairs, a leader in civic causes, in education, in charity, and in philanthropy." Lou Ella Jones was buried at the Rose Hill Cemetery in Corpus Christi.[20]

Despite the loss of his wife, W. W. Jones continued his ranching and business pursuits. In an interview with the *Corpus Christi Times* on November 13, 1938, the paper described W. W. Jones as "one of the few remaining Texas cattlemen who rode the long trail to Kansas cattle markets long before existing railroad lines were built." Jones was a "Cattleman all his life, riding the range since he was 12 years old." The article also noted that after all the years, he still raised cattle on the Alta Vista ranch in Jim Hogg County. Jones still wore his wide-brimmed hat and "he never goes 100 feet from the house without it. He loves a good story and is a good story teller." His motto was "Hew to the line and let the chips fall where they may. Labor always wins."[21]

In addition to his ranching activities, Jones held a number of positions in South Texas banks. In this role, he essentially served the South Texas region as a "merchant-capitalist." The lack of available and affordable credit and capital were an ongoing issue among rural and small town business and political leaders. Becoming involved in both finance and business in local communities (particularly in the American West and South) allowed these individuals to assume a level of importance in civic and local political affairs.[22] Jones assumed most of these board positions after his move to Corpus Christi in 1905. Local banks and positions he represented were: President and Director of Alice State Bank and

Trust; Director, Corpus Christi National Bank; Member, Nueces County Navigation Board; Member, Texas and Southwestern Cattle Raisers Association; Owner, the Nueces Hotel and the Jones Building in Corpus Christi; and Organizer and Director of Hebbronville State Bank, 1915. As an illustration of the growth in the community, the Corpus Christi National Bank expanded with the city. From deposits of $380,000 in 1904, the bank grew to over $12 million in deposits by 1940.[23]

Brooks and Jim Hogg Counties, which comprised a portion of the Jones family ranches, were among the latest counties formed in Texas. Their creation was due to a series of events that involved W.W. Jones with the major South Texas political and business leaders of the era. The land that now composes these two counties was originally part of Starr County. Named for James Harper Starr, a Land Commissioner and Treasurer during the Republic of Texas, Starr County formed after the end of the Mexican War in 1848. Rio Grande City became the county seat. From Starr County's founding in 1848 until the late nineteenth century, the region's economy centered on sheep, cattle, and trade along the international border. Fort Ringgold near Rio Grande City served as a major military post along the U.S./Mexico border. The population was overwhelmingly Hispanic and many ranching families traced their roots back to the ranchos between the Rio Grande and Nueces River.

From the end of the nineteenth century into the twentieth century— the era when W. W. Jones assembled his ranch—a small group of men exercised control over their counties and politics in South Texas. James B. Wells in Cameron County, Archer Parr in Duval County, and Manuel Guerra in Starr County were the dominant figures in both politics and commerce in the region. All three leaders were contemporaries of W. W. Jones and he had contact with them in business and ranching affairs. After his election in 1902, Congressman John Nance Garner served as the representative of South Texas in Washington, D. C. and maintained a close alliance with these local political leaders. Each of these men had an extensive network of supporters and friends that extended into the ranching and commercial community of the region. As South Texas grew in population and business, their influence extended beyond county politics and local affairs. They utilized their influence to control local elections and create business opportunities for themselves and their friends. The domination of politics and business in the Rio Grande Valley became known as "Boss Rule." All of these leaders engaged in more than politics. Ranching, land speculation, railroads, business promotion, and commerce formed the foundation for each to promote their interests alongside those of the communities they represented.[24]

Cameron, Hidalgo, Duval, and Starr Counties were the dominant political jurisdictions in South Texas in this era. County governments provided basic social and economic services to residents. This included roads and bridges, law enforcement, local courts, schools, and the repository for records involving land transactions and other legal records. As each of these counties remained predominantly rural and agricultural with only a handful of cities, county government served as the most visible and accessible government. Wells, Guerra, Parr, and the counties where they lived and worked served as the center of their political organizations and business activities.

All of these individuals played a role in the formation of Brooks and Jim Hogg Counties. With Starr County rancher Edward C. Lasater's open support of opposition candidates to Guerra in Starr County, combined with ongoing investigations into Guerra's political organization, the ongoing friction created problems for the political bosses in South Texas. Lasater also issued similar challenges and supported opposition candidates to Parr in Duval County. In an effort to quell the uproar, James Wells intervened and provided a recommendation: Lasater and his supporters in Falfurrias would have their own county. Wells apparently convinced Guerra and Parr that carving out the eastern portion of Starr County and establishing a new county would effectively remove Lasater from the scene.

The Texas Legislature adopted a law that created Brooks County with Falfurrias as the county seat. Named for former Texas Ranger and State Representative John Brooks (the author of the legislation), Brooks County was organized in 1911. The legislation to create Brooks County stated: "The great inconvenience to which the people are subjected, living in the territory from which said new county is created, by being compelled to travel extraordinary distances to attend to their private and public business at the county seats of the respective counties in which they now reside, creates an emergency and an imperative public necessity." While this explanation gave credence to the supporters of the new county, its creation was an attempt to calm the troubled South Texas political waters. The legislation also called for Ed Lasater, F. S. Rachel, Amando Garcia, A. C. Jones, H. H. McCampbell, H. D. Thomas, and E. R. Rachel to be appointed commissioners to organize the county government. The law went into effect on March 11, 1911.[25]

Brooks County was still in its organizational process when W. W. Jones made his move in the following state legislative session. Jones apparently worked an agreement with Lasater to have his son A. C. Jones included as one of the first appointed Brooks County Commissioners. But Jones apparently had his own ideas for a separate county and made his wishes known as the Brooks County legislation moved forward. Jones recalled: "The new county was created over my protest." Having observed Lasater's success in forming Brooks County, Jones vowed that he would come back to the legislature with his own proposal. "This time, I built my fences right," he stated.[26]

Two years later, Jones convinced first-term State Representative D. W. Glasscock to file legislation in the 1913 regular session to establish Jim Hogg County from part of the newly created Brooks County and the southern portion of Duval County. Named for popular Governor Jim Hogg who had passed away in 1905, Jones and his supporters realized that naming the new county after the late chief executive was an astute move. Many state representatives and senators held the late Governor

Hogg in high esteem. Other members expressed opinions that new South Texas counties would protect ranches and the economy from the growing violence of the Mexican Revolution along the Rio Grande border. But getting legislation passed to create the new county proved to be challenging for the proponents of Jim Hogg County.

Sponsors for the proposed Jim Hogg County used some of the same arguments utilized in the successful approval of Brooks County in 1911. The legislation stated that they needed to avoid the domination of factions in Starr County. They also argued that they were too far removed from the new Brooks County seat of Falfurrias, which placed ranch owners like Jones at a disadvantage. As Jones stated in a letter to legislators in February 1913: "It is extremely inconvenient for those living in that portion of the county now sought to be created into Jim Hogg County, to go to the County seat to attend Court and to matters connected with the business of the County administration to private business in the County." Jones also noted that the proposed Brooks County $45 million bond issue was costly and designed "exclusively for the northeastern portion of the county. People living in the western portion of the county did not have voting boxes."[27]

The proposed Jim Hogg County also met with opposition from Ed Lasater and Representative Brooks who had become the new Brooks County Judge after leaving the legislature. In an open letter opposing the division of the county, Brooks stated that if Jim Hogg County came into existence, it would be "absolutely dominated by men who are wholly concerned in holding it as mere ranch properties and in perpetuating intolerable conditions which have existed and now exist in Zapata and Starr Counties." However, Lasater's opponents in Brooks County noted that he had adopted some of the same tactics that he criticized Parr and Guerra of using: paying the poll tax of hundreds of Tejano constituents. In his counter argument Jones maintained, "The new county will have no political boss and all will be found working together for the welfare of the entire County." To reinforce his argument, Jones declared: "I, as well as others, have gigantic plans on foot to make Jim Hogg County the banner county of Southwest Texas. [28]

Confronting Lasater and Brooks' opposition, Jones succeeded in moving his plan forward. He enlisted the support of his friends in the Texas and Southwestern Cattle Raisers Association to support the bill. He also had his son-in-law Lee Blanchette, "one of the ablest and most popular men in the state," to assist with passage. Jones said at one point during the process that he inadvertently "almost ruined things: in a poker game staged during our fight." Playing cards with three influential State Senators, Jones recalled that they "lost more than they ought—and all to me—it nearly alienated their influence." In retrospect Jones said, "I didn't know I was supposed to let those fellows win."[29]

In spite of the ill-timed poker game, Jones had sufficient support. The legislature passed and the governor signed the bill to create Jim Hogg County. The legislation called for an election to establish the county and elect county officers. With the creation of Jim Hogg County in 1913, elections for county officials were held in July. At that time the school system was organized, and construction of a county courthouse was started. At the first meeting of the county commissioners on August 13, 1913, A. C. Jones presided as county judge, receiving an annual salary of $600. A. C. Jones was also appointed as County Superintendent of Schools at a $600 annual salary. The commissioners considered a site for location of the courthouse in Hebbronville, as well as a jail location. Notably, the first meeting was held in the W. W. Jones Building. The first county officials were: Precinct 1: H. C. Yaeger; Precinct 2: R. H. McCampbell; Precinct 3: R. Holbein; Precinct 4: J. F. Hardcastle; Sheriff: Oscar Thompson; County Clerk: W. A. Dannelley. Sheriff Oscar Thompson was Jones's long-time ranch foreman at Alta Vista, who also became a respected rancher and public official in Jim Hogg County. The other elected officials knew W. W. Jones and his family and undoubtedly understood the role they played in creating Jim Hogg County.[30]

W. W. Jones took a unique approach to achieve his political goals that he adopted throughout his later life. He shunned publicity and public confrontations whenever necessary, and pointedly avoided involvement in the violent political acts that occurred in Starr and Duval Counties. He prepared his son A. C. Jones to take public positions in both Brooks and Jim Hogg Counties. W. W. Jones also avoided costly legal suits against other South Texas political bosses who continued to exert strong interest in the region. Not unlike his approach to business and ranching, W. W. Jones followed a successful path as he navigated the treacherous political waters of South Texas. He focused on consolidating his family ranch and cattle ranching business in Jim Hogg County. This lessened his financial risk and also allowed him to diversify his business and banking interests in Corpus Christi.

While Jones was assembling his ranching and business empire, the Texas oil industry expanded throughout the state by the 1920s. Beginning with the Spindletop discovery near Beaumont in January 1901, both independent and large corporations began exploration of new fields in all areas of the state. With less news coverage than the East Texas oil fields, production began in South Texas with a series of oil discoveries in McMullen, Calhoun, and San Patricio Counties. The opening of the *Piedras Pintas* field in Duval County in 1907 just north of Jim Hogg and Brooks Counties marked the southernmost strike in the early decades. The oil business in Texas accelerated with the outbreak of World War I in 1914 and the pressing need for petroleum for the war effort. Thereafter, petroleum prices soon increased as exports flowed to England and France to fuel the Allied war machine. Many new discoveries throughout the state added to oil production, while large refineries, pipelines, and other petroleum-related businesses organized and expanded during the war years. The Texas Company (later known as Texaco), Gulf, Sun, Magnolia, and Humble Oil (later known as Exxon) all diversified as they saw their profits rise faster than a new gusher. During the 1920s, new discoveries in Southwest Texas included government wells in Duval County, adjacent to the Jennings gas field, and smaller gas production in the Agua Dulce,

Kohler, and Three Rivers fields. By 1927, natural gas production in the region passed four billion cubic feet a day, with pipelines linking these sites to Houston the year before. Lines also moved natural gas from Mirando City near Laredo to the lower Rio Grande Valley.[31]

The port city of Corpus Christi and the surrounding area played a major role in the development of oil and gas in South Texas. Following completion of the Corpus Christi Ship Channel in 1926, the city attracted new refineries for exporting petroleum. Humble Oil built a refinery at Ingleside on the Corpus Christi Bay. Other facilities opened in Corpus Christi, Refugio, and Port Lavaca during the 1930s. The Taylor Refining Company, the Pontiac Refining Company, and the Southwestern Oil and Refining Company all selected Corpus Christi, which helped stimulate exploration and drilling in South Texas. During the 1930s, other strikes expanded oil production in South Texas. In 1933 Humble Oil leased one million acres on the King Ranch and the company launched its successful drilling and production that same year. Additional refineries in Corpus Christi and the surrounding region added to production. As he served on the board of the Corpus Christi Navigation District, Jones had a bird's eye view of the oil and gas development and its impact on the economy. [32]

The impetus from oil and gas discoveries in South Texas caught the attention of the Jones family. In spite of the ongoing Great Depression, oil and gas production provided a much-needed injection of jobs and money into the Texas economy. The construction of oil refining facilities in Corpus Christi and the extension of pipelines into South Texas also encouraged exploration and production. With the King Ranch lease and other nearby discoveries, W.W. Jones began to consider alternatives for how they could expand beyond the cattle business into oil and gas production.

W. W. Jones had initially resisted any extensive oil and gas exploration on his ranches prior to the Great Depression. Clarence McElroy Hocker, an oil attorney from Oklahoma and Texas, changed his approach. Hocker married Kathleen Jones Blanchette, the daughter of W. W. and Lou Ella.

Jones trusted Hocker and agreed that pooling the mineral interests into a company managed by his son-in-law might be a good idea. Jones, unsure of the future in his advanced years, "wanted all his children and grand-children to benefit—if there was any substance to this oil and gas frenzy." In 1935 this led to the creation of the Mestena Oil and Gas Company for the Jones family.[33]

The name "Mesteña" was taken from a series of Mexican land grants from 1835 and patented in 1858 by the State of Texas. These grants contained several names: *La Mesteña, Las Mesteñas,* and *La Mesteña Y Gonzalena.* As mentioned earlier, Mesteña means "wild horse" and early maps of Texas tagged the whole area as the "wild horse desert." The name reflected the heritage that the Jones family held for the ranch that the patron of the family—W. W. Jones— had assembled by 1930.

The first Mesteña organizational meeting, held on January 5, 1935, in San Antonio, stated the purpose for the Jones family:

> The establishment and maintenance of an oil company to establish and maintain an oil business with authority to contract for the leases and purchase of the right to prospect for, develop and use coal and other minerals, petroleum and gas, and the right to erect, build, and own all necessary oil tanks, cars and pipelines necessary for the operation of the business.

The first Board of Directors meeting of the Mesteña Oil and Gas Company was held at 616 Bedell Building in San Antonio, January 17, 1935. Members of the Jones family assumed the board positions: A. C. Jones as chairman of the board and vice president; second vice president, Alice Eshleman; secretary-treasurer, Kathleen Hocker; and assistant secretary-treasurer Lorine Spoonts. Clarence Hocker served as president and the active manager, under the control and direction of the Board of Directors.[34]

The first oil lease occurred the day after the charter was granted and ratified on January 18, 1935. On March 1, 1935, the company signed with The California Company (Standard Oil). Over forty producing wells resulted from this lease on the Alta Mesa Field—a few of which are still producing to this day. Unfortunately, Clarence Hocker died unexpectedly in 1937. Urged by her father and friends to manage the business, Kathleen Hocker assumed the presidency, thus becoming one of the first female corporate oil and gas executives in the state. She signed her first major lease that same year with Humble Oil. Later, W. W. Jones joined the Board of Directors before his death in 1942. Kathleen remained the president until 1969 and chairman of the board for the following three years. The Mesteña Company prospered along with the growth of the oil and gas business in Texas. By 1940 the value of oil and gas in Texas was greater than the value of all crops in the state. Within a generation, oil and gas replaced ranching and agriculture to become the dominant economic force in Texas. World War II (1939-1945) brought increased demand for petroleum for the armed forces. The boom continued in the postwar era as the American economy experienced significant growth and expansion. From the day of its founding in 1935, the company has remained under family ownership and control with its modern headquarters operation in Corpus Christi.

W. W. Jones died at age eighty-five years, bringing to a close a ranching era in South Texas history. In his July 17, 1942, obituary, the *Corpus Christi Times* described Jones as a "Pioneer Rancher and Capitalist." He was a "capitalist, rancher, industrialist, and hotel manager." The honorary pallbearers included many ranching and business leaders in South Texas: Richard King, J. H. Frost, Richard Kleberg, George Farenthold, Robert Kleberg, John Kenedy, Horace Guerra, Archie Parr, Garland and Thomas Lassiter, Victor Garcia, and Alvino Canales. The funeral was held at the First Methodist Church in Corpus Christi. Prior to the service, his body was taken to the Lou E. Jones Building at the First Methodist Church, which served as a memorial to the late Mrs. Jones. W. W. Jones was buried alongside his wife Lou Ella in the Rose Hill Cemetery.[35]

Figure 12. W. W. Jones in the center with his six grandchildren

left to right: W. W. (Bill) Jones, II, Jeanne Gertrude Jones Hause, Alice
Cathryne Jones Thompson, Louella Jones Borglum, and the two younger chil-
dren in front are Lorine Jones Eshleman and Benjamin Eshleman, Jr.
Courtesy Jones Family Archives, Corpus Christi, Texas

W. W. Jones left his estate to his six grandchildren, explaining that
his four children had already received bequests prior to his death. The
Mesteña Oil and Gas Company, established in 1935, consolidated the
subsurface mineral holdings into the family-held corporation. As directed
in W. W. Jones's last will and testament, the entire surface acreage of
the ranch was given or sold to his four children in the 1930s and it was
the remainder of the estate that was divided six ways among the six
branches of the Jones grandchildren: Jones, Eshleman, Vogt, Thompson,
Hause, and Borglum. Since 1942 these families and their descendants
continue in the ownership and operation of the Jones Family Ranches.
While managing the surface acreage separately, each of the families still

values the heritage and the historic integrity that make the Jones Family Ranches a tribute to the vision of W. W. and Lou Ella Jones.

The life of W. W. Jones provides more than a family ranching legacy; it also adds to the image of the traditional Texas cattleman. Jones was not only a "pioneer rancher" with admirable traits such as self-reliance and a strong work ethic, but also a "capitalist" who had much in common with northeastern industrialists. Jones served as a model for the modern business leader through his diversification of interests and properties combined with his civic involvement. He introduced modern technology and management to his sizable ranching properties. His political skills in negotiating with the South Texas bosses and Corpus Christi community leaders illustrated a learned sophistication in working with a number of very adept and influential leaders. At the same time, Jones broadened the persona of the mythical Texas cattle rancher by furthering the industrialization and modernization of South Texas. This aspect has been often ignored or forgotten in the traditional public memory of Texas. Nonetheless, his work led to the creation of one of the most significant ranching operations and the economic diversification of Corpus Christi, Texas, and the larger region of South Texas, thereby contributing to the emergence of a nationally significant trade and financial center.

SELECTED BIBLIOGRAPHY

Anders, Evan. *Boss Rule in South Texas.* Austin: University of Texas Press, 1982.

Cox, James M. *Historical and Biographical Record of the Cattle Industry and the Cattlemen of Texas and Adjacent Territory.* St. Louis: Woodward & Tiernan Printing Co, 1895. Reprinted: New York: The Antiquarian Press, 1959. With new introduction by J. Frank Dobie.

Gilliland, Maude T. *Rincon: Remote Dwelling Place.* Brownsville, TX: Springman-King Lithograph Company, 1964.

Gressley, Gene M. *Bankers and Cattlemen.* Lincoln: University of Nebraska Press, 1966.

Hause, Burt, and Jeanne Hause. *The Interview.* Beeville, TX: Hause Family Publication, 1985.

"The History of the Port of Corpus Christi: 1926-2001," (http://www.portofcc.com/index.php/general-information-155/history-a-highlights), accessed January 5, 2015.

Holmes, Vivienne. *Historic Corpus Christi: A Sesquicentennial History.* San Antonio, TX: Historical Publishing Network, 2002.

Lasater, Dale. *Falfurrias: Ed C. Lasater and the Development of South Texas.* College Station: Texas A&M University Press, 1985.

Montejano, David. *Anglos and Mexicans in the Making of Texas, 1836-1986.* Austin: University of Texas Press, 1987.

O'Rear, Mary Jo. "Silver-Lined Storm: the Impact of the 1919 Hurricane on the Port of Corpus Christi." *Southwestern Historical Quarterly* 107 (January 2005).

Tijerina, Andres. *Tejano Empire: Life on the South Texas Ranchos.* College Station: Texas A&M University Press, 1998.

NOTES

1. Vivienne Holmes, *Historic Corpus Christi, A Sesquicentennial History* (San Antonio, TX: Historical Publishing Network, 2002), 138.

2. Christopher Long, "CORPUS CHRISTI, TX," *Handbook of Texas Online* (http://www.tshaonline.org/handbook/online/articles/hdc03), accessed January 06, 2015. Uploaded on June 12, 2010. Published by the Texas State Historical Association.

3. Burt and Jeanne Hause, *The Interview* (Beeville, TX: Hause Family Publication, 1985), 6-12; Grace Bauer, "BEEVILLE, TX," *Handbook of Texas Online* (http://www.tshaonline.org/handbook/online/articles/heb0 4), accessed February 11, 2014. Uploaded on June 12, 2010. Published by the Texas State Historical Association.

4. Marion A. Knight, "Last of the Cattle Barons," unpublished manuscript and interview with W. W. Jones, October 10, 1941, 4, Jones Family Ranches Archives.

5. Ibid.

6. Knight, "Last of the Cattle Barons," 5.

7. Long, CORPUS CHRISTI, TEXAS.

8. Maude T. Gilliland, *Rincon: Remote Dwelling Place* (Brownsville, TX: Springman-King Lithograph Company, 1964), 67.

9. Ibid.

10. Mary Jo O'Rear, "Silver-Lined Storm: The Impact of the 1919 Hurricane on the Port of Corpus Christi," *Southwestern Historical Quarterly* 107 (January 2005); Holmes, *Historic Corpus Christi,* 57-58.

11. Ibid.

12. "The Port Was the People," *Port of Corpus Christi 1926-1976,* Corpus Christi Public Library Archives.

13. Ibid.; "Port Rededicated to Citizenship of Tomorrow at Fets," *Corpus Christi Caller Times,* September 15, 1926; "The History of the Port of Corpus Christi: 1926-2001,"

14. (http://www.portofcc.com/index.php/general-information-155 history-1-highlights). Hause, *The Interview,* 29, 30, 34.

15. W. W. Jones letter to Lorine Jones Spoonts, November 12, 1907, Family Letters Scrapbook, Jones Family Ranches Archives.

16. Ibid.

17. Hause, *The Interview,* 102-103.

18. Knight, "Last of the Cattle Barons," 17.

19. Hause, *The Interview*, 34-35.

20. *Corpus Christi Times*, December 1, 1932.

21. *Corpus Christi Times*, November 13, 1938.

22. Gene M. Gressley, *Bankers and Cattlemen* (Lincoln: University of Nebraska Press, 1966), 30-31.

23. Facts Concerning William Whitby Jones, 1855-1942, Jones Family Ranches Archives; *Corpus Christi Caller Times*, November 13, 1938.

24. Evan Anders, *Boss Rule in South Texas* (Austin: University of Texas Press, 1982), 6-20.

25. Alicia A. Garza, "JIM HOGG COUNTY," *Handbook of Texas Online* (http://www.tshaonline.org/handbook/online/articles/hcj06), accessed October 28, 2013. Published by the Texas State Historical Association.

26. Knight, "Last of the Cattle Barons," 13.

27. W. W. Jones Statement to the Texas House of Representatives, February 24, 1913, Papers of the Jones Family of South Texas, Jones Family Ranches Archives.

28. Jones Statement to the Texas House of Representatives; Anders, *Boss Rule*, 181-182.

29. Burt Hause interview with Kathleen Jones Alexander, "The Interview," January 15, 1967, Jones Family Ranches Archives, Corpus Christi, Texas, 71-72; Knight, *Last of the Cattle Barons*, 14.

30. Minutes of Commissioners Court, Vol. 1 (Jim Hogg County, Jim Hogg County Courthouse, Hebbronville, Texas), 1.

31. Roger M. Olien, "OIL AND GAS INDUSTRY," *Handbook of Texas Online* (http://www.tshaonline.org/handbook/online/articles/doogz), accessed October 29, 2014. Published by the Texas State Historical Association.

32. Ibid.

33. Robin Carter Kennedy, "*Mesteña*, Inc. —a brief history of six families united by an uncommon purpose for 63 years," unpublished manuscript, Jones Family Ranch Archives, 2012. The King and Lasater loans are documented in Note Data, May 1928 and September/October 1929, Box 3, A. C. Jones IV files, Jones Family Ranches Archives.

34. Ibid.

35. *Corpus Christi Caller-Times*, July 17, 1942.

CHAPTER 7

DELGADO V. BASTROP

CIVIL RIGHTS AND IDENTITY IN TEXAS HISTORY

by
Gene B. Preuss

Editor's Note: The tendency to view the past as a series of distant events that happened long ago with little relevance to the present is part of the myth and memory of the civil rights movement. First generation participants in the movement reconstruct their memories based on immediate and personal experiences, while second and third generations remember and interact with its legacies or benefits. In this essay Gene Preuss relates the social and legal significance of the Delgado v. Bastrop *(1948) case that held Mexican American students, although technically considered white, could not be segregated in Texas public schools. But integration was never quick or easy and even court decisions did not necessarily change habits. School districts and other facilities found creative ways to avoid desegregation across the state. As a consequence, this landmark decision has long been overlooked and almost forgotten in the scholarship of the civil rights movement in Texas until now. It has also been absent from Texas school textbooks where people learn the content of public memory. In this essay the author corrects this historiographical oversight by describing events from recent civil rights history of discrimination and segregation that have occurred within our lifetimes. In doing so, the author reminds us that collective or historical memory is not just a passive process, but an active one. It involves identity creation, in this case Tejano identity, selective remembering or forgetting, and the promotion of a particular version of the past. In short, this essay drives home the essential reality that Texas identities change over time and that today a powerful Mexican-based identity is part and parcel of significant Texas identities. The legal case discussed in this essay, notably absent from the myth and public memory familiar to most Texans, constitutes an important building block of that identity.*

In 2010, while visiting a small-town cemetery in West Texas, I chatted with the caretaker, an older Hispanic man. He asked me if I had noticed that all the Spanish surnamed people were buried outside of the road surrounding the cemetery. Of course, as a historian, I understood that the cemetery, like the town, had been segregated. In West Texas, when white settlers came to the Southern Plains in the early 1900s segregation was a way of life, as it was in the rest of the state, and in many other states. The caretaker told me that his predecessor had tried to plot all of the graves, the marked and unmarked, in order to preserve the history of the cemetery. He told me about a map he found which had the names of the plot owners, and written in large letters on the side: "No Niggers! No Meskins!" He donated it to the local museum.

The caretaker then proudly announced that his father and brother were the first Mexican Americans buried within the cemetery proper. He said he bought the plots for $500, but when town fathers found out that the plots were for Mexican Americans, they offered him $5,000 to buy the plots back. He refused. I asked him if this happened in the 1960s or '70s. He said, "No, it happened in 2000!"

As a historian, I am accustomed to discussing segregation issues in the past, but was surprised that such blatant segregation would occur so recently. When I tell my students this story, they are equally surprised.

From their perspective, the victories of groups like the NAACP and LULAC during the Civil Rights Era, led by heroic figures like Martin Luther King and Cesar Chavez, ended minorities' struggle against discrimination and segregation in the mid-twentieth century. Yet, sadly the battle for Civil Rights did not end; prejudice, segregation, and discrimination still exist across Texas and the nation, perpetuating somehow in the popular mind of some people the Anglo-American myth as discussed in the introduction to this volume. Fortunately for Texas, there have been people who have refused to bow to community practice and who have broken the "color barrier," like the cemetery caretaker in the tiny West Texas community.

At its heart, the study of history is an analysis of change—or the lack of it—across time. The stories of those who effected change, both small and large, form the fabric from which the tapestry of myth and memory are constructed. How the story is woven becomes our communal story —our memory if not our myth. In Texas, our public school curriculum exposes children to the constructed story at various intervals, especially the fourth, sixth, seventh, eighth, and eleventh grades. This exposure helps students form a sense of membership in our state's community and identity. As a result, the school history curriculum has been the focal point of the so-called Culture Wars of the late twentieth century. The opponents in the Culture Wars have debated in the 1990s with discussions about the National History Standards over the interpretation of the role of the *Enola Gay* exhibit at the Smithsonian American History Museum, and later various issues over the roles played by the Founding Fathers, and their intentions in drafting the Constitution. In Texas, the hearings by the State Board of Education's (BOE) from 2009-2010 over revision to the public school history curriculum drew considerable national and even international attention.[1]

As a result of the deliberations, the BOE included lists of historical events and people, some more well-known than others, in the curriculum. For example, eleventh graders enrolled in the required US History Since

1877 course are expected to learn about the Civil Rights Movement and are expected to be able to:

> evaluate changes and events in the United States that have resulted from the civil rights movement, including increased participation of minorities in the political process; and describe how litigation such as the landmark cases of *Brown v. Board of Education*, *Mendez v. Westminster*, *Hernandez v. Texas*, *Delgado v. Bastrop I.S.D.*, *Edgewood I.S.D. v. Kirby*, and *Sweatt v. Painter* played a role in protecting the rights of the minority during the civil rights movement.[2]

Many of these historical cases are familiar, especially the 1954 *Brown* decision, which challenged the "separate but equal" doctrine of segregation in public schools. Some students may be familiar with the earlier *Sweatt* case (1950), which had previously overturned segregation in graduate and professional schools. Although the *Hernandez* decision came two weeks before *Brown*, few would recognize the case that declared unconstitutional the Texas practice of excluding Mexican Americans from trial juries. The 1984 *Edgewood v. Kirby* case over Texas public school funding, an issue which had first come to the Supreme Court's attention in the 1970s *Rodriguez* case, and had been addressed with the Lone Star State's "Robin Hood" plan. A few might know that the issue resurfaced in 2013 when almost every school district in the state filed lawsuits over the issue of school funding. Even if not all of the cases were immediately identifiable, most might assume that the cases were US Supreme Court decisions.

In fact, two of the cases were not Supreme Court cases, but opinions issued by federal district court judges, the *Mendez* and *Delgado* cases. Both cases originated in the mid-1940s and challenged the practice of segregating Mexican American children in public schools in California and Texas, respectively. Because they were district cases, however, their rulings did not apply to all states, but only within the particular districts.

Nonetheless, it is easy to see how some students, or teachers, might misunderstand the cases' results and their significance.

Figure 13. Minerva Delgado

After she graduated from Howard Payne University, Minerva Delgado Lopez became a public school teacher in San Antonio. In 1973, the *San Antonio Light* featured her photographed in her classroom on January 22, 1973.
Photo courtesy of the Hearst Corporation

One of the challenges of teaching history, whether in grade school or at the post-secondary level, is to help students understand the past not simply as a series of events that happened long ago, but that it is still relevant to the present. Historians challenge students to apply the "five Cs of historical thinking": change over time, context, causality, contingency, and complexity, to past events and people. By examining one of the cases in the eleventh grade curriculum, *Delgado v. Bastrop,* we come to understand the case as a micro-history of the Hispanic educational experience in post-World War II United States. By helping students see the case with a historical perspective, they can understand that the significance of the case is not only that it was an important civil rights decision, but that it also ties into the larger history of the state, region, and nation. Finally, the *Delgado* case, which originated with a grandmother's request for her granddaughter to attend a better school, helps us unravel the complex narrative of minorities who sought to access the benefits of US citizenship, and share in the hope reflected in the Preamble to the US Constitution and secure the blessings of liberty for themselves and their families.[3]

The chain of events that ultimately led to the *Delgado v. Bastrop* case started when Nanamensia García tried to get the Bastrop school superintendent to allow her granddaughter, Minerva Delgado, to attend the school for white children. In April 1948, Pickett James Dodson, the superintendent of Bastrop schools, recalled the telephone call he received. He sat in Norwood Tower on Congress Avenue in downtown Austin, in the offices of the Capital National Bank, just blocks from the State Capitol and the Governor's Mansion during the deposition.[4]

During his deposition his school district's attorneys, Ireland Graves and his son-in-law J. Chrys Dougherty, advised Dodson. Joe Greenhill, from the Attorney General's Office, was also present. Gus A. García, a San Antonio lawyer who often filed civil rights suits on behalf of the League of United Latin American Citizens (LULAC), was the lead attorney for the plaintiffs. Los Angeles attorney Abraham Lincoln Wirin, council for the American Civil Liberties Union, assisted Garcia. Opal Looke, a court reporter and notary public, was present to record the testimony.[5]

After a few preliminary questions, Wirin asked Dodson about the number of elementary schools in the Bastrop school district. "We have, I guess you would call it three," the superintendent replied. "We have the colored school that has a grade school; then we have a grade school incorporated with the White school, in with the high school, a so-called White building; and then we have the Mina Ward School." Wirin asked who attended that school. "That," Dodson said, "is the school for Latin-American children primarily." He then went on to briefly relate the history of schools for Mexican American students in Bastrop, and explained that a few attended the White school, if they could speak English well enough. Wirin wanted to know how he determined if the children spoke English. "We haven't made a practice of giving them an examination," Dodson said, "I recognize that we should have, but I have never thought of it; but all who want to come, come over." When the ACLU attorney tried to determine how the superintendent qualified students' English ability, Dodson provided one example:

> This past fall, the first day of school, one of our Latin-American students in the freshman class in high school called me that afternoon and said, "Mr. Dodson, Mama wants Minerva Delgado to go to the 'White' school." I said, "Why?" He says, "She is too far from the Latin-American school." I said, "Does she speak English?" He says, "No, sir." "Does your mother speak English?" He says, "No, sir." I says, "She will have to go up there until she can speak English well enough to do the work."[6]

Following the disappointing telephone conversation, Nanamensia and her husband Samuel García, Sr., met with San Antonio civil rights attorney Gus García, who filed the lawsuit on behalf of twenty students and their families against the Bastrop, Elgin, and Martindale independent school districts, as well as the Travis County's Colorado common school district. Of the twenty students, he named six-year-old Minerva Delgado as the principal plaintiff.[7]

Garcia and the other attorneys for the plaintiffs hoped to use the recent California 9th Circuit Court's decision, *Mendez v. Westminster*, where the court ruled that discrimination against Mexican American students was unconstitutional, as the basis for their case. Although Texas Attorney General Price Daniel had previously agreed that the *Mendez* ruling should apply to Texas, segregation persisted. According to the complaint García initially filed, the plaintiffs accused the defendants of violating their constitutional rights by segregating children into "Mexican Schools" solely because they were Latin American. By excluding the students from attending school with the white children, García contended, school officials effectively "prevented... school children of Mexican descent, from receiving the educational, health and recreational benefits which such other white children received" and violated their 14th Amendment constitutional rights. School districts' attorneys Graves and Dougherty warned the school districts that they would almost certainly lose the case. Both defense and plaintiff attorneys requested that Judge Rice issue a summary decision. The case took less than ten minutes. Judge Rice ruled that the *Mendez* decision applied to Texas schools, and that segregating Mexican American schoolchildren was unconstitutional.[8]

Although the case was handled quickly, the decision has been widely considered a historical milestone. Following the *Delgado* decision, Texas Superintendent of Public Instruction Littleton A. Woods drafted instructions for public schools to comply with the ruling. He stated that segregating Mexican American students was unconstitutional, but he allowed it was "permissible to have separate classes in the first grade for any students who have language difficulties, whether the students be of Anglo American, Latin American, or any other origin." While Spanish-speaking children could be separated "for instruction purposes," he explained: "These separate classes should be formed only for students who clearly demonstrate that they do not understand English sufficiently to follow even the simple class-room teaching process." While it was unclear exactly how schools would determine whether children understood English —the depositions revealed that most school districts did not use any standardized testing to evaluate language proficiency—Woods cautioned school administrators that he would "take whatever steps are necessary to enforce these instructions and regulations and to prevent segregation of Mexican or other Latin American descent in the public schools."[9]

Figure 14. Gus Garcia

Mexican-American attorney Gustavo C. "Gus" Garcia of San Antonio filed
the case *Delgado v. Bastrop* on November 17, 1947, supported by LULAC and
American GI Forum. He sought to apply the recent *Mendez* decision from Cali-
fornia that segregating by Mexican-descent was illegal in Texas.
Photo from UTSA's Institute of Texan Cultures, no. L-4303-1, courtesy of the Hearst
Corporation

Due to Superintendent Woods's stringent proclamation, the League
of United Latin American Citizens (LULAC) concluded that the case
was a victory in their timeline of historically significant events. Since
the 2010 State Board of Education's decision to include the case in the
revised public schools Social Studies standards, archives have made more
primary source material related to the *Delgado* case available online for
teachers who want to use the case in their lesson plans. Yet there has been
neither articles nor monographs focusing on the *Delgado* decision, and
the case has not drawn significant attention in Texas history textbooks.
As a result no one has undertaken a thorough analysis of the case's

significance. A void in the critical historical analysis of an event attracts attention and sympathy, and that a group deems significant to its ethnic identity incubates the growth of myth. Indeed, now that the case is included in the public school curriculum, it is increasingly important to focus academic attention to the case's interpretation and significance rather than allow simplistic interpretations to arise that can result from cursory discussion of a topic. [10]

An examination of the changing demographic conditions of the Central Texas region during the World War II period sheds light on the context in which the case took place. Because of the depopulation of rural farming areas resulting from the Great Depression of the 1930s, Central Texas urban areas experienced an increase in population, especially in the state capital of Austin. By 1940 there were 6,418,824 people living in Texas. Of those the majority, or 6,179,296 (96.23 percent), were born in the U.S. Of the foreign-born white population, 159,266 (2.5 percent) were born in Mexico. This was down from the 266,046 Mexican-born reported in the 1930 census, probably due to the outmigration caused by Repatriation in the 1930s that sent almost a half-million Mexican residents and Mexican Americans citizens to Mexico during the Depression. World War II attracted even more people to urban areas like Austin. By 1947 the capital's population was estimated to be at 112,000. To the east of the city, Elgin's population was about 3,600. On the other hand, in Martindale— near San Marcos to the southwest of Austin—the population was less than 600. South of Austin, in Del Valle, the population was 125.[11]

This swelling of the Austin population, and the corresponding decline in the rural areas surrounding the capital, correspond to the decline in agricultural Texas as a result of the Great Depression, as well as the general trend toward increasing urbanization that occurred during the war years. The labor shortage in agricultural areas was exacerbated by the number of men enlisting or drafted into the military. The agricultural labor shortage threatened the home front economy, and the US sought to take advantage of officially neutral Mexico's labor force to fill the gap. In 1942 the US and Mexico agreed to the Bracero program, allowing Mexican laborers to temporarily come to the US to work primarily in the labor-intensive agriculture industry.

Discrimination and segregation against Mexican laborers, however, stymied the program in Texas. Complaints flowed into the Mexican consulates and government offices, and in response Mexico blacklisted Texas from participation in the Bracero program. The problem of discrimination was not limited to Texas, however. In the wake of the Sleepy Lagoon Case and the Zoot-Suit riots in Los Angeles, California, in the summers of 1942-43, University of Texas professor George I. Sánchez found that "vicious economic exploitation directed against the 'Mexican'" existed across the Southwest. The Sleepy Lagoon case sprang from the discovery of a body near the Sleepy Lagoon reservoir. The murder was assumed to be the result of Mexican American youth gang violence. During the trial, witnesses blamed the violence on racial characteristics. "The pseudo-science of the Los Angles official who is quoted as reporting to the Grand Jury on the Sleepy Lagoon murder case that 'Mexican' youth are motivated to crime by certain biological or 'racial' characteristics," Sánchez responded, "would be laughable if it were not so tragic, so dangerous, and, worse still, so typical of the biased attitudes and misguided thinking." The next year US Navy sailors and Marines in Los Angeles attacked Mexican American and Filipino youth who wore zoot suits, attire often associated with gang members.[12]

In May 1943 as a result of the Bracero boycott, the Texas Legislature sought to address accusations of racial discrimination by passing a concurrent resolution aimed at eliminating prejudice. House Concurrent Resolution 105, known as the Caucasian Race Resolution, which stated that, "All persons of the Caucasian Race [which ostensibly included Mexican Americans since they were not considered Negro nor Asian] are entitled to the full and equal accommodations, advantages, facilities, and privileges of all public places of business or amusement." The Resolution went on to state that "Whoever denies to any person the full advantages, facilities, and privileges" including anyone who "aids or incites such discrimination, distinction, or restriction shall be considered as violating the good neighbor policy of our State." The Caucasian Race Resolution was essentially a recapitulation of Article VIII of the 1848 Treaty of Guadalupe Hidalgo. The treaty stated that those Mexican citizens who resided in the region ceded to the United States following the US–Mexican War would become US citizens "to the enjoyment of all the rights of citizens of the United States, according to the principles of the Constitution."[13]

Despite the intent of the Legislature, segregation and discrimination against Mexicans and Mexican Americans persisted in Texas. Sánchez received numerous reports of discriminatory incidents against Mexicans and Mexican Americans. Although he did not name the individual towns where discrimination occurred, civil rights attorney and diplomat Alonso S. Perales compiled a similar list of discrimination reported across the state. For example, in one case swimming pool attendants near San Antonio denied access to a Mexican American. Even the Legislature's Caucasian Race Resolution and a proclamation by Governor Coke Stevenson that the Resolution was official state policy had no legal weight. Jacob I. Rodríguez, who later served as LULAC Executive Secretary, subsequently took the owners of the pool to court citing the Caucasian Race Resolution. Ultimately, however, the courts ruled that the Resolution was a legislative resolution and not a law. "We must presume that if the Legislature of this State had desired to change the common law as it has always existed in this State and enact a 'civil rights' law regulating who should be admitted to private places of amusement," the appeals court ruled, "that it would have done so by the well-known and exclusive method of enacting a 'Bill' to that effect and would not have passed only a resolution." In the absence of an actual civil rights statute, the court ruled that a private owner could deny service to anyone he wished.[14]

In 1945 Texas state senator J. Franklin Spears proposed Senate Bill 1, which stated that no person or business could "deny to any person because of his or her Mexican or Latin-American origins equal facilities, privileges, accommodations or services with any other person who is a member of the public." Spears appealed to the national emergency posed by World War II:

> The fact that there are thousands of men and women in our armed services of Mexican or Latin-American origins and millions of such persons in the armies of the United Nations who are giving their lives that others may enjoy freedom and liberty and that fact that the prejudice and the lack of understanding on the part of some of our citizens are denying to those fine soldiers in Texas the things that they are fighting for abroad, creates an emergency and in imperative public necessity.

Despite clearing the Senate with only two "Nay" votes, the proposed legislation died in the Texas House.[15]

In 1945 several discrimination cases drew national attention to Texas. In September 1945, just a month after receiving the Medal of Honor from President Truman, Staff Sargent Marcario (or Macario) García was involved in an altercation in a Sugar Land café after the owner refused him service because of his ethnicity. National reporter Walter Winchell reported the incident and Sugar Land was labeled as the most racist city in the nation. On September 1 Ben Aguirre was severely beaten by a white gang, but the incident appeared to be part of a larger pattern of violence against Mexicans and Mexican Americans. Local pastors urged the state police to investigate a gang of white boys "who have been and continue to threaten, abuse, beat, maltreat and waylay Latin Americans." On September 11, 1945, in San Angelo, Texas, police charged ten young white gang members with attempted murder of a veteran and two other men. [16]

In 1947 President Truman's Committee on Civil Rights further collaborated the discrimination encountered by minority service personnel. The Commission's report stated: "the uniform is not always accorded the esteem it warrants. Some of our servicemen are all too often treated with rudeness and discourtesy by civil authorities and the public." The report went on to indicate that "they have been forced to move to segregated cars on public carriers. They have been denied access to places of public accommodation and recreation. When they attempt to assert their rights, they are sometimes met with threats and even outright attack."[17]

Other cases of discrimination also occurred, such as the one in August of 1948. In this instance a Mexican American Methodist pastor, who served several congregations in Brady and the Southern Plains of Texas, reported that he and other pastors were denied service in San Angelo.

The overwhelming number of cases of reported discrimination and the continued barring of Bracero workers in the Lone Star State led Texas Governor Coke Stevens to call for a state Good Neighbor Commission. The commission's name, based on President Franklin Roosevelt's Latin American policy, sought to reduce discriminatory practices, and encourage cultural understanding around the state. In August 1948, *West Texas Today*, the magazine of the West Texas Chamber of Commerce, reported that the Chamber had received the promise of some fifty mayors and Chamber of Commerce presidents from the region, to cooperate with the Texas Good Neighbor Commission in eliminating discrimination against Mexican nationals. The West Texas Chamber even created a Latin-American Commission of its own. The Chamber delivered the collected pledges of cooperation to Tom Sutherland, executive director of the Texas Good Neighbor Commission, in hopes of "extending every possible aid to your honorable body in overcoming discriminations against Mexican Nationals and in assuring a continued flow of seasonal agricultural labor across our international border." The Chamber also included a map to demonstrate the widespread geographical territory represented by the pledges, which "came from the bulk of counties in the West Texas area customarily using migratory and seasonal agricultural labor."[18]

The Chamber requested that the state Good Neighbor Commission urge Governor Beauford Jester to urge all Texas chambers of commerce to work together to end discrimination against Mexican laborers. Furthermore, they wanted the governor to charge state agencies "to exercise their every legal power to prevent discriminations and to establish a definite good neighbor practice." They asked that the Good Neighbor Commission be made aware of these efforts so it could assure the Mexican government that efforts were being taken across the state to stop the discrimination that prevented Bracero workers from coming to Texas. While the efforts to improve conditions in order to gain Bracero workers in Texas were promising, some members of the Mexican American community were wary. Mexican American pastors argued that their congregations wanted more than empty promises from politicians. "We take promises back to our people," Methodist pastor Antonio Guillen stated, "but they ask us for demonstrations and facts."[19]

In July 1948 the West Texas Chamber of Commerce again requested assistance from the governor's office to lift the ban, although now the plea came from the West Texas business organization's new Latin-American Relations Commission. In response Governor Jester proclaimed November 15–20 as "Good Neighbor Week" across the state. In his proclamation Jester stated:

> May I offer some of the reasons why solidarity and friendship in Texas, and elsewhere on the American Continent, are a matter of concern to us:

> Because of the proximity of Texas to lands occupied by Latin Americans and the enormous potential of modern industry for the development of the resources of the earth we have this choice: either work out our destiny in mutual happiness and prosperity, or to cast away opportunity for unfortunate and unnecessary divisions that keep us in stagnation and fear.

> The power and speed of information today has made individuals responsible not only to their immediate neighbors, but to all the world, which is now one neighborhood.

> We, in Texas, and in the rest of the Western Hemisphere, are today the keepers of faith in democracy. It is our special privilege

and duty to carry forward for a troubled world our ideals of self-government with justice to all and freedom under the law, which have proved their worth to mankind wherever they have been applied in this State, in the Nation, and in this Hemisphere.

The governor urged town leaders, whom he apparently presumed were Anglos, to include Mexican American community leadership in their Good Neighbor Week plans.[20]

Jester also sent a message to all state agencies to support and participate in Good Neighbor Week activities. He suggested that they recognize Mexican American employees, and inform the Mexican American community about the services their organizations provided. "Undoubtedly there are many positive acts of good neighborliness in your office, or known to your office, which could be valuable in giving a fair picture of the growth of good relations in this State," the governor prompted. "It is part of our job as the government of the State of Texas to see that the progressive side of our State is known, as well as the items requiring correction." Perhaps he intended a list of positive interactions between Texas whites and Mexican and Mexican American residents as a counter to the reports of discrimination and segregation that were being tallied. In any case, the governor closed with the hope that the activities would encourage Texans to "Treat all Latin Americans as fellow citizens and Americans."

As a result of the Great Depression and World War II, Texas saw a population shift from the rural areas towards more urban areas, and during the war years this created an economic threat to Texas agriculture production. The repatriation of Mexican and Mexican American residents during the Depression deepened the agricultural labor shortage. The Bracero agreement between the US and Mexico was one solution, yet reports of discrimination denied this relief to Texas farmers. The state government, as well as local chambers of commerce and other agencies, worked together to change white Texans' attitudes towards Mexican workers and residents. These discriminatory attitudes and practices, however, persisted in and were evident in public schools. [21]

"Schools do not exist in a vacuum," S. Trevor Hadley, a university administrator, wrote. "They are a reflection of the society in which they exist. They hold, promote, and value the same aspirations as the society they mirror." Historian Gilbert G. González noted that, "Although there were no laws that mandated the practice of segregation, educators did invoke the state power granted to school administrations to adapt educational programs to the special needs of a linguistically and culturally distinct community." As the testimony from Superintendent Dodson at the beginning of this chapter reveals, segregation of Mexican and Mexican American schoolchildren was a tradition, neither codified in law, nor practiced uniformly across the state or the Southwest, as several have pointed out. One of the earliest recorded separate schools for Mexican children in Texas was in Seguin, when one of the members of the school board made a "Motion that the Mexican children be allowed a separate school" on June 9, 1902.[22]

As the twentieth century progressed, the Mexican population of Texas increased, especially following the Mexican Revolution of 1910. Discrimination against Mexican residents increased as the population grew. In response Mexican and Mexican American citizens formed mutual aid societies. Several of these *mutualistas* advocated for Mexican American civil rights and urged resistance to discrimination. In 1929 several joined to form the League of United Latin American Citizens (LULAC). The groups were able to strengthen support for their struggle against inequality by combining it with the national and international concerns that racism was negatively affecting the economy. Following World War II, a variety of individual reformers and activists were able to leverage a growing concern that ethnic discrimination was un-American and un-patriotic. Still, they faced a daunting challenge because as the Mexican population grew, segregation continued to increase in Texas public schools and other venues.[23]

Besides attorneys such as Gus García and the ACLU's A. L. Wirin, a network of other prominent individuals worked together to challenge segregation in ways that historians have not fully examined. While there is no record of Congressman Lyndon Johnson's participation in the *Delgado* case, part of Bastrop County was in the 10th Congressional District, which he represented. We do know that soon after the *Delgado* case, Johnson, who won a controversial election to the US Senate in 1948, worked closely with Good Neighbor Commission Executive Director Thomas Sutherland on the Felix Longoria incident, which resulted in LBJ being closely associated with Mexican American civil rights activism.[24]

No incident in Mexican American civil rights history drew more national and international attention than the refusal of a funeral home in Three Rivers, Texas, to open its facilities for a Mexican American serviceman killed in the Philippines. When Private Felix Longoria's remains were returned home, the funeral home proprietor refused to allow Longoria's widow to hold a wake service because he feared it would upset the local white residents. The case became an international scandal, and Senator Johnson arranged for Longoria's remains to be interred at Arlington National Cemetery with full military honors.[25]

As part of the Senator's investigation into the particulars of the Longoria incident, LBJ sent two aides to investigate the case: future Texas governor John Connolly and Liz Sutherland—his aide and later Lady Bird Johnson's speechwriter. It was not by chance that Johnson sent Sutherland to investigate. She was also Tom Sutherland's sister. Moreover, Johnson was a friend of Robert C. Eckhardt, an attorney and later US Congressman who worked on civil rights cases with Gus García. Both were also friends with Thomas Sutherland. Eckhardt was also a cousin to Congressman, and King Ranch heir, Richard Kleberg—whom LBJ worked for as a congressional aide. It was this network of reformers, attorneys García, Eckhardt, and Wirin, supported by their associations with Good Neighbor Commission director Sutherland, and politician Lyndon Johnson, who formed an effective collaboration that enacted numerous reform measures during their careers. LBJ would also portray the public school classroom as an incubator where society could inculcate American democratic values into future generations. [26]

These reformers challenged a gauntlet of societal rationales supporting segregation of Mexican and Mexican American children. In 1944 Wilson Little prepared a report for the Committee of Inter-American Relations in Texas to study the educational characteristics of Latin-American students in the state. He surveyed superintendents to ascertain the reasons behind the practice of school segregation for Spanish-speaking children. Among the responses he received were the following reasons: "We think that in the elementary schools we can give them better opportunities to learn English and other fundamentals so difficult to get otherwise. Evidently, the Latin-American parents thought likewise for they wanted their own school for their elementary youngsters." Another was even simpler: "Local prejudice and inability to speak English." Another explained: "The school board has had this arrangement for several years and does not want to change the plans." One reported: "Children cannot speak English, and are very irregular in attendance." An example of a more blatantly segregated response was: "School board is antagonistic toward housing in the same building." A lengthier response seemed to sum up the other responses: "These children need five or six years of Americanization before being placed with American children. Their standard of living is too low—they are dirty, lousy, and need special teaching in health and cleanliness. They also need special teaching in the English language." [27]

Another study of ten Texas school districts a few years later revealed some similar rationales, yet found that the segregation was not beneficial, but "discriminatory and prejudicial to their educational developments." The report authors concluded: "The practices disclosed were in no way conducive to their Americanization, better health and social habits, better language development or better school attendance." In 1947, University of Texas professor and coordinator of the Texas Study on Secondary Education J. G. Umstattd was even blunter about segregation practices.

He wrote: "It is a crime against the future of America, one that approaches treason, deliberately to keep any segment of the population in ignorance through discrimination against that segment in our educational program." He suggested that the states should withhold funds from schools that discriminated against minority students.[28]

In Bastrop the Mexican American school was the Mina Ward School. It was a small school on 2.5 acres near the railroad tracks on Main Street. One teacher taught first through eighth grade. Superintendent Dodson said the Mina Ward School was an improvement from previous buildings that housed the Mexican American students:

> Well, this one-teacher Latin-American school was a separate school when I went there; you see, we didn't have many Latin-Americans in town, only 15 or 16, but there were Latin-American schools all around us that had a large enrollment. One had fifty some-odd; one had 90 some odd with one teacher and very few pupils going, I made an agreement with the County Superintendent, if he would transfer them to me, I would take the State money and buy a bus, give them a building and give them a good school; so we took our 16 out of that tumble-down building, and about 125 from the rural districts surrounding us, and created a good school for the Latin Americans.[29]

Former State Senator Gonzalo Barrientos likewise attended the Mina Ward School. He recalled that "the school room was *pura raza, puros Mexicanos* [solely Mexican children]. . . And all I can remember is the teacher almost every day giving us a sheet of paper and telling us to draw with a crayon." In an earlier interview, Barrientos complained, "We didn't learn a damn thing at Mina Ward except survival tactics. You had to really watch out or you'd get your lunch ripped off. Even cold tortillas or boloney was important to you when that's all you had."[30]

We do not know whether the Garcías were concerned about the quality of education their granddaughter would receive. Beyond the facts of the case, we know little of Minerva Delgado's family. The 1940 U.S.

Census roll lists Samuel García, Sr., then 52 years old, and his 47-year-old wife Nanamensia in the household. Both were farmers, had no income the previous year, and neither had been to school. Four children lived at home with Samuel and Nanamensia, 22-year-old daughter Sulima, who had three years of high school; 17-year-old Gloria (who would become Minerva's mother) who had a seventh-grade education; 11-year-old Samuel, Jr., who had three years of schooling; and nine-year-old Gamaliel, who had been to school for one year. Felix Garcia, Samuel Sr.'s, 31-year-old brother, who also lived with them, had a fifth-grade education. The low levels and uneven educational achievement reflect the effect of segregated schooling on the García family.[31]

While we do not know if the Garcías hoped for a better educational opportunity at the white school, we do know that Mexican American parents rarely made such a request. One former student remembered: "We never even thought about going to the Anglo school; it just didn't occur to us." We do know, however, that there was another concern that may have urged Mrs. García to ask her son to seek Superintendent Dodson's permission to allow Minerva to transfer to the white school —the Mexican school was farther, and Mrs. García was concerned for her granddaughter's safety.[32]

A tragic crime that shocked Bastrop around the time Minerva was born served to aggravate her fears. In October 1942, the abduction and murder of eight-year-old Lucy Rivers Maynard, daughter of the Bastrop county judge, shocked the Bastrop community. The suspect, George S. Knapp, a 38-year old soldier stationed at nearby Camp Swift, admitted to kidnapping and strangling the girl. Knapp had a long criminal history and had been committed to mental hospitals for several attempts to strangle his mother and sister. "I just can't help it," he stated during the investigation. "When women start to yell, I just want to choke them." He was sentenced to hang following his court martial.[33]

Gus García's pursuit of segregation cases, an interest by state government and business leaders in reducing incidents of desegregation, Judge

Rice's quick decision based on California's *Mendez* case, and Texas State Superintendent of Public Instruction Littleton A. Woods's strongly worded instructions for schools to comply with the ruling have led many to conclude that the *Delgado* case ended school segregation for Mexican American students. Contemporary newspaper headlines also reflected this belief. For example the June 17, 1948, *Sweetwater Reporter*'s article reporting the case carried the headline: "Latin Segregation Ended in Texas School Districts." The case's inclusion in the school history standards further reinforces that perception.

Yet even at the time of the decision, there was some question over the actual effectiveness of the *Delgado* judgment and Superintendent Woods's enforcement of the ruling. *Austin American* columnist Virginia Forbes described the decision as an attempt to calm concerns the Mexican government had about discrimination against migrant workers, especially since the reports of segregation had caused Texas's exclusion from the Bracero program. The ruling "may be an opening wedge toward getting back on hat-tipping labor relations with Mexico," she opined. On the other hand, the editor of the *Dallas Morning News* did not agree that concerns about the Bracero program had influenced Judge Rice's decision. "Some at a distance may wonder just how sincere Texans are in this matter. Is it all due to the fact that the Mexican Government has blacklisted Texas as a place where migratory farm laborers may not work? The *News* does not think so." Incredibly, despite the extensive coverage of the West Texas Chamber of Commerce's attempt to end discrimination and have the ban on Braceros lifted, the Dallas newspaper editorialist dismissed the suggestion, writing, "Most Texans don't know what the word bracero means, much less have need of such transient labor."[34]

The *Dallas Morning News* editorial is even more surprising, especially considering that the newspaper itself had reported on the concerns over the Bracero ban. Austin reporter Forbes's column took a more analytical approach in questioning the effectiveness of the *Delgado* ruling. Woods had threatened that a school in violation of the ruling would lose accreditation, but Forbes wondered whether the loss of accreditation would indeed be a detriment for any Texas school. She reported that Woods even admitted that he could not "legally take away per capita apportionments as a penalty. For rural aid schools lack of [accreditation would] mean funds for an eight month semester instead of nine months. That's the only financial threat." The only tangible effect students would suffer if they graduated from an unaccredited school would be that they would have to take an entrance exam before they enrolled in a college. Furthermore, it is unclear whether Woods was interested in withholding funds at all. Earlier in 1948, when Good Neighbor Commission executive Sutherland stated that the school in the South Texas town of Mathis would lose accreditation for discrimination, Woods quickly countered that no schools had lost accreditation.[35]

In early January 1949, a complaint against the Del Rio ISD prompted an investigation that led Woods's assistant state superintendent to suggest removing the school's accreditation. Woods held off this punishment pending a review from Judge Rice. But Rice warned Woods that he would not constantly revisit each individual case. The next month, during an American G. I. Forum inspection of the George West schools in Live Oak County, Texas, the principal of the segregated Mexican school continued to admit students despite Woods's instructions to cease because the school district had no approved plan to integrate students.[36]

In fact historian Carl Allsup noted that after the *Delgado* ruling, "Many schools paid little or no attention to these instructions due to an unwillingness to correct years of 'practice, custom and usage' or while professing ignorance of the law." Allsup was not the first to question the significance of the *Delgado* case. In 1971, Guadalupe Salinas wrote in the *Houston Law Review* that school districts had found creative ways of avoiding integrating Mexican American students into their classes. Jorge C. Rangel and Carlos M. Alcala stated in an article in 1972 that the judgment "Should have put an end to the tri-ethnic system," but it did not. They blamed Superintendent Woods for ineffective actions, a lack of enforcement, and even stated "that the state's decrees were not even communicated to all affected districts." In fact, the *Delgado* case and Woods's subsequent instructions, did allow for segregation for language differences. This allowed school districts across the state to continue to use to language proficiency as a rationale for segregating Mexican American students. Even after the 1954 and 1955 *Brown* decisions, segregation for both African American and Mexican American students continued in Texas schools. In 1957 the American G. I. Forum filed a suit in federal district court against the Driscoll Consolidated Independent School District, and in 1971 federal district judge William Wayne Justice's ruling in *US v. Texas* held the Texas Educational Agency responsible for integrating Texas schools.[37]

Although schools continued to segregate Mexican and Mexican American in the wake of the *Delgado* decision, the Mina Ward School in Bastrop closed as Mexican American students were integrated into the white schools. More importantly, Minerva Delgado directly benefitted from Judge Rice's ruling. Five years after the case, as a sixth grader, she performed at a recital at the First Baptist Church. The next year, she and forty-six other students in her Texas history class traveled to San Antonio to visit the missions, Fort Sam Houston, Brackenridge Park and Zoo, and the Witte Museum. In high school Minerva played the clarinet in the band, and performed in the Austin Band Day Parade in November 1955. Later, she and her classmates toured the University of Texas campus, attended the UT-Texas Christian University football game, and performed during the half-time show. In 1956 she started in the Beginning Band along with classmate Gonzalo Barrientos. Next year, they both played in the sixty-piece Concert Band. On May 28, 1959, Minerva Delgado's name appeared in a list of thirty-two graduating seniors in a full-page advertisement congratulating the class of 1959. A few weeks earlier, she had attended a wiener roast provided by some of her classmates' parents, complete with hot dogs and potato salad, cookies, punch, and tea.[38]

Following her graduation from high school, in 1960 Minerva Delgado began her freshman year at Howard Payne. As a freshman, she joined *La Hora Bautista* (The Baptist Hour), a student organization that provided a Spanish-language religious radio program in Brownwood. The college newspaper, *Yellow Jacket*, reported that two women's football teams would "take to the gridiron" at Brownwood's Lion Stadium for that year's Powder Puff football game. Minerva "Dealing" Delgado was a tackle for the Titanic Tacklers. In the 1962 yearbook, a smiling Minerva Delgado is listed as a senior Elementary Education major.[39]

After graduating from Howard Payne, Minerva Delgado married and began teaching school. In 1965, the *Bastrop Advertiser* carried her wedding announcement, and noted that she taught for San Antonio's Harlendale ISD, while fiancé Dan Lopez, from North Platte, Nebraska, worked in San Antonio for Sears, Roebuck & Company. Minerva and Dan married on December 31 at the Bastrop Mexican Baptist Church, the same church who gave her a scholarship to attend Howard Payne. In 1973 the *San Antonio Light* carried a photo of Minerva Delgado Lopez in her classroom. When asked about the importance of her case, she said, "I hope that my civil court case opened many gateways for my fellow Mexican-Americans and that they, as well as myself, use these gateways to help others through education, just like the late Gus García did with his."[40]

If the significance of the Delgado ruling was not that it ended segregation, certainly the relevance of the *Delgado v. Bastrop* case is the immediate and obvious effects it had on the life of Minerva Delgado Lopez, and by extension, it reveals how segregation sealed so many children from the opportunities available to others. Instead of being forced to remain separate from other children, Minerva Delgado was able to attend an integrated school where she was able to fully participate in school activities, including band, prom, and graduation. She became the first person in her family to complete twelve years of public school and go on to complete a university education, which allowed her entre into a

profession as a teacher. Classmates like Gonzalo Barrientos were able
to take advantage of similar opportunities.

The story of the *Delgado* case opens up many questions for historians.
Educational history, in general, is neglected by most Texas historians.
LULAC attorneys such as Gus García and John J. Herrera, have no
monograph-length biographies. The Texas Good Neighbor Commission
has received little historical attention since the 1960s. The connections
between reformers such as Lyndon Johnson, Thomas Sutherland, Bob
Eckhardt, Gus García, and other political figures needs further exploration.
Other important factors missing from the historical record are the names
of those residents of Bastrop, and other communities across the state,
who stepped forward to affect integration. Although discrimination and
bigotry certainly continued, the story of Minerva Delgado reveals that
some parents and other community members were willing to participate
in integration of Mexican American students. In his 1993 essay, "Our
Gringo Amigo: Anglo Americans and the Tejano Experience," Historian
Arnoldo De León points out that the history of civil rights and minorities
often presents simplistic portrayals of, or even overlooks, Anglos.[41]

The case of *Delgado v. Bastrop* is an important event in Texas and
Mexican American history, but not for the reasons implied in the state
history standards. Students may think that the case resulted an end to
segregation, or mistake it for a Supreme Court decision. Instead, *Delgado*
is important because of what it teaches about the Civil Rights Movement
in general. It demonstrates that the common perception that civil rights
activism was limited to the 1960s, or limited to African-Americans civil
rights, is simplistic and inaccurate. The case provides Mexican American
students with the opportunity to see that members of their community
played an active role early in the Texas civil rights movement. It helps
underscore that the *Brown* and *Sweatt* decisions originated in educational
settings because schools are a microcosm and reflection of the society
that creates them, and it helps us understand why civil rights groups like

LULAC, NAACP, and American G. I. Forum believed that educational opportunity opens doors otherwise closed.

More importantly, the *Delgado* case illustrates the importance of agency in understanding the civil rights struggle. Such cases originated in the daily experiences of normal people, and the actions they took to build a better world for themselves and their children. Had Minerva Delgado's grandparents done as so many others and not ask whether she could attend the white school; had superintendent Dodson agreed to the request; or if Minerva's grandparents had not agreed to Gus García's request to litigate in the case, how different might her education and life have been? Would she have been welcome at the piano recitals, or even learned to play? Would she have marched in the band? Would she have gone to the prom and wiener roast? Would she have graduated high school and attended college? Would she have become a teacher? Because of these series of contingent events, Mexican American children like Minerva Delgado Lopez and Gonzalo Barrientos were able to overcome decades of uneven schooling and educational neglect, and were able to have the opportunity for professional careers, and achieve the American Dream of social mobility. Like the cemetery caretaker in West Texas, Minerva Delgado became an agent of change, helping forge her identity as both a Texan and an American. Her story, and others like hers, deserve to have a larger role in the collective memory of Texas because they help to define what it means to be Texan.

SELECTED BIBLIOGRAPHY

Carroll, Patrick James. *Felix Longoria's Wake: Bereavement, Racism, and the Rise of Mexican American Activism.* Austin: University of Texas Press, 2003.

Erekson, Keith A. *Politics and the History Curriculum: The Struggle Over Standards in Texas and the Nation.* New York: Palgrave Macmillan, 2012.

Gonzalez, Gilbert G. *Chicano Education in the Era of Segregation.* Cranbury, NJ: Balch Institute Press, 1990; Reprinted, Denton: University of North Texas Press, 2013.

Keith, Gary. *Eckhardt: There Once Was a Congressman from Texas.* Austin: University of Texas Press, 2007.

Kibbe, Pauline R. *Latin Americans in Texas.* Albuquerque: University of New Mexico Press, 1946.

Preuss, Gene B. *To Get a Better School System: One Hundred Years of Education Reform in Texas.* College Station: Texas A&M University Press, 2009.

San Miguel, Guadalupe, Jr. *"Let All of Them Take Heed": Mexican Americans and the Campaign for Educational Equality in Texas, 1910-1981.* Austin: University of Texas Press, 1987. Reprinted, College Station: Texas A&M University Press, 2000.

Sánchez, George I. *Concerning Segregation of Spanish-Speaking Children in the Public Schools.* Austin: University of Texas, 1951.

Strum, Philippa. *Mendez v. Westminster: School Desegregation and Mexican-American Rights.* Lawrence: University Press of Kansas, 2010.

Wollenberg, Charles. *All Deliberate Speed: Segregation and Exclusion in California Schools, 1855-1975.* Berkeley: University of California Press, 1976.

NOTES

1. See, for example Gary B. Nash, Charlotte A. Crabtree, and Ross E. Dunn, *History on Trial: Culture Wars and the Teaching of the Past* (New York: A.A. Knopf, 1997); Edward T. Linenthal, and Tom Engelhardt, *History Wars: The Enola Gay and Other Battles for the American Past* (New York: Metropolitan Books, 1996); and more recently Jill Lepore, *The Whites of Their Eyes: The Tea Party's Revolution and the Battle Over American History* (Princeton, N.J.: Princeton University Press, 2010). The Texas State Board of Education battle over the 2010 history curriculum is examined by various authors in Keith A. Erekson, *Politics and the History Curriculum: The Struggle Over Standards in Texas and the Nation* (New York: Palgrave Macmillan, 2012).

2. *Texas Essential Knowledge and Skills*, §113.41, c, 9, H and I.

3. Thomas Andrews and Flannery Burke, "What Does It Mean to Think Historically?" *Perspectives on History*, January 2007, accessed January 20, 2015, http://www.historians.org/publications-and-directories/perspectives-on-history/january-2007/what-does-it-mean-to-think-historically.

4. Amy Standifer, "Services Held for P. J. Dodson, Bastrop's Beloved Superintendent of Schools for 37 Years," *Bastrop Advertiser*, July 25, 1968.

5. Depositions of Gus F. Urbantke, I. W. Popham, P. J. Dodson, Claud E. Brown, C. R. Akin, F. Kenneth Wise (April 30, 1948), *Minerva Delgado, et al. vs. Bastrop Independent School District of Bastrop, et al.*, Civil Action 388, US District Court, Western District of Texas, Austin Division, National Archives and Records Administration, Southwest Region Archives, Fort Worth, TX, 1-2.

6. Ibid., 44–49.

7. Mary Katherine Serrill, "Minerva Delgado, et al., v. Bastrop Independent School District, et al.," term paper, July 3, 1975, 8; "Latins File School Suits," *Dallas Morning News*, November 18, 1947.

8. Charles Wollenberg, "*Mendez v. Westminster*: Race, Nationality and Segregation in California Schools," *California Historical Quarterly* 53 (Winter, 1974), 317-8, 329; *Digest of Opinions of the Attorney General of Texas*, v-128 (1947). Accessed 12/10/2014 https://www.texasattorneygeneral.gov/opinions/opinions/40daniel/op/1947/pdf/pd0128.pdf; Complaint to Enjoin Violation of Federal Civil Rights and

for Damages, 17 November 1947, *Minerva Delgado, et al. vs. Bastrop Independent School District of Bastrop, et al.*, Civil Action 388, US District Court, Western District of Texas, Austin Division, National Archives and Records Administration, Southwest Region Archives, Fort Worth, TX., 9–10; Newspaper Clipping, "Fallo De La Corte Federal En Contra De La Segregación," n.p., n.d., John J. Herrera Papers, Houston Metropolitan Research Center at Houston Public Library, Houston, Texas. Accessed January 19, 2015 (http://texashistory.unt.edu/ark:/67531/metapth24886 6/), University of North Texas Libraries, The Portal to Texas History, http://texashistory.unt.edu.

9. L. A. Woods, "Instructions and Regulations to All School Officers of County, City, Town and School Districts," found in George I. Sanchez, *Concerning Segregation of Spanish-Speaking Children in the Public School* (Austin, TX: Study of Spanish-Speaking People, University of Texas, 1951), 75; "Latin Segregation Ended in Texas School Districts," *Sweetwater Reporter*, June 17, 1948.

10. "LULAC Milestones" Accessed 12/10/2014 http://lulac.org/about/history/milestones/

11. *Texas Almanac, 1947-48*, 124 - 142.

12. George I. Sanchez, "Pachucos in the Making," *Common Ground*, September 1943, p. 14.

13. H.C.R 105, Expressing The Policy of the State in Regard to the Caucasian Race, *Texas House Journal*, 48th Legislature, April 15, 1943, p. 1725; *Treaty of Guadalupe Hidalgo*, February 2, 1848; Perfected Treaties, 1778-1945, General Records of the United States Government, 1778-1992, Record Group 11, National Archives, accessed January 21, 2015 http://www.ourdocuments.gov/doc.php?doc=26&page=transcript, Article VIII.

14. Alonso S. Perales, "List of Locations Where Mexicans Have Been Denied Service." (ca. 1944), ID 05/2010-002, Box 8, Folder 5, Alonso S. Perales Papers, Special Collections, University of Houston Libraries; *Terrell Wells Swimming Pool v. Rodriguez*, 182 S. W. 2nd 824 (Tex Civ. App. 1944).

15. J. Franklin Spears, "Draft of Texas Senate Bill 1, Elimination of Discrimination of Public Utilities Against Hispanic Americans," n.d., John J. Herrera Papers, Houston Metropolitan Research Center at Houston Public Library, Houston, Texas, found in University of North Texas Libraries, The Portal to Texas History, http://texashistory.unt.edu. Accessed January 19, 2015 (http://texashistory.unt.edu/ark:/675 31/metapth248737/); Neil Foley, *Mexicans in the Making of America* (Cambridge, MA: Belknap Press, 2014), 88-89.

16. "Anglo-Americans Charged in Beating Latin-Americans," *Dallas Morning News*, September 12, 1945, p. 4.

17. President's Committee on Civil Rights, *To Secure These Rights* (New York: Simon and Schuster, 1947), 46.

18. "Latin-American Commission Offers Help in Mexican Worker Discrimination Fight," *West Texas Today*, August 1948: 3.

19. Ibid.

20. "Good Neighbor Week!: Governor Takes Action on WTCC Latin-American Commission Request; Calls for Cooperation," *West Texas Today*, September 1948, 7; "Good Neighbor Week Proclaimed by Jester," *Dallas Morning News*, August 13, 1948, p. 16; "Good Neighbor Week," *Sweetwater Reporter*, November 14, 1948, p 8.

21. Ibid.

22. S. Trevor Hadley, "Education Reflects Desires of Society," *The Pittsburgh Press*, March 8, 1965; Gilbert G. Gonzalez, *Chicano Education in the Era of Segregation* (Denton: University of North Texas Press, 1990, 2013), 2, 12-13; Wilson Little, *Spanish-Speaking Children in Texas* (Austin: University of Texas Press, 1944), 59; Virgil E. Strickland and George I. Sanchez, "Spanish Name Spells Discrimination," *The Nation's Schools* 41, no. 1 (January 1948): 22–23; Pauline Kibbe, *Latin Americans in Texas* (Albuquerque: University of New Mexico Press, 1946; New York: Arno Press, 1974), 96; George I. Sánchez, *Concerning Segregation of Spanish-Speaking Children in the Public Schools*, Inter-American Education Occasional Papers IX (Austin: The University of Texas, 1951), 9; David Montejano, *Anglos and Mexicans in the Making of Texas, 1836-1986* (Austin: University of Texas Press, 1987), 160; Seguin Independent School District, Minutes of the Board of Trustees, 12 July 1892 - 8 January 1915, Administrative Offices, Seguin, Texas.

23. Guadalupe San Miguel, Jr., *"Let All of Them Take Heed": Mexican Americans and the Campaign for Educational Equality in Texas, 1910-1981* (Austin: University of Texas Press, 1987), 19–25.

24. "Latin-American Commission Offers Help in Mexican Worker Discrimination Fight," *West Texas Today*, August 1948, 3.

25. *Felix Longoria's Wake: Bereavement, Racism, and the Rise of Mexican American Activism* (Austin: University of Texas Press, 2003).

26. See Gary Keith, *Eckhardt: There Once Was a Congressman from Texas* (Austin: University of Texas Press, 2007); Patrick James Carroll and Julie Leininger Pycior, *LBJ and Mexican Americans: The Paradox of Power* (Austin: University of Texas Press, 1997).

27. Wilson Little, *Spanish-Speaking Children in Texas* (Austin: University of Texas Press, 1944), 60–61.
28. Virgil E. Strickland and George I. Sanchez, "Spanish Name Spells Discrimination," *The Nation's Schools* 41, no. 1 (January 1948): 23; J. G. Umstattd, "The Extension of the Program of Public Education," in *A Desirable Educational Program for Texas* (Austin: State Department of Education, 1947), 15 – 16.
29. Depositions, *Delgado v. Bastrop*, 45-6.
30. Ken Kesselus, "Mina Ward School Alumni Gathered Here," *The Bastrop Advertiser*, October 31, 2009; Oral History Interview with Gonzalo Barrientos, 1996, by José Angel Gutiérrez. CMAS No. 93, University of Texas at Arlington. Accessed 12/10/2014 http://library.uta.edu/tejanovoices/interview.php?cmasno=093; Serrill, "Minerva Delgado," 7.
31. US Bureau of the Census, Bastrop, Texas, Precinct 1, SD no. 10, ED no. 11-4, page 5A.
32. Serrill, "Minerva Delgado," 7.
33. "Soldier Held in Connection with Death of Child," *Bastrop Advertiser*, October 8, 1942; Frank Levine, "1942 Child Murder Stunned Bastrop," *Bastrop Advertiser*, June 16, 2007.
34. Virginia Forbes, "Your Capital City: School Ruling Helps Restore Latin Relations," *Austin American*, June 16, 1948; "Texas Eliminates False Prejudice," Editorial, *Dallas Morning News*, June 18, 1948.
35. Ibid.; Ray Osborne, "Woods Denies Schools Lose Accreditation," *Dallas Morning News*, February 15, 1948.
36. Carl Allsup, "Education Is Our Freedom: The American G. I. Forum and the Mexican American School Segregation in Texas, 1948-1957," *Aztlán* 8 (1977): 34-35.
37. Guadalupe Salinas, "Mexican-Americans and the Desegregation of Schools in the Southwest," *Houston Law Review* 8 (1971): 941; Jorge C. Rangel and Carlos M. Alcala, "Project Report: De Jure Segregation of Chicanos in Texas Schools," *Harvard Civil Rights-Civil Liberties Law Review* 7 (March 1972): 316.
38. Ken Kesselus, "Mina Ward School—Part 1," *Bastrop Advertiser*, October 8, 2009; "Students Are Presented in Recital," *Bastrop Advertiser*, June 25, 1953; "Seventh Grades Make Trip to San Antonio," *Bastrop Advertiser*, December 10, 1953; "Bastrop High School Band to Take Part in Band Day Parade in Austin," *Bastrop Advertiser*, November 10, 1955; "Beginners Band Consists of 49," *Bastrop Advertiser*, October 4, 1956; "Large Crowd Attends Concert Tuesday Night," *Bastrop Advertiser*, December 26, 1957;

"Graduates of 1959," *Bastrop Advertiser*, May 28, 1959; "Wiener Roast Given for Members of Senior Class," *Bastrop Advertiser*, Thursday, May 28, 1959.

39. Howard Payne College (Brownwood, Tex.). *The Lasso, Yearbook of Howard Payne College*, 1960, 149, 188; Don Newbury, "Sports Call," *The Howard Payne Yellow Jacket*, December 11, 1959; "Women Try Men's Game," *The Howard Payne Yellow Jacket*, December 11, 1959, *The Howard Payne College Yellow Jacket*, December 11, 1959.

40. "Wedding Plans Announced for December 31," *Bastrop Advertiser*, November 11, 1965; Merrisa Brown, "S.A. Back in the Day, January 1973," January 6, 2013. Accessed 12/10/2014 http://www.mysanantonio.com/news/local/history-culture/slideshow/S-A-Back-in-the-Day-January-19 73-54765/photo-3993201.php

41. Arnoldo de Leon, "Our Gringo Amigo: Anglo Americans and the Tejano Experience," *East Texas Historical Association Journal* 32, no. 2, (1993): 72-79.

CONTRIBUTORS

Figure 15. The Contributors

The contributors to this volume: (l. to r.) Jesús F. de la Teja, Gene B. Preuss, Kay Goldman, Stephen L. Hardin, Light Townsend Cummins, Mary L. Scheer, Patrick Cox, Jody Edward Ginn

Patrick L. Cox is an historical consultant after having retired as Associate Director of the Dolph Briscoe Center for American History at the University of Texas at Austin. He received a B.A. from the University of Texas, an M.A. in History from Texas State University, and a Ph.D. from the University of Texas. His books include *The First Texas News Barons, The House Will Come to Order, Writing the Story of Texas,* and *Ralph Yarborough: The People's Senator.*

Light Townsend Cummins is the Guy M. Bryan, Jr. Professor of History at Austin College. He received a B.S. in Ed. and an M.A. from Texas State University, and a Ph.D. from Tulane University. He was named a Minnie Stevens Piper Professor in 2006. Cummins served as the official State Historian of Texas from 2009 to 2012. He has been a Fulbright Scholar to Spain. Cummins is the author or editor of twelve academic books and several dozen scholarly articles dealing with Texas and Gulf Coast history along with two best-selling college textbooks, popular-oriented essays, and numerous book reviews. His most recent book is *Allie Victoria Tennant and the Visual Arts in Dallas.*

Jesús F. de la Teja is Jerome H. and Catherine E. Supple Professor of Southwestern Studies, Regents' Professor of History, and Director of the Center for the Study of the Southwest at Texas State University. He is an authority on Spanish and Mexican Texas, along with the era of the Texas Revolution. His books include *Faces of Béxar: Early San Antonio and Texas; Tejano Leadership in Mexican and Revolutionary Texas;* and *San Antonio de Béxar: A Community on Spain's Far Northern Frontier.* He was the official Texas State Historian from 2007-2009 and has served as President of the Texas State Historical Association. De la Teja is a fellow of the Texas State Historical Association and the Texas Catholic Historical Society in addition to serving on the board of directors of Humanities Texas. He is an elected member of the Philosophical Society of Texas and the Texas Institute of Letters. The contributors to *Texan Identities* are honored he provided the foreword to this book.

Jody Edward Ginn received a B.A. and M.A. from Texas State University and a Ph.D. in History from the University of North Texas, where Professor Richard McCaslin served as his dissertation director. Ginn was for many years an investigator with the Hays County Criminal District Attorney's Office in San Marcos, Texas. He has contributed book reviews on volumes dealing with the Texas Rangers to the *Southwestern Historical Quarterly.* He has also presented academic papers at the Texas State Historical Association and the East Texas Historical Association. He has twice won the Fred White Jr. Research Award in Texas History. Ginn is the historical consultant for the Bryan Museum in Galveston.

Kay Goldman lives in Houston, Texas. She is retired from Texas A&M University, where she was a program coordinator. She received a B.A. and M.A. from Texas State University, and a Ph.D. in History from Texas A&M. She is a specialist in the history of Jewish Texans. She has presented a number of conference papers on topics related to her interests and is a member of the Texas Jewish Historical Society. Her book *Dressing Modern*

Maternity: The Frankfurt Sisters of Dallas and the Page Boy Label (Texas Tech University Press, 2013) won the initial Lou Halsell Rodenberger Prize in Texas History and Literature.

Stephen L. Hardin is Professor of History at McMurry University. Hardin is a specialist in Texas, military, and social history. He received a B.A. and M.A. from Texas State University and a Ph.D. in History from Texas Christian University. His numerous publications range from the award-winning *Texian Iliad: A Military History of the Texas Revolution* to the *Texian Macabre: The Melancholy Tale of a Hanging in Early Houston*, a fascinating study of early Houston society. In addition to his writing and teaching activities, Hardin has also provided specialist commentary on the A&E Network, the History Channel, the Discovery Network, and NBC's TODAY show.

Gene B. Preuss is Associate Professor of History at the University of Houston-Downtown and currently serves as the Special Assistant to the President of that institution. He received his B.A. and M. A. from Texas State University, and a Ph.D. in History from Texas Tech University. His research interests center on the history of American Education, Texas History, Public History, and the American South. He is the author of the award-winning book *"To Get a Better School System": One Hundred Years of School Reform in Texas* (Texas A&M University Press, 2009) and articles dealing with the history of education in Texas. These include "Public Education in West Texas," in The Giant Side of Texas and "'As Texas Goes, So Goes the Nation': A History of the History Culture Wars in the Lone Star State," in *Politics and the History Curriculum.*

Mary L. Scheer is Professor of History and chair of the History department at Lamar University. She received a B.A. and M.A. from Texas State University, later earning a Ph.D. from Texas Christian University. She has authored *The Foundations of Texan Philanthropy* (Texas A&M University Press, 2004), co-edited *Twentieth-Century Texas: A Social and Cultural History* (University of North Texas Press, 2008), and edited the award-winning *Women and the Texas Revolution* (University of North

Texas Press, 2012). Scheer was a Fulbright scholar at the University of Potsdam, Germany, in 2004.

INDEX

abolitionists, 148n9

Abrahms, W. H., 137

academic history, 2, 18–19

accreditation of schools, 239

Act of January 20, 1840, 77–78

Adams, Abigail, 65, 79

Adjutant General Department, 93

African Americans, 19

Aguirre, Ben, 229

The Alamo (2004), 48

The Alamo.
  breach-in-the-wall myth, 42–44
  disobeying orders myth, 37–38
  embellishment of narrative,
    33–35
  failure to send reinforcements
    myth, 38–39
  historical re-inspection of, xii
  impact on Santa Anna's
    advance, 42
  "last stand" myth, 46–48
  "line in the sand" myth, 39–41,
    50, 53n3 55–56n27, 56n28
  mythic status in Texas history,
    30–33
  in popular culture, 13–14, 48–49
  role in Texas independence,
    49–51
  strategic significance of, 35–36
  and symbols of Texas identity,
    15, 36
  and the Texas Constitution, 70
  "three-waves-of-attack" fallacy,
    44–46

The Alamo (1960), 14, 33–34, 43,

The Alamo (1960) (*continued*),
  58n36

The Alamo (Myers), 42

Alcala, Carlos M., 239

Alexander, Donald, 191

Alice State Bank and Trust,
  200–201

Allred, James V., 176

Allsup, Carl, 239

Almonte, Juan, 45

Alta Mesa Field, 211

Alta Vista Ranch, 192, 194–95, 202,
  207

American character, 30

American Civil Liberties Union
  (ACLU), 222–23, 234

American Federation of the Arts,
  167

American G. I. Forum, 239, 243

American Indians.
  and the "battle" of Pease River,
    97–98
  and the Texas Rangers, 90, 92,
    97, 103, 106–7
  and the Texas Revolution, 42
  and visual arts in Texas, 157–58

American Jewish Year Book,
  153n45

American Revolution, 6

Andrade, Juan José, 43

Anglo identity.
  and Alamo mythology, 53n2
  and male Anglo-centrism, 64–65
  and Manifest Destiny, 13
  and patriarchy, 7–9

Anglo identity. (*continued*)
  and the Texas constitutional
    convention, 80
  and Texas identity, 7–8, 10, 13,
    18–19, 80
  and the Texas Rangers, 9–10,
    87–90, 94, 96–98, 102–5,
    107–8, 115
  and voting rights in Texas,
    66–67
  and women of Texas, 80–81
Annales School of historiographical
    interpretation, 4–5
annexation of Texas, 61
anthropology, 12–13, 14, 125
anti-government separatists, 114
anti-Semitism, 143
archival research, 18
Arpa, Jose, 165, 169
Art and Artists of Texas (O'Brien),
    157
art collections, 162
Atascosito Road, 35, 36
athletic clubs. *See* Verein
    movement
Attwater, A. P., 169
Attwater Collection, 169–70
Austin, Moses, 13
Austin, Stephen F., 90
Austin, Texas, 141, 226
Austin American, 238
Austin German Free School
    Association, 149n18
Ayres and Ayres (architectural
    firm), 170
Bailey, Thomas A., 12
Balduras Ranch, 194–95
"Ballad of Davy Crocket" (Bruns),
    54n10
"Ballad of the Alamo" (Robbins), 44

"The Ballad of the
    Alamo" (Tiomkin and Webster),
    58n36
bandits, 101
Barnard, Joseph, 43
Barnston, Henry, 139, 146n1,
    152n40
Barrientos, Gonzalo, 236, 240,
    242–43
Barse, George, 191
Bastrop, Texas. *See Delgado v.
    Bastrop I.S.D.*
Bastrop Advertiser, 241
Battle of Pease River, 97–98
Battle of Salado Creek, 103
Battle of San Jacinto, 13, 43, 75,
    79–80
Bedichek, Roy, 9
Beretta, J. K., 183n18
Berg, Henry, 132
Beyond Texas Through Time
    (Buenger and De León), xiv
bilingual education 148–49n12, 224
Blackburn, Thomas W., 54n10
Blake, J. Edmund, 43–44
Blanchette, Kathleen Jones, 208–9
Blanchette, Lee, 191, 207
The Blood of Heroes (Donovan), 41,
    56n28
Blumenthal, Julius, 136
B'nai Brith, 142
border conflicts, 102, 193, 203, 206
Borglum, Gutzon, 161, 175
Borglum, Louella Jones
    (photograph), 212
Bourne, Daniel, 50
Bowie, Jim, 33, 35, 37
Bracero program, 227, 230–32, 238
Brackenridge, Eleanor, 162
Brackenridge Park, 171

Branch Davidians, 114
"branding" of Texas, 8
Brear, Holly Benchley, 30
Brennan, Mary, 22
Brooks, John, 100, 205–6
Brooks County, 192, 203–8
Brown, James, 50
Brown, John Henry, 97
Browne, Sybil, 172
Brown v. Board of Education, 220, 242–43
Brundage, Fitzhugh, 17
Bryan Museum Collection, 178
Buenger, Walter L., xi–xii, xiv, 18
Bulfinch's Mythology (Bulfinch), 25n11
Burnet, David G., 75
Burnett, Samuel "Burk," 186
California Company (Standard Oil), 211
Calvert, Robert A., xi–xii
Cameron County, 204
camino real, 35
Campbell, Randolph B., 17, 50
Camp Swift, 237
Canales, Alvino, 211
Cantrell, Gregg, xii, 16–17, 20
capitalism, 20
Carlson, Paul H., xii, 98
Carnegie Public Library, 160, 163–64, 167
Caro, Ramón Martínez, 45
Casino Clubs, 126, 131–34, 143, 150n23
Castrillón, Manuel Fernández, 47
Catholic Women's Association, 160
cattle ranching.
    and Anglo-American myth of Texas, 4, 9, 14
    cattle drives, 155, 190–91

cattle ranching. (*continued*)
    and cattleman stereotype, 186–87, 198
    cattlemen as capitalists, 20, 186, 188, 192, 202, 211, 213
    and symbols of Texas identity, xiii, 15
    and visual arts in Texas, 157–58
    wild cattle, 192
    and W. W. Jones, 186–93, 196, 200–203, 208–9, 213
Caucasian Race Resolution, 227–28
cemeteries, Jewish, 139, 146n1
Center for the Study of the Southwest, 22
Central Texas, 226
Chambers, C. M., 175
Chambers of Commerce, 230–31
Chautauqua Hill, xiv
Chavez, Cesar, 219
Cherokee Indians, 42, 103
Cherry, E. Richardson, 169
Chisholm, Jesse, 14
Churchill, Lady Randolph, 161
citizen soldiers, 39
Civil Rights Movement, 220, 242–43
Civil War, 129 152–53n44, 157, 190
Clemons, Leigh, 8
Coahuila y Tejas, 66, 83n8
Cohen, Percy S., 12
Cohen, Rebecca, 149n13
Cohuila y Texas, 66–67
Colquitt, Oscar B., 93
Coman, Charlotte B., 169
Comanches, 92
Committee of Inter-American Relations in Texas, 235
Committee on Civil Rights, 229–30
common law, 77–78, 228

Commonwealth, 44
compañías volantes (flying companies), 90, 107
Confederate battle flag, 16
Congregation Beth Israel, 129–30, 136
Congregation Emanu-El, 130
Congregation Rodef Sholom, 130
Congress of the Republic of Texas, 90–91
Connolly, John, 234
Cooper, Collin Campbell, 169
Coppini, Elizabeth diBarbieri, 164
Coppini, Pompeo, 164–65
Cordova, Vincente, 103
Corenblith, Michael, 48–49
Corman, Charlotte B., 164
"Corps of Rangers," 90
Corpus Christi, San Diego, and Rio Grande Narrow Gauge Railroad, 189
Corpus Christi, Texas.
    and cattle ranching, 192
    civic life in, 200–201
    economic development of, 187–90
    and hurricanes, 196–97
    and the Jones family legacy, 201–2
    and Jones's business interests, 195–98, 202–3, 211, 213
    oil and gas industry, 208–9
    population growth, 185–86
    and port facilities, 187–90, 196–98, 209
Corpus Christi Deep Water Committee, 197–98
Corpus Christi National Bank, 203
Corpus Christi Ship Channel, 208
Corpus Christi Times, 202, 211
Cortez, Gregorio, 104

Cortina, Juan Nepomuceno, 103
Courtman, Henry, 50
coverture, 78
Cowan, Louise, 13
cowboy identity, 20
Cox, Patrick, xiii
creation myth of Texas, 30
Crisp, James, 30
Crockett, David, 34, 44 (drawing) 46, 47, 53n3, 59n42
Crum, Tom, xii, 98
Culberson, Charles Allen, 100
cultural constructionists, xiv
Culture Wars, 219
Cummins, Light, xiii, xiv, 7, 23
Cummins, Victoria Hennessey, 23
Curran, Charles, 172
Daily Express, 44–45 55–56n27
Dallas, Texas.
    and German cultural institutions, 125, 130, 137–39, 142, 153n45
    and urbanization, 189
    and the visual arts, 158–59, 172
Dallas Morning News, 238–39
Dallas Saengerfest, 137
The Dallas Weekly Herald, 137
Daniel, Price, 223
Dannelley, W. A., 207
Darst Field, 173
Davis, Edgar, 173, 174
Davis, J. Frank, 176
Davis, William C., 41, 56n28
Davis Wildflower Competitions, 159, 173–75
Davy Crockett, King of the Wild Frontier (1955), 44
Dawson-Watson, Dawson, 175
D-Day invasion, 113
Declaration of Rights, 73

Del Valle, Texas, 226
De León, Arnoldo, xiv, 242
Delgado, Minerva, 221, 222–23, 236–37, 240–43
Delgado v. Bastrop I.S.D., 217, 220–25, 225, 234, 236, 238–43
Del Rio I.S.D., 239
demographic shifts, xi, 153n45, 217, 226, 232–33
desegregation, 217, 237–38. See also *Delgado v. Bastrop I.S.D.*
DeShields, James Thomas, 97
Despujols, Jean, 172
Diaz, Porfirio, 102
Dibrell, Joseph E., 163
Dickinson, Susanna, 44–45
Diner, Hasia, 122
discrimination.
    and German-Jewish immigrants, 123, 131, 150n21
    and Mexican labor, 227
    and segregation in Texas, 218–19, 223, 227–33, 235, 238–39, 242
    and the Texas Constitution, 68, 72, 75
    and the Texas Rangers, 89
    See also segregation.
Dobie, J. Frank, 9, 25n10
Dodson, Pickett James, 222–23, 233, 236–37, 243
Donelson, Jackson, 32
Donovan, James, 41, 56n28
Dougherty, J. Chrys, 222
Dowling, Dick, 14
Downs, Fane, 64
Driscoll, Robert, 198
Driscoll Consolidated Independent School District, 240
Drought, Anna, 177

Drought, Ethel Tunstall.
    and the Carnegie Public Library, 160, 163–64, 167
    and civic culture of Texas, 159–60, 162–63
    and the Davis Wildflower Competitions, 159, 173–75
    illness and death, 177
    legacy of, 177–78
    portrait, 176, 179
    rural estate, 161–62
    and the San Antonio Arts League, 159, 163–72, 166, 174–77
    San Antonio home, 160–61, 182n5
    and the San Antonio Museum Association, 169–70, 183n18
    and the San Antonio Woman's Club, 159, 162–63, 167, 176
    and the Texas Fine Arts Association, 159, 162–63
    and the Witte Museum, 171–77
Drought, Frederick Gerald, 176
Drought, Henry P., 160
Drought, Kathleen, 177
Droughtfels estate, 161–62
droughts, 189, 191, 194
due process, 76–77, 83n8
Duty, Michael W., 178
Duval County, 204, 205
Duvall, Robert, 110
Eagle Pass, Texas, 133
Eastern European Jews, 124, 142–43
Eberly, Angelina Peyton, 79
The Echo, 130
Eckhardt, Robert C., 234, 242
economic conceptualizations of identity, 6
economic frames of reference, 4–5
Edgewood I.S.D. v. Kirby, 220

education in Texas.
　　and art contests, 167
　　and causes of independence,
　　　　83n8
　　and challenges of history
　　　　education, 221–22
　　and *Delgado v. Bastrop*, 222–26,
　　　　234–43
　　and Drought's influence, 169
　　and German-Jewish immigrants,
　　　　121, 126–31, 137–38, 143,
　　　　148n10, 149n14
　　and history of segregation in
　　　　Texas, 218–19, 226–33
　　key court cases, 219–21
elections, 32, 64–68, 75, 204, 207
Elgin, Texas, 226
El Monte, 185
Ely, Glen Sample, 88
Emmich, Zachariah, 152n38
English common law, 77–78
Enlightenment, 72
Epstein, Y., 132
Eshleman, Alice, 210
Eshleman, Benjamin, Jr.
　　(photograph), 212
Eshleman, Benjamin, Sr., 191
Eshleman, Lorine Jones
　　(photograph), 212
Esparza, Enrique, 40–41, 56n28
Esparza, Gregorio, 50
ethnocentrism, 64, 96. *See also*
　　Anglo identity
European Jews, 123 147nn4–5
Everett, Edward, 43–44, 48
executions, 105
Falcón, Cesario, 107
Fannin, James Walker, Jr., 35,
　　38–39
Farenthold, George, 211
Federal Art Commission, 183n12

Federal Bureau of Investigation
　　(FBI), 89
Feinberg, Sigmund, 128
Fenwick, Marin B., 162
Fields, Caroline Jane, 190
filibustering, 102, 103–4
Filisola, Vincenté, 43, 45
Finley, Rebecca, 73
Flanders, John, 50
Flores, Richard R., 30
Flores, Salvador, 107
flying companies *(compañías
　　volantes)*, 90, 107
folk tales, 11. *See also* myth
Forbes, Virginia, 238
Formosa gallery, 163
Forsyth, John Hubbard, 50
Fort Ringgold, 203
Founding Fathers, 219
14th Amendment, 223
Fox, S., 139
"Framing of the Constitution of the
　　Republic of Texas" (Richardson),
　　64
Frank, A. B., 129, 132
Freemasons, 127–28
Freund, Henry, 140
Fries, John, 48
Frohsinn, 137
Frontier Battalion/Frontier Force,
　　91–93
frontier heritage.
　　and cowboy myth, 14, 18, 20
　　and cultural hegemony, xii, 9
　　and gender relations, 78–80
　　and the Texas Rangers, 87,
　　　　90–96, 106–7, 113
　　and the visual arts in Texas,
　　　　157–58, 159, 178
Frontier Thesis, 94–95

Frost, J. H., 211
Frost, T. C., Jr., 168
Frost Bank Building, 170, 171
Frost National Bank, 168, 183n16
Galveston, Texas, 130–31, 136,
    141–42
Galveston Saengerfest, 136
Gans, Rachel, 133
Garcia, Amando, 205
García, Felix, 237
García, Gamaliel, 237
García, Gloria, 237
García, Gus A., 222–23 **225**, 234,
    237–38, 241–43
García, Marcario, 229
García, Nanamensia, 222–23, 227,
    237
García, Samuel, Jr., 237
García, Samuel, Sr., 223, 237
García, Sulima, 237
Garcia, Victor, 211
Garner, John Nance, 197, 203
Garrison, George P., 8
Gawenda, Peter-Bodo, 149n14
Gazley, Thomas J., 75
gendered conceptualization of
    identity, 6, 9, 20, 77, 80–81
General Provisions, 72–73
German associations, 126
German English Day Schools,
    128–30, 143 148–49n12, 149n18
German-Jewish immigrants.
    and Casino Clubs, 126, 131–34,
        143, 150n23
    German heritage of Jewish
        immigrants, 146n1
    misconceptions in historical
        research, 123–24
    origin of German immigration,
        124–25
    and Saengerbunds, 126, 128, 134,

German-Jewish immigrants.
    and Saengerbunds (*continued*),
        136–37, 143 147–48n8
    and Vereins, 126, 128, 133–34,
        136, 138–41 147–48n8,
        152n41
Gilded Age, 20
Gillian, Maude, 196
Ginn, Jody, xiii, xiv
Glasscock, D. W., 205
Goldberg, Theresa, 137
Goldfrank, M., 132
Goldman, Kay, xiii
Goliad, Texas, 13, 35–36, 190
González, Gilbert G., 233
Gonzalez, Xavier, 169
Gonzaullas, Manuel "Lone Wolf,"
    98
Goodnight, Charles, 14, 186
Grainger, Percy, 161
Grand Saengerfest, 137
Graves, Ireland, 222
Gray, William Fairfax, 71
Great Depression, 94, 176, 200–201,
    208, 226, 232
Green, Tom, 14
Greenberg, Mark, 150n21
Greenhill, Joe, 222
Grimes, Jesse, 39
Grumbach, Charles, 140
Guerra, Horace, 211
Guerra, Manuel, 203–4, 206
Guillen, Antonio, 231
Gutzeit, Emma, 183n18
Hadley, S. Trevor, 233
Halbwachs, Maurice, 16
Halff, L., 132
Halff, Solomon, 132
Halff & Levy, 129
Hamer, Frank, 112
Hancock, John Lee, 48

Hanning, Susanna Dickinson, 40–41, 45 55–56n27
Harbor Island, 197
Hardcastle, J. F., 207
Hardin, Steve, xiii, 41, 159
Harlendale I.S.D., 241
Harris, Adolph, 137–39, 142
Harris, Charles H., 89
Hause, Jeanne Gertrude Jones (photograph), 212
Hawaii 5-O (television), 109
Hays, Jack, 107
Hays, John C., 112
Heifetz, Jascha, 161
Herff, William, 163–65, 167
Hernandez v. Texas, 220
heroic history, 80. *See also* myth
Herrera, John J., 242
Hertzberg, Eli, 132
Hidalgo County, 192, 204
"The Hill," 21–22
Hill Country, 161–62
Hirschfeld, Henry, 137–38
historiography.
    and *Delgado v. Bastrop*, 218
    described, 2
    French Annales School, 4
    and public memory, 18–20
    and the Texas Rangers, 87–89, 94–96, 107, 115
History Channel, 109
History of Texas (Yoakum), 8
The History of Texas from 1685 to 1892 (Brown), 97
H. Mayer and Co., 128, 132
Hobby, William P., 197
Hocker, Clarence McElroy, 191, 208–11
Hocker, Kathleen, 210–11
Hoffman, Josef, 161

Hogg, Jim, 205
Holbein, R., 207
Hollywood, 109–10, 118n9
Houston, Elizabeth, 183n12
Houston, Sam, 37–38, 42
Houston, Texas, xiii, 10, 140–41
Houston Law Review, 239
Houston Saengerbund, 136–37, 143
Houston Schutzen Verein, 140–41, 152n41
Houston Turnverein, 139
Howard Payne University, 241
Howe, Irving, 123
Huddle, Nannie, 157
Huddle, William Henry, 157
Hughes, John, 100
Humble Oil, 208, 211
hurricanes, 196–97
Hutton, Patrick, 18
Hyman, Harold, 141–42
Independence Hall (photograph), 63
Indianola, Texas, 197
Indian Wars and Pioneers of Texas (Brown), 97
individualism, 9
industrialization, xiii, 20, 193–94, 213
integration, 16, 124, 239–42. See also *Delgado v. Bastrop* I.S.D.
Intracoastal Canal, 197
Jackson, Andrew, 32, 160
Jackson, Joaquin, 110, 114, 118n9
Jacksonian heritage, 68–69
Jahrmacht, 139
Jeffersonian heritage, 68
Jester, Beauford, 230–31
Jewish immigrants. See German-Jewish immigrants
Jim Hogg County, 192, 203–8
"Joe" (Travis's body servant), 45

Johnson, Lewis, 50
Johnson, Lyndon, 234–35, 242
Jones, Alice, 191
Jones, Allen Carter (A. C.), 190–91, 205, 207, 210
Jones, Kathleen, 191, 198, 201
Jones, Lorine, 191, 200
Jones, Lou Ella Marsden, 192, 195, 197, 200–202, 209–13
Jones, Margaret Whitby, 190
Jones, Tommy Lee, 110
Jones, William Whitby (W. W. photographs), **199, 212**
    banking and finance, 187–91, 193, 195, 200–203, 208, 213
    cattle ranching, 186–93, 196, 200–203, 208–9, 213
    and Corpus Christi port facilities, 187–90, 196–98, 209
    and county politics, 202–8
    death, 211
    estate, 212–13
    legacy, 213
    oil/gas interests, 188–90, 208–12
Jones, W. W. (Bill), II (photograph), 212
Jones Building, 195
Jones Family Ranches, 192–93, 196, 212–13
Journals of the Convention, 71
jury trials, 83n8
justice, 88–89, 92, 99, 101, 103
Justice, Wayne, 240
Justified (television), 110
Kamin, (A. or H.), 141
Kamphoefner, Walter, 149n12
Keeth, Kent, 122, 150n23
Kellam, John W., 198
Keller, Jacob, 140
Kempner, Dan, 126
Kempner, Harris, 126, 142

Kempner, Ike, 126
Kenedy, John, 211
Kenedy, Mifflin, 185, 201
Killer Women (television), 109
King, Martin Luther, Jr., 219
King, Richard, 14, 185, 201, 211
King Ranch, 107, 208, 209, 234
Kleberg, Richard, 211, 234
Kleberg, Robert, 211
Knapp, George S., 237
Knight, Marion, 190–91, 195
Koenigheim, Alexander, 132
Koenigheim, Eliza Levyson, 149n15
Koenigheim, Marcus, 128–29, 132 152–53n44
Koerner, Freda, 183n12
Kökény, Andrea, 7
Kopperl, Moritz, 131
Koresh, David, 114
Krueger, Max, 168, 169
Kuykendall, Bill, 190–91
labor shortages, 226–27, 230–32, 238
Lack, Paul, 79
La Hora Bautista, 241
Lambert, Ray, 170
Landa, Harry, 134, 147n6
Landa, Joseph, 125, 127, 134, 142 152–53n44
land grants, 191–92
Landsberg, Clara, 136
land titles, 64
La Retama Public Library, 195
Lasater, Ed C., 201, 204–6
Lassiter, Garland, 211
Lassiter, Thomas, 211
The Last Command (1955), 43
Latin-American Relations Commission, 231
lawlessness, 193
Lawrence, A. B., 32–33, 50

League of United Latin American
    Citizens (LULAC), 219, 222, 225,
    228, 233, 242–43
Lebman, R., 137
legal analysis, 61
legendary history, 80
Lévi-Strauss, Claude, 12–13
Levy, A., 132
Levy, Emil, 128
Levyson, Albert, 149n15
Lewis, C. S., 50
Lewis, Frank Morton, 191
Lewis, Lorine Jones, 197
Libo, Kenneth, 123
"Life of Captain Bill
    McDonald" (Paine), 99
"line in the sand" myth, 39–41, 50,
    53n3 55–56n27, 56n28
Little, Wilson, 235
Live Oak County, 191
Locke, John, 65
Loewenstein, Joseph, 136–37
London, Jack, 113
Lonesome Dove (McMurtry), 14
Lone Star Justice (Utley), 99, 106–7
Lone Star Lawmen (Utley), 102,
    106–7
Lone Star Pasts (Cantrell and
    Turner, eds.), xii, 19–20
Lone Star symbol, 15
Long, Jane, 79
longhorn cattle, 15
Longoria, Felix, 234
Lopez, Dan, 241
Lopez, Minerva Delgado. See
    Delgado, Minerva
Lord, Walter, 40, 42–43, 53n3
Los Angeles Times, 100–101, 112–13
Lou E. Jones Building, 211
Loyalty Rangers, 92, 105

Maas, Louis, 141
Maas, Max, 141
Maas, Samuel, 126, 131
Manifest Destiny, 13, 87–88, 94–95,
    108
Mann, Pamelia, 79
The Man Who Shot Liberty Valence
    (1962), 12
Marcus, Jacob Rader, 148n9
marital law, 78
market economy, 68
Marsden, Lou Ella, 191
Martindale, Texas, 226
Martinez, Ray, 101
Mason, Tyler, 99–100
Mathis, Texas, 239
Maverick, Lucy, 165
May Day, 131
Mayer, Henry, 128–29, 132, 149n13
    152–53n44
Maynard, Lucy Rivers, 237
McAllister, Lena, 183n18
McArdle, Henry A., 33, 157
McCampbell, H. H., 205
McCampbell, R. H., 207
McCullough, Ben, 14
McDonald, Bill, 98, 99, 100
McFaddin, Al, 201
McLane, M. Jean, 169
McMurtry, Larry, 14
Medal of Honor recipients, 229
Meican Constitution of 1824, 66
Meinig, D. W., 153n46
Méliès, Georges, 13–14
memory.
    collective, xi–xii, 15–19, 80, 89,
        99, 108–9, 112, 115, 124, 243
    and construction of Texas
        identities, 15–18
    creation of, 17, 111

memory. (*continued*)
  and intellectual
    conceptualizations of
    identity, 3–5
  myth and historical memory, 18
  public memory, 16–20, 30, 155,
    158, 213, 217–18
Mendez v. Westminster, 220, 223,
  238
mentalités, 4–5
Mesteña land grants, 191
Mesteña Oil and Gas Company,
  209–13
Mexican American students. See
  Delgado v. Bastrop I.S.D.
Mexican Revolution, 193, 206, 233
Milam, Ben, 160
military conscription, 123
Mina Ward School, 236, 240
Mission San Jose, 160
Mix, Tom (photograph), 111
modernization, 193–94, 213
Moke, Emmanuel, 132
Moke, L., 129
Moke, M., 132
Moore, Jacqueline M., 20, 186
Moore, Stephen, 106–7
Morgan, Theodore, 172
Morris, Chistopher, 7
Mother's Clubs, 162, 165, 167,
  183n12
Municipal Auditorium (San
  Antonio), 175
mutual aid societies (mutualistas),
  233
Myers, John, 42
myth.
  academic study of, 11–12
  Alamo myths, 29–35, 37–44,
    46–51, 53n3 55–56n27, 56n28
  Anglo-Texan myth, 13

myth. (*continued*)
  anthropological construction of,
    14
  and collective memory, 15–17
  and cowboy myth, 14, 18, 20
  defined, 12
  and historical memory, 18
  and identity, 15–16
  and intellectual
    conceptualizations of
    identity, 3–5
  "line in the sand" myth, 39–41,
    50, 53n3 55–56n27
  mythic history, 80
  and popular culture, 13–14
  as reflection of history, 50
  social construction of, 16–17
  symbols and objects of, 15
  and Texas identity, xi
  and the Texas Rangers, 88–90,
    94–96, 98–102, 106, 108,
    113–15
Myth, Memory, and Massacre
  (Carlson and Crum), xii, 98
Napoleonic Wars, 123
National Association for the
  Advancement of Colored People
  (NAACP), 219, 243
National Council of Jewish
  Women, 142
National History Standards, 219
Native Americans. *See* American
  Indians
natural environment of Texas, 9
natural rights, 78–79
Nazi Germany, 122
Neill, James Clinton, 35, 38
New Braunfels, Texas, 125, 134
  152–53n44

A New History of Texas for Schools (Pennybacker), 44

New Jersey, 79

newspapers, 32, 130

New York Times, 105

Ney, Elisabet, 157, 163

Nile, Rosamond, 176

norias, 194–95

Norris, Chuck, 110

Nueces County Courthouse, 197

Nueces County Navigation District Commission, 187–88, 198

Nueces Hotel, 187, 195, 197–98, 201

Nueces Strip, 103

Nueva Santander, 185

O'Brien, Esse Forrester, 157

Offenbach, Isabella, 126

oil and gas industry, 188–90, 208–12

Old Market House, 170

Old San Antonio Road, 35

Olson, James S., 41

Onderdonk, Eleanor Rogers, 173, 183n12

Onderdonk, Julian, 164–65, 173

Onderdonk, Robert Jenkins, 33, 157, 162–65, 173

O'Neal, Bill, 109–11

One Ranger Returns (Jackson), 114

"One Riot, One Ranger" myth, 98–100, 112

opinion-making process, 16

Oppenheimer, Anton, 132, 150n24

Oppenheimer, Barney, 132, 150n24

Oppenheimer, Dan, 132, 150n24

Oppenheimer, M. L., 126, 132–33, 150n24

oral tradition, 94

Orozco, Pascual, 105

"Our Gringo Amigo" (De León), 242

Owens Valley vs. Los Angeles, 113

Paine, Albert Bigelow, 99

paramilitary units, 90

Paredes, Americo, 104–6

Parker, Cynthia Ann, 97–98

Parker, Fess, 34–35

Parker, Quanah, 97–98

Parlin, H. T., 176

Parr, Archer, 203–4, 206, 211

Parsons, Jim, 178

patriarchal social structure, 7, 9, 68–69, 72, 77, 80

patriotism, 32

Pavilion Hotel and Pier, 197

Peine, Louis, 136

Peña, José Enrique de la, 45, 47, 57n33

Pennybacker, Anna J. H., 44, 58n36

Peoples, Clint, 98–99

Perales, Alonso S., 228

Perez, Antonio, 107

Permanent Council, 67

Perry, Geroge Sessions, 20

physical objects of myth, 15

Piedras Pintas field, 208

Pierce, J. Stuart, 183n18

Pierce, Shanghai, 190–91

Plains Indians, 92

Plan De San Diego, 103

Podet, Mordecai, 130

politics and political partisanship. county politics, 202–8

and German-Jewish immigrants, 125–26, 131–32, 134, 142–43

and Loyalty Rangers, 92, 105

and societal norms, xii

and the Texas Rangers, 108

poll taxes, 206

Ponselle, Rosa, 161

Pontiac Refining Company, 208

popular culture.
 and the Alamo, 13–15, 48–49
 and Anglo-American identity,
  8–9
 and physical symbols of Texas
  identity, 15
 and public memory, 17, 19
 and the Republic years, 80
 and the Texas Rangers, 88–89,
  94–95, 102, 108–13, 115
Port Aransas, Texas, 197–98
Port of Corpus Christi, 187–90,
 196–98, 209
posses, 104–5
Potter, Reuben Marmaduke, 33,
 43–44
Presidio La Bahía, 35
Preuss, Gene, xiii–xiv
property requirements for voting,
 69
property rights, 78
Providence High School, 182n5
Provisional Government, 67, 77
public education, 127–28, 190. See
 also Delgado v. Bastrop I.S.D.;
 desegregation
public memory, 16–20, 30, 155, 158,
 213, 217–18
Rabba, Ernst, 165
Rachel, E. R., 205
Rachel, F. S., 205
racism and racial conflict, xii,
 19, 104, 227, 229. See also
 discrimination; segregation
railroads, 92, 185, 189–90, 193–96,
 202, 204, 236
Railway Killer, 114
Ramírez y Sesma, Joaquín, 47
Rangel, Jorge C., 239
Ranger Force, 93
Raphael, E., 136

Rather, Aline, 169
Rather-Gonzalez Art Class, 169
Ray, Frederic, 42
Reaugh, Frank, 155–57
Reaves, William E., Jr., 159, 173
Reel Rangers (O'Neill), 109
regional conceptualizations of
 identity, 5–6
Reichman, John, 136
religious conceptualizations of
 identity, 6. See also German-
 Jewish immigrants
"Remember the Alamo", 31
representation, 83n8
republican government, 64–65
Republic of Texas.
 declaration of independence, 62
 and male Anglo-centrism, 64–65
 and paramilitary units, 90
 Provisional Government, 77
 and the Texas Rangers, 87–91,
  96–97, 103–4, 110, 114
 See also Texas Constitution.
Republic of Texas (Davis
 Mountains separatists), 114
Reséndez, Andrés, 7–8
revisionism, xiv, 88, 106–7
revolutionaries, 106
Rice, Ben H., 224, 237–40
Richardson, Rupert, 64
Riding for Texas (Mason), 99–100
right of petition, 72
Rio Grande Valley, 101–3, 105–6,
 185, 204. See also South Texas
Robbins, Marty, 44
Roberts, Randy, 41
Robinson, James W., 38
rodeos, 15
Rodríguez, Jacob I., 228
Rogers, John H., 100

Roos, Simon, 140
Roosevelt, Franklin D., 230
Rose, Louis "Moses," 40, 56n28
Rose Hill Cemetery, 202, 211
Rosenberg, J., 132
Rosenspitz, A., 130–31
Ross, Lawrence Sullivan "Sul,"
    97–98
Royal Canadian Mounted Police, 89
Runaway Scrape, 70
rural areas, 9. *See also* frontier
    heritage
Rusk, Thomas J., 73
Russell, Anna Gertrude, 191
Russi, David, 48
Russian Jews, 124
Sadler, Louis R., 89
Saengerbunds, 126, 128, 134,
    136–38, 143 147–48n8
Salinas, Guadalupe, 239
San Angelo, Texas, 229–30
San Antonio, Texas.
    and civil rights activism,
        222–23, 228
    and railroads, 195
    role of women in civic life,
        158–62
    urbanization and
        industrialization, xiii, 189
    and the visual arts in Texas,
        162–78
San Antonio, Uvalde and Gulf
    Railway, 195
San Antonio and Aransas Pass
    Railway, 195
San Antonio Art League, 159,
    163–72, 166, 174–77
San Antonio Casino Club, 132–33
San Antonio City Council, 170
San Antonio Conservation Society,
    171

San Antonio de Béxar, 35–36
San Antonio German English Day
    School, 128–30 148–49n12
San Antonio Light (photograph
    from), 221
San Antonio Museum Association,
    169–70, 183n18
San Antonio Public Schools, 165
San Antonio Woman's Club, 159,
    162–63, 167, 176
Sánchez, George I., 227, 228
Sánchez-Navarro, José Juan, 45, 49
Sanger, Alex, 125–26, 137, 146n1,
    147n6
Sanger, Cornelia, 137
Sanger, Fannie, 137, 139
Sanger, Philip, 125, 137
San Javier Casa Mayor, 194
Santa Anna, Antonio López de,
    35–36, 42, 44–45, 47, 49–50, 103
Savage Frontier series (Moore),
    106–7
Schasse, Agnes, 165
Scheer, Mary, xiii, 23
Scheer, Richard L., 23
Schipa, Tito, 161
Schultz, Ellen D., 169–71, 172–73,
    183n18
Schwarz, Benito, 128, 129
Scotland Yard, 89
secular mythology, 13
segregation.
    and cemeteries, 217–19, 243
    and federal interventions, 230
    and German-Jewish immigrants,
        134–36
    and key court cases, 219–20,
        223–24
    and Mexican laborers, 227–28,
        230–32, 238
    in recent years, 218–19

segregation. (*continued*)
  and social reform in Texas,
    232–38, 240–42
  See also Delgado v. Bastrop I.S.D.;
    discrimination.
Seguin, Juan, 107
Seguin, Texas, 233
self-identification, 6
"separate but equal" doctrine, 220
shape of Texas, 15
Shurtleff, Stella, 168
slavery, 49, 64 152–53n44
Slayden, James L., 165, 183n12
Sleepy Lagoon Case, 227
Smith, Henry, 37–38
Smithsonian American History
  Museum, 219
social compact, 65
sociological conceptualizations of
  identity, 5
southern identity, 6–8
Southern States Art League, 175
South Texas.
  and banking, 202
  and cattle ranching, 186–92, 201
  and civic life, 200–202
  and county politics, 202–8
  and cultural diversity, 193–94
  and industrial development, 189
  See also Rio Grande Valley.
Southwestern Oil and Refining
  Company, 208
Southwest Texas State Normal
  School, xiv
Southwest Texas State Teachers
  College, xiv
Southwest Texas State University,
  xiii–xiv, 21–22
Spanish colonial era, 194
Spaulding, Albert, 161
Spears, J. Franklin, 228–29

"Special Rangers," 92
Spindletop discovery, 208
Spoonts, Lorine, 210
Spoonts, Marshall, 191, 200
sports teams, 15
Standard Oil, 211
Starr, James Harper, 203
Starr County, 191–92, 203–4
state-based identities, 6–7
State Board of Education (BOE),
  219–20, 225
State Historian of Texas, xiii
State of Texas Constitution
  (proposed 1833), 66–67, 83n8
states' rights, 148n9
steam ships, 189
Steinfeldt, Cecilia, 173
stereotypes, 3–4, 88, 186–87, 198
Stevenson, Coke, 228, 230
St. Louis, Brownsville and Mexico
  Railway, 195
Stock Market Crash of 1929, 174
The Story of the Alamo (Ray), 42
suffrage, 69, 75–76, 83n7, 162
Sugar Land, Texas, 229
Suhler, A., 130
Sun and Mist (Corman), 164
Sutherland, Liz, 234
Sutherland, Thomas, 230, 234–35,
  239, 242
Sweatt v. Painter, 220, 242–43
Sweetwater Reporter, 238
Tashima, T. J., 113
Taylor, Rolla S., 165
Taylor Refining Company, 208
Teja, Jesús F. de la, xi–xv, 22
Tejano identity.
  and cattle ranching, 193–94
  compañías volantes (flying
    companies), 90

Tejano identity. (*continued*)
  and electoral politics, 206
  and school integration, 218 242
    (*see also Delgado v. Bastrop
    I.S.D.*)
  and the Texas Rangers, 90, 97,
    101–8, 114–15
  and Texas Revolution, xiii, 80
Temple Beth El, 122
Temple Beth Israel, 136, 138,
    152n38
Temple B'nai Israel, 131
Temple Emanu-El, 139
tequileros (smugglers), 106
*Terrell Wells Swimming Pool v.
  Rodriguez*, 220, 228
Texana, 1
Texas: A Contest of Civilizations
  (Garrison), 8
Texas Almanac, 40
Texas and Southwest Cattle Raisers
  Association, 201, 207
Texas Centennial Celebrations, 95,
  176
Texas Constitution (photograph),
  74
  and Alamo myths, 49–50
  and brevity of the Republic,
    79–80
  and citizenship, 76
  convention adopting, 38–39, 42,
    62–68, 79, 84n11
  and emergency relief policy,
    70–71
  and English common law, 77–78
  and first elections, 75–77
  and gender-neutral language,
    64, 70–72, 75–76
  inconsistencies and confusion,
    70, 73

Texas Constitution
  (*continued*)
  and natural rights, 78–79
  and patriarchal social structure,
    68–69, 72–73, 77
  and petition rights, 72
  and political rights of women,
    69–70, 75–77, 80
  preamble, 65
"Texas Declaration of the Causes
  for Taking up Arms against
  Santa Anna," 67
Texas Department of Public Safety,
  90–91, 94, 107
Texas Educational Agency (TEA),
  240
Texas Federation of Women's
  Clubs, 159
Texas Fine Arts Association
  (TFAA), 159, 162–63
Texas General Exhibition, 172
Texas General Land Office, 192
Texas German and English
  Academy, 137–38
Texas Good Neighbor Commission,
  230–32, 234–35, 239, 242
Texas Independence Convention,
  38–39, 42, 62–64, 67–68, 79
Texas Jewish Burials, 146n1, 152n39
Texas Mexican Railway, 189, 195
Texas Monthly, 101
Texas Rangers.
  and Anglo identity, 9–10, 88,
    107–8
  and controversial subjects,
    100–101, 114–15
  and county names, 205
  creation of, 90–91
  legal issues surrounding, 92
  linguistic confusion of term,
    105–6

Texas Rangers. (*continued*)
  mythical status, 14, 89
  "One Riot, One Ranger" myth,
    98–101, 112
  origins of, 90
  peace-keeping and law
    enforcement duties, 92, 104
  photographs of, 91, 111
  and popular culture, 110–14
  public perception of, 108–9
  reputation problems, 93–94
  role in Republic of Texas, 87–91,
    96–97, 103–4, 110, 114
  and tensions with Tejanos,
    102–3
  and Webb's Frontier Thesis,
    94–95
The Texas Rangers (Webb), 95, 110
*The Texas Rangers and the Mexican
  Revolution* (Harris and Sadler),
  89
Texas Rangers Heritage Center, 110
Texas Revolution, xiii, 13, 33, 35,
  67–68, 126–27. *See also* The
  Alamo
Texas Rising (television), 109–10
Texas State University, xiv–xv,
  21–22
Texas Through Time (Calvert and
  Buenger, eds.), xi–xii
Texas War for Independence,
  49–51
"Texas Women" (Downs), 64
Texas Youth Commission, 114
Texian Iliad (Hardin), 41
Texians, 7, 14, 31–33, 35–42, 47, 160
13 Days to Glory (Tinkle), 42–43
Thomas, H. D., 205
Thomas, Manetta, 183n12
Thompkins, Mrs. Frank A., 202

Thompson, Alice Cathryne Jones
  (photograph), 212
Thompson, Oscar, 207
Three Rivers, Texas, 234
Three Roads to the Alamo (Davis),
  41
A Time to Stand (Lord), 43, 53n3
Tinkle, Lon, 42–43
Tiomkin, Dimitri, 58n36
Tobin, John, 170–73
tourism, 195–96
traditionalists, xiv
Travis, William Barret, 35–39, 45,
  49–50, 53n3, 70
Treaty of Guadalupe Hidalgo, 103,
  228
Truman, Harry, 229–30
Turner, Elizabeth Hays, xii, 17, 20
Turner Frontier Thesis, 94–95
Turner Hall (photograph), 140
Turner Societies, 134–36, 139–41
Turnstall, Ethel, 160
Umstattd, J. G., 235–36
United Farm Workers Strike, 101–2
University of Texas at Austin, 21
urbanization, xiii, 226, 232
Urrea, José, 36
Urwitz, Max, 139, 146n1
US Army, 92
US Army Corps of Engineers, 198
US Congress, 198
US Constitution, 65, 68, 71
US Marines, 101
US-Mexican War, 89, 103–4, 109,
  228
US Navy, 227
US Neutrality laws, 105
US Supreme Court, 242–43
US v. Texas, 240
Utley, Robert, 99–100, 102–3, 105,
  107–8, 115

Veith, Ignatz, 139, 146n1, 152n39
Verein movement, 126, 128, 133–34, 136, 138–41 147–48n8, 152n41
"Views from the Hill" (symposium), xiv
visual arts in Texas, 155–79
Volksfests, 138, 152n38
Von Blucher, Friedrich Herman, 134
Vonnah, Bessie Porter, 172
Voorsanger, Jacob, 135, 136, 143, 146n1
voting rights, 61–62, 66–70, 75–77, 79, 81, 83n7, 162
Waco, Texas, 130
Waco *Examiner*, 130
Waggoner, W. T., 186, 187
Walker, Nancy, 73
Wall, Bernhard, 161
Washington-on-the-Brazos, 62–64, 68
Wayne, John, 14, 33–35, 38, 58n36, 80
Webb, Walter Prescott, 9, 94–96, 100, 108, 110, 118n9
Webster, P. F., 58n36
Weinbaum, A., 136
Weiss, Harold, 100
Weiss, J. J., 141
We Lived There Too (Libo and Howe), 123
Wells, James B., 203–4
Westheimer, Sid, 136
West Texas Chamber of Commerce, 230–31, 238
West Texas Today, 230
widows, 71–72
wild cattle, 192
Wild Horse Desert, 185, 210
Wilson, Kathleen, 6
Winchell, Walter, 229

Wirin, Abraham Lincoln, 222–23, 234
Witte, Alfred G., 171–72
Witte Museum, 159, 171–77
Woeltz, Julius E., 169
women in Texas history.
    and construction of public memory, 19
    and coverture, 78
    and gender-neutral language of the Texas Constitution, 64, 70–72, 75–76
    and German cultural institutions, 132, 142
    and male Anglo-centrism, 64–65
    and promotion of the visual arts, 155–78
    and voting rights, 61–62, 66–70, 75–77, 79, 81
    See also Drought, Ethel Tunstall.
Wood, John, 102
Woods, Littleton A., 224, 238–40
Woodward, Ellsworth, 175
World War I, 92, 158, 167
World War II, 8–9, 113, 211, 226, 229, 232–33
Wulff, Marie, 128–29
W. W. Jones Building, 207
W. W. Jones Ranch, 189, 192
Yaeger, H. C., 207
yeshivas, 127, 148n10
Yoakum, Henderson, 8
Zagarri, Rosemarie, 69
Zanco, Charles, 50
Zoot-suit riots, 227
Zork, Abraham, 132, 150n24
Zork, Leon, 142
Zork, Louis, 122, 128–29, 132
Zuber, Abraham and Mary Ann, 40